The Colours of Life -
through the eyes of a blind man

My true life story

The Colours of Life - through the eyes of a blind man

Published by The Conrad Press Ltd. in the United Kingdom 2022

Tel: +44(0)1227 472 874

www.theconradpress.com

info@theconradpress.com

ISBN 978-1-914913-66-2

Copyright © David John Forrest, 2022

All rights reserved.

Typesetting and Cover Design by: Charlotte Mouncey, www.bookstyle.co.uk

The Conrad Press logo was designed by Maria Priestley.

Printed and bound in Great Britain by Clays Ltd, Elcograf S.p.A.

The Colours of Life -
through the eyes of a blind man

My true life story

David John Forrest

Author's note

Before you read my story, I would like to elaborate on my chosen book title. Blindness as we all know, is defined as the inability to see. While I am not visually impaired physically, I have used the term 'blind' as a figurative expression to decribe my mental blockage to unfortunate happenings in my life.

You will note through these pages, why I was struck by mental blindness, to the actions of persons within my immediate orbit. But it did not stop there, as I have also always been consciously blind to race, colour, culture, caste and creed, age, sexual orientation and social standing. I believe all of us come from the same place and as such we are all equal, irrespective of who we are.

For all who have been a part of my inner circle, you will know that though I can tell a good tale, I could never put it all together into a story book format.

When you read this story of my life, I want you to know that every incident experienced as well as thoughts, recollections, language, meanings and views expressed are solely mine.

Every aspect of my story has been thoroughly vetted by me personally. Anne has in a totally unbiased way, only helped me to compile and write my story to make sense and bring my world to 'Life' in print.

David John Forrest – July 2022

Dedication

For my (late) parents John (Jack) Forrest and Maria Nicolina Suvali Forrest:

Who could not give me the start in life they would have liked to. But they gave me something far richer. They were instrumental in moulding and making me into the man I am with an abundance of inner strength, 'titantic' proportions of 'self-belief' and a macro vision of our wonderful but fickle and easily swayed world.

They taught me by example the importance of not only honesty, integrity and respect, but that we are all 'one people' and discrimination of any kind, is only in the minds of small minded people and in the eyes of tunnel visioned people.

With all my love till we meet again, your only son.

For all my grandchildren:

To my current grandchildren - I would have loved to have met, known and had you in my life. But you do not even know I still exist. While I may never know you or even get the chance to ever meet and have my future grandchildren in my life, maybe one day you will all read this story of my life's journey. You will learn about your history as well as the simple and uncomplicated grandfather you never met, who led an unusual and colourful life for just a common man.

Through my life story, you will note from my personal experiences, the mystery about life is the fact we have absolutely no clue as to what cards it will deal us from one day to the next. Yes, the future holds the unknown, but if you don't take the risk to pursue your dream or anything you love, as well as accept the challenge to explore it, you would hamper your own happiness and stop really living your life.

I have demonstrated that love never sails smoothly, as it occasionally runs into stormy weather and involves making tough decisions. But never let the hurt and disillusionment which are invariably collateral damages of love, to stop you from following your heart, as life is too short to be miserable.

I hope you will try to prepare yourselves for every eventuality. Enjoy and share the good times with family and friends who make you laugh and feel loved, making memories to last your lifetime. At the same time, accept the bad times that will surely cross your path, with inner strength and fortitude.

Don't ever forget the road ahead is yours alone and though several people may walk it along with you, no one can ever walk it for you. Learn to love all of you first, as unless you love yourself, you will not be able to experience the power of love that comes knocking on your door.

Always make time for your parents as life is unpredictable and one day when you want or need them in your life, they will no longer be around. Do remember your folk who gave you a start in life and come what may, be appreciative of the people who contribute to your life long success.

Whatever life has in store for you, I hope you will always ensure to conduct yourselves with honesty, grace, dignity and respect for all. It is an undisputed fact we will leave our world in the same way we entered it - with nothing. Treat our world well so that our future generations can enjoy it, and never forget the ground we walk on today will ultimately be the roof over us tomorrow.

Finally, may you always be happy, not just because everything in your life is good but because you can see the good side of everything in your life.

With all my love, Grandad

Contents

Author's note	5
Dedication	7
Preface	13
Chapter 1 - The Russian and Italian connection	16
Chapter 2 - World War II – the dark days	26
Chapter 3 - Breaking free on the high seas	47
Chapter 4 - The return of a man	55
Chapter 5 - Warm hearth – cold heart	62
Chapter 6 - Gaziantep – Turkey (Europe)	**71**
Chapter 7 - A new life through a magnifying glass	78
Chapter 8 - The call of the Indian Ocean – Mauritius	87
Chapter 9 - Barbados, St. Lucia, Grenada (West Indies)	94
Chapter 10 - Fremont, California (USA)	99
Chapter 11 - Addis Ababa – Ethiopia (East Africa)	106
Chapter 12 - Kampala – Uganda (East Africa)	111
Chapter 13 - Kitwe – Zambia (East Africa)	123
Chapter 14 - A cockney Down Under (Australia)	127
Chapter 15 - The draw of the desert – Dubai (United Arab Emirates)	134
Chapter 16 - The land of the pharaohs – Cairo (Egypt)	167
Chapter 17 - A woman of substance – La Puttana to La Buttana	169
Chapter 18 - My high octane pleasurable toys	182
Chapter 19 - Sharon and Tony – through the years	199
Chapter 20 - Marie – my parents' daughter	231
Chapter 21 - The colours of my first marriage – the secrets of a scarlet woman	267
Chapter 22 - The colours of my second marriage – my blindness creates blunders!	290
Chapter 23 - The colours of my third and final marriage – the best is saved for last!	302
Chapter 24 - Conclusion: A life worth living – (you know what I mean?)	339

Preface

Our world to me, is a rainbow that never quite ends with the elusive pot of gold. Just like me, every individual searches for the ultimate life has to offer with the intention of making impossible dreams, possible.

I have realised the journey of our life through this world we call home, can be either a positive or negative one depending on how we look at life; choose to experience it and what we make of it; how we embrace the time we spend living a self-satisfying life; and being the best person we can possibly aim to be while on our spectacular road of discovery.

I was born into a multi-cultural family, and having since travelled and lived in several fantastic countries around our world, I have experienced the various colours of life right from gory through to glory, which not only had positive and negative effects on my life but it affected my view of our world as total figurative blindness impaired me.

Based on my personal experience, I feel our views of the world, its citizens and our life, goes through a series of changes through time, due to individual experiences, perspectives, travel and cultural education, as well as the state of the mind.

I have always led a busy life - working, socialising, travelling and enjoying my family time. But I have never had much personal free time to sit and read a book, get lost in my favourite music, appreciate the view, or just relax and do absolutely nothing.

It is said retirement is the exclusive club you join after years of graft and toil, to wind down and smell the roses. However,

I totally disagree as I find since I officially retired, I not only work more, but when I am not working, I am travelling or busy with the odd job I should have done yesterday.

Life works in mysterious ways. The years 2020, 2021 and 2022 we are living through, will definitely go down in infamy as the years that darkened our horizons and changed our world. A world we love, but will never be the same from now going forward. The Covid-19 pandemic which unleashed the greatest infectious disease our world has experienced since the 1918 influenza outbreak, has taken the lives of millions of loved ones, put citizens around our world under strict lockdown for months, changed the way we live, turned our lives topsy turvy, crushed global economies and literally brought our world to a halt, to make me realise that I had many months of lockdown free time to do something I would normally never have attempted.

I never did plan on putting my life out of the confines of my home for all the world to see, as I did not see my life as anything out of the ordinary. But it took a close look into my life by the very savvy woman by my side, to see that what I regard as normal, is actually exciting, adventurous, dangerous, fun, disastrous, crazy, sad, extraordinary and definitely not normal.

Over the past twenty-five years, I have regaled Anne with stories from my colourful past. I would like my memories to communicate an accurate picture of my life as I have no doubt that with the passage of time, I may lose them as they will either fade, or get embellished along the way.

As such, I realised the time has come for me to release the burden from my mind to my eyes, by collating the numerous memories I have been carrying around with me so far, for all of us to see instead. While I hope to be around for a long time, I am writing this story of my life now, as I know it will survive whatever plan God has for me.

Truth is stranger than fiction and there is no doubt that cathartic as it may be, I would certainly prefer to leave out some of my immediate family members, to avoid dredging up and reliving painful memories. However, being family, they are so finely interwoven into the fabric of my life, that my story would never be complete without their inclusion.

For the couple of people on the edge of my periphery, you are enmeshed in my story because you are the 'Judas Iscariots' in my life. As you know, I have the hard proof and I hope this story brings you within my orbit so I can finally get my due from you the legal route. However, do not worry, I will ensure you receive the comeuppance you so greatly deserve. I believe truth is a major factor in the accuracy of my life story, and while you may find the truth of my words a bitter pill to swallow, I hope it will energise you to change your life for the better and never use or treat people the way you wronged me.

Through these pages, my readers have the opportunity to glean that just as I learned through my journey, making a hundred friends is no miracle. Like I eventually did, the miracle is finding just a single person who will stand by your side even when a multitude desert you.

Life is never black and white but a myriad of colours that appear different to every individual. Infact, life is just what colour you want to make of it. While many melodies may make up the song of our life, we all have just one 'life story' and, this is my story.

David John Forrest – July 2022

Chapter 1

The Russian and Italian connection

It is said that all children grow into the image and likeness of their parents. However, I do believe the likeness stops there, as every person needs to see and experience various aspects outside their own family perspective, to know whether they would appreciate it or dislike it. They have to live their own life, form their own opinions, make their own mistakes, achieve their own accomplishments and follow their own chosen path in life.

My paternal grandparents were English, and it has always been my greatest disappointment that they passed on before I was old enough to get to know them well, as it would have been wonderful to have grown up and been spoilt rotten by two sets of doting grandparents.

My maternal grandfather Angelo was born on 25 November 1871 in Monte Cassino, Italy, while my maternal grandmother Anna was born in Moscow, Russia on 29 April 1879. Love knows no boundaries and I am here because they did not follow the dictates of distance or borders when they met and married.

I have never quite figured out how they met, considering that during the time period, the main mode of travel was by horse and carriage or oxen and carts. Journeys through countries across Europe took weeks if not months, depending on the season and climatic conditions. Even with the advent of the railway in the mid-nineteenth century, the rail network system through Europe was limited and not everyone could afford to travel by the railway.

It was only in 1886 that Karl Benz the renowned German inventor, patented his Benz Motorwagen which paved the way for the glorious start of the world's first mass produced automobiles in the early twentieth century, which is an important accessory in our daily lives today. Though, I have no doubt it was out of the financial reach of my grandparents during their early life.

When my grandparents got married, they lived in the Italian town of Monte Cassino, about a hundred and thirty kilometres south east of Rome. After their first born daughter Anna died in infancy, they moved from Italy to Great Britain in 1902, purchased their own home and settled into their new life in Croydon on the south east border of London.

My nonna started an Italian ice-cream business from their home, while my nonno did the rounds of the town selling the ice-cream from a trundling barrow. Their business did well enough for them to expand their family as time passed, to include another four daughters, my aunts Concetta and Lena, my mum Nicolina and the youngest, my aunt Nell.

When the First World War started, life was difficult for people. But on the 7 May 1915 the Cunard ocean liner 'RMS Lusitania' when making its way from New York to Liverpool, was attacked and sunk just off the coast from the 'Old Head of Kinsale' in Ireland, now the Republic of Ireland. Around one thousand two hundred innocent passengers were killed in the attack by a German submarine, or U-boat as they were called.

This escalated the war and life suddenly got very much harder. All men of European origin between seventeen and fifty-five years, were sent to internment camps for 'enemy aliens'.

My European origin grandparents, along with their four young daughters who were all naturalised British citizens, were uprooted from their home in Croydon, and sent to an internment camp on the coast to wait out the war. A host of other European British citizens were also rounded up from all over the country, and treated not as British citizens, but prospective 'enemies of the state'. When I heard of this from my mum, I was aghast. I could not believe my country would forceably imprison and treat its own people in such a discriminatory manner.

But it seemed war hysteria was virulent among the general English population, and the government decided action had to be taken. And even though most of the people were just innocent law abiding citizens, they all had to pay the price because of their heritage, and live in the internment camps till 1919. However, England was not the only country to treat its citizens with such blatant unfairness, as the United States of America and even Canada did the same to its European citizens during the war.

Many European families in England were separated from their men-folk, and the men were imprisoned in specially built and securely protected internment camps for 'enemies of the state'. My grandparents and their four young children were however allowed to remain together for the duration of the war, in the area specified by the authorities, which was good because my grandmother could not look after all the four young children on her own. While they were given regular food rations for the family, my grandmother had to home-school the older children. Neither my grandparents nor my mum spoke much about this period, except to say their life was difficult but not unbearable, and that like everyone else, they dreamed of a normal post war life.

But it was not to be, and my grandparents could not return permanently to their home in Croydon after the war. They could not believe even their long time friends and neighbours were now instilled with paranoia, due to the widespread negative propaganda during the war. War brings about unusual changes in people and as such, friends and neighbours were extremely wary about my grandparents returning to the neighbourhood. The stigma, pain and humiliation at being ostracized by the people who knew them for so many years, was instrumental in my grandparents' decision to sell their home in Croydon. They moved and started a new post-war life in Kent, a county in the southeast of England also known as the 'garden of England', an expression that has remained since it was first used by King Henry VIII.

They settled in the small but beautiful coastal town of Herne Bay, meaning 'a place on a corner of land'. As history relates, the name Herne came from the old English word 'hyrne' meaning 'corner'. The town was a seaside resort with quaint shops on its only high street, colourful beach huts along the sea front, a wonderful pier walkway going right out into the sea, old attractive buildings and rows of terraced residential houses. Over the past one hundred years, despite its population explosion, not much has changed in Herne Bay, and it has managed to retain its casual seaside charm. The demographic shift however leaned towards the senior citizens, and Herne Bay has locally been known as 'God's waiting room' with tongue-in-cheek humour.

My grandmother was an extremely enterprising woman for her times. The family moved into a large house, and she opened and managed a very successful 'bed and breakfast' and also continued their business selling home made Italian gelato from trundling barrows. She kept a brood of hens in the rear garden to provide her with eggs for a wonderful English breakfast for her guests, and her feathered friends never let her down. As their four daughters grew up, they did not have a lot of free time out of their school hours, as each girl was given a trundling barrow to sell their gelato to specified localities in Herne Bay, and my nonna's reputation and her gelato business grew, as her ice-cream was second to none.

However, each daughter eventually did find the time to meet and marry her Englishman. They eagerly pushed their trundling barrows into the garden shed where the barrows died a natural death, along with the eventual demise of my grandmother's gelato business. My nonna did continue with her thriving 'bed and breakfast' operation, but I do think it was a pity none of their daughters inherited my nonna's grit and business acumen, nor her passion to continue to expand her European dream.

My grandfather was very patient with me when I was a young child, as my constant chatter and unintelligible questions would have tired out a less tolerant person. I used to sit at the foot of the stairs and often chat with him as he sat in his favourite chair by the back door, looking out as the world went about its daily business, and smiling at me every now and then, though he probably did not heed nor understand my childish gibberish.

Nonno unfortunately passed on when I was just nine years

old and as such, my memories of him are sweet but extremely short. He was a man with a quiet and thoughtful demeanour and easy-going disposition. Considering he was surrounded by five women in his own casa (as he called his home), I am certainly not surprised. He was totally outnumbered and he probably could not get a word in edgeways, or even allowed to have an opinion or say on any matter in the home. But he must have been a strong-willed, broad-minded man to have not only accepted it, but survived it.

Having moved to a foreign country, learned a foreign language and adapted to the life in England, would have been a culture shock for both my nonno and my nonna during that time period. But to see their own daughters grow up as English women, must have seemed totally alien to them and yet they welcomed the blending of cultures, embracing it with grace.

My grandparents never spoke much about their families or life prior to reaching the UK. When Anne and I went to Italy, I found out from old family documents that my grandfather's family were rich land owners in Monte Cassino, and obviously lived a very comfortable and good life. However, for reasons known only to them, they left Monte Cassino and familiarity, travelling into the unknown to start a new life together, away from their well-to-do family and their past. A past that was left behind and of no importance or relevance to them, as they were into the here and now.

The documents also indicated my grandfather's Italian family name was Soave. But when they lived in England, while my nonno was still known as Angelo Soave, all their daughters were known as Suvali. I have till today, never received the answer to my question about their change in family name. What was their reason for going so far as to change their identity?

Why was their past a closed chapter in their lives? Did their families not want them to get married? Did they have a falling out with their families? Why did they never keep in touch with any of their respective families? Do I have relatives in Russia? Did any of my grandfather's family survive one of the bloodiest and longest engagements of World War II, during the battles of Monte Cassino in 1944? Or did the total decimation of Monte Cassino eliminate any family I may have had? The quick-fire questions keep coming but unfortunately, there will never be any answers, and this part of my history will continue to remain a mystery to me.

Like most children growing up, heritage and family history was way down the list of my interests and priorities. Subsequently, life and its daily plans for me took over a great many years, and I not only lost the inclination but I did not have the time to pursue the matter. Eventually, when I came across a copy of my grandparents official documents relating to the period before they left Italy, I decided to look into it. But I could not get any further information from the authorities in Monte Cassino. By this time my grandparents, parents and my mum's siblings were all no more and my most genuine source of information had just slipped from my grasp.

However, the Monte Cassino comune or town municipality, said they were extremely happy to receive a copy of my grandfather's birth certificate, as all the records in their archives were destroyed during the war. They had never seen an original birth certificate issued during that period and it is now placed on display at their premises.

My grandparents had integrated extremely well into the

English lifestyle. Though, unlike their daughters who were brought up as regular English women and spoke like all English folk, my grandparents' command of the English language was far from perfect. Considering I do not speak Russian and my command of the Italian language is extremely basic, who am I to judge them?

As an overactive mischievous child, I used to be chased around the property by my nonna, a wonderful and caring woman, who started berating me in English for my misdemeanours, saying 'I'm going to put fire on you' in a foreign accent, and continuing in a foreign language when she either forgot or ran out of English words to use. I laughed at her as I did not understand a word she said and this made her more cross, while I just burst a gut laughing. I loved my grandparents and even though they spoke differently it did not bother me. Being a child I did not realise it was their European accents, and the fact they spoke English with that fascinating foreign intonation. To me they were just my nonno and my nonna.

My nonna was a great cook and I thoroughly enjoyed the food and gelato she prepared at home. At that time, gelato was just ice-cream to me. I had alsolutely no concept of the authenticity of the Italian gelato she made and as far as I am aware, as she did not have any of her recipes in writing, she took the recipes of all the delicacies she created, with her when she passed on.

I have carried extremely fond memories of my nonno and my nonna throughout my life, and even though my memories of them have faded with the passage of time, they have never disappeared, and I absolutely enjoy reviving them on occasions like this.

My grandparents Angelo and Anna Soave in Monte Cassino, Italy

Nonno and Nonna Soave with daughters
Concetta, Lena, Nicolina and Nell

Nonno Angelo and Nonna Anna Soave in England

Nonna Anna Soave with monty, at the beach in Herne Bay

Chapter 2

World War II – the dark days

My mum Nicolina was the third daughter born to my grandparents, on 5 November 1909 in Croydon. She married John Forrest my dad, who was born on 15 June 1910, in the coal mining town of Silksworth, Sunderland in the north east of England. Like most residents of Silksworth, and following in his father's footsteps, my dad worked down the mines as well. He had facial scars as a result of accidents in the mines. Over time, the coal dust had formed a dark blue tinge under the skin of his scars making them very pronounced, but he carried them with pride.

My parents started their married life at 18 Beddington Terrace, West Croydon, in Surrey and Marie my sister followed soon after. Five years later, just after the start of World War II, I joined the family on 31 January 1940. While my dad belonged to the Church of England, my mum was a Roman Catholic and my sister and I were baptised into the Catholic faith.

In any part of the world, war forces young children to grow up quickly and take on responsibilities within the family. Like many families, my mum took care of Marie and myself when my dad enrolled and joined the military to serve in World War II. He was commissioned into the British Eighth Army and was a despatch rider stationed in the North African deserts of Egypt and Libya.

The horror of war leaves a permanent mark on the mind of a young child. Instead of rainbows, laughter and happy times, my early childhood memories were of sirens, bombs and disaster. But it was not a frightening time for me. Instead, like most young lads I guess, I found it exciting looking at the planes flying overhead, and the bombs whizzing across the sky, without having any concept of danger and the disaster waiting to happen.

Everytime the sirens screamed (day or night), my mum ran with us to the Anderson air raid shelter my dad had installed in our back garden, before he joined the war. It was only a small shelter approximately ten foot in length by five foot in width, and had benches along the length of the shelter on the left and the right side. She had covered the narrow floor area between the benches with a mattress and a few pillows, as I was just a toddler and it was a safe play area.

My mum also equipped the shelter with blankets for the three of us as very often like everyone in our neighbourhood, we had to spend the night in the shelter. In addition, my mum kept some books, toys and items to keep Marie and me occupied, as well as food, water and a couple of oil lanterns since there was no electricity in the shelter. We stayed in the shelter till the sirens gave us the signal it was safe to return to the house.

Every home was required to have blackout curtains over all the windows. If the curtains were not drawn properly and even if a sliver of light shone through, we could guarantee there would be a knock on the door, and the night wardens patrolling the area would enter the house to ensure the curtains were closed completely. They were very strict as any light however dim, would act as a beacon and could get the area bombed by the Germans. Every day the bombing brought new distruction to areas all around us.

When I was around four years old, the age when children see things, remember it and have an over-load of questions about it, I regularly looked up at the sky along with my mum and other residents, and followed the path of the silent doodle bugs. These pilotless flying bombs looked like small planes with wings, and we watched their flight paths after the sound of their engines stopped, to see where it would hit and cause a firestorm of distruction.

The German Luftwaffe had once again commenced bombings from June 1944 to the end of the war in 1945. Over one hundred doodle bugs were aimed at London every day. To protect the British Isles, the defence measures adopted by the British comprised of several batteries of anti- aircraft land to air Bofors guns. However, as the range of guns could not hit all the flying bombs which moved so fast across the sky, barrage balloons as well as fighter aircraft assisted in shooting very many of them down before they reached their targets.

There were around three thousand massive unmanned non-rigid air ships or blimps across the skies, which were commonly known as barrage balloons. Nearly one-third of them were over the London area. These huge kites were tethered with a long steel cable, and posed a severe risk to incoming bombs and enemy aircraft flying at lower levels, before they reached their targets.

Croydon was also the home to two airfields called the Beddington and Waddon Aerodromes, which were not far from where we lived. These twin aerodromes were combined to form the largest aerodrome near London, and became the main terminal for international freight into London, with all cargo and subsequently, commercial aircraft using its services.

But World War II saw the airport's status elevated to that of a fighter airfield, and it was renamed as RAF Croydon during the Battle of Britain. Thousands of troops were transported into and out of Europe from this airfield. The airfield was still in use occasionally long after the war, as I noticed the odd plane when I went with my friends to the public swimming pool located next to it.

I found out when I was older, that during the blitz on England which initially spanned over an eight months period from 7 September 1940 to 11 May 1941, the German Luftwaffe bombed London consecutively for fifty-seven nights. Many of the bombs missed their targets and caused distruction in our London borough of Croydon instead, due to its proximity to London. My mum said we spent more time in the Anderson air raid shelter than in the house during this period.

Compared to other cities in England, Croydon was the city most bombed by German bombs and doodle bugs and suffered extensive distruction. The Luftwaffe initially were targeting London but unfortunately, now that Croydon's airfield was being used as a military air base, Croydon was one of the most bombed cities in England. As is well recorded, these bombs and doodle bugs or flying bombs wrecked havoc and caused immense distruction to the country's infrastructure, with thousands of innocent people dying during these attacks. We were extremely lucky as though our home was located close to the Croydon airfield, our area was saved from any major tragedy.

As in any war time, food was heavily rationed and many

items were hard to come by. Every family was provided with a ration book and they could only purchase what they were permitted to buy, based on the size of their family. Food continued to be rationed for many years even after the war ended.

From the time I started school, I used to have my lunch in school. There were very many poor families like mine who relied on the meals supplied to the children in schools. For some families living way below the poverty line and in a worse situation than us, these free meals were a life saver and was the only meal the children had in a day.

After the war when I was a bit older, I went rabbit hunting with Freddy Walker, a friend of mine who lived a few doors away from my home. We crossed the railway tracks to the industrial area where there was a considerable number of rabbits in the small woodlands. Both of us had good Milbro catapults and we were top-notch with our sling shots. Rabbits are very quick animals and scamper around like lightening. We aimed our catapult at a rabbit and followed it till it slowed down on reaching its burrow, and shot it at the precise moment it was entering its abode.

A good many families were forced to eat rabbit in those days, as meat was still expensive and like them, it was beyond our affordability. As such you could say that when I was still in short pants, and before I even reached double digits, I provided for my family and was responsible for putting food on our table, since my mum frequently cooked the rabbits I caught.

A friend John Wilkinson lived according to me, in a house of plenty in Tankerton Terrace which was a few houses from us. John had said his father's trade as a window cleaner was regarded as essential to the country and it was the reason his father was exempted from joining the war services. Being children, we naturally did not question nor give his explanation a second thought. As his father was paid in cash for his window cleaning services, their family was in a position to purchase luxuries on the black market like non-basic and non-essential food.

John always had chocolates with him but being a rare and expensive commodity, he ate it around us but never ever shared it with the rest of us friends. Like my other mates, I too as a young child, felt that being so poor was terrible since we could not buy chocolates. I had never even tasted a chocolate and like all kids in my age group, it was all we were interested in.

But my mum explained to me that life would get better after the war, and we would have to manage without complaining till then. I knew my family could not afford these little luxuries, but even at that tender age, I was determined to eat as much chocolate as I could when the war was over. I guess it was the juncture in the road, which took me directly to the diabetic club as lifetime president. My sweet tooth has been with me ever since and infact, just like me it only gets better with age.

When I was growing up, I did not have toys or get presents for birthdays or even Christmas, like our children expect and receive in our modern day world. There was no Christmas tree or decorations in our home, nor a special Christmas family lunch. I never did experience the excitement of a child trying to stay awake for the midnight arrival of Santa Claus, or even leaving old Saint Nick a serving of milk and cookies.

I never had my friends over for a party to celebrate my birthday, or experience the joy at ripping open the wrapping paper on my birthday and Christmas gifts to see what was inside, or even the simplistic pleasure of blowing out the candles on my birthday cake in front of my friends. My mum always did her best to give us a normal life within her resources. She never failed to bake a small cake for Marie and me on our birthdays as like most people, money was extremely tight and my mum had to literally count the pennies to look after us.

It makes me wonder about my elder two children, who were always whining about not having everything they wanted during their growing up years. As in contrast to my upbringing, they had an extremely comfortable life in the lap of luxury. I presume they are the epitome of the 'spoilt child', who is unable to differentiate between wants and needs.

Growing up in the 1940s World War II period, posed its own sort of discrimination. I was too young and naturally I did not recognise it as discrimination, but my mum did. We led a satisfactory life for that period in time, but we were not a family of any great means. When a child cannot reciprocate a friend's birthday party invitation with a return invitation, you just get knocked off the invitee list and will never receive an invite again.

Yes, as a young child I was at the receiving end of discrimination from our fellow English neighbours, on the basis of my family's lack of financial and social standing. Ofcourse I was upset whenever it happened. As a child, it did hurt like hell to be shunned by the young lads I regarded as my mates. But my friends Leonard Offed who lived in a foster home at 19 Beddington Terrace, and Margo Flight who lived in the foster home at 17 Beddington Terrace, were also never invited, and we three just put on a brave face, learned to overlook the exclusion, and carry on with our daily life.

The one gift I enjoyed as a child was a rocking horse my parents bought us. Both Marie and I used it and while it was not a new horse, it was our new rocking horse and I loved it. My parents would have liked to give us gifts on occasions, just as we give our children. However, it was a luxury they could not afford, over the cost of basic family living expenses. But I never complained, and nor did my friends living in the foster homes on either side of our home. Leonard and Margo were my good friends and both of them had no other family of their own.

We played together in our gardens or on the street and as we had no toys, we made up games and had fun in our own way with sticks, stones and home made rustic toys. As we did not know any different, it did not bother us not having toys and presents. One day we were playing on the street, and decided to have a competition as to which of us would be the quickest to climb up a tree on the pavement outside our homes. I was the last to have my turn and just as I made my way nearly half way up the tree, a man passing by thought I was having trouble getting down. He reached up and pulled me down literally by the seat of my short pants, with a big smile on his face and a pat on my head. Leonard and Margo were laughing ever so hard, as I now had to start climbing the tree all over again and needless to say, I did win the competition from the rear.

At the end of the day, I had a home and family to go to, though my dad was away in the army. But Leonard and Margo lost their complete families and the authorities kept moving them from one foster home to another. As such during my childhood years, I made and lost more friends than I care to remember. Initially I would get very upset at losing a close friend. But as I grew up, though it was hard for all of us kids, we understood their situation and accepted the fact that we would never be life long friends, as even they never knew where they were being sent to next.

I was a grown up five years old with an old soul in 1945, when the war ended and my dad returned home. It was like meeting and having a strange man living in our home. But more importantly, getting to know my dad for the first time was not easy for the young lad in me, and it involved strategising on my part, just to converse with him.

Further, I also did not find him a very communicative man. On my return from school he never asked me how my day was and what I had done in school. He never ever played any games with me, read me a story or even spent time to chat with me. I could understand if he did not have the time due to a busy work schedule. But he had yet to find a post-war job, and despite having so much free time, trying to engage him in my life was a non-starter.

The first father-son bonding session we had was when I helped my dad dismantle the Anderson air raid shelter, and earned a momento for life to prove it. In my eagerness to help, I tripped and fell on the corrugated sheeting, cutting my leg. Instead of concern, the first words my dad expressed was of his displeasure at me for injuring myself and requiring hospital attention. Irrelevant of the fact I was just five years old, he expected me to behave like a grown up, be more careful and not cry like a child.

Life slowly reached a new normal as my parents said. But then, I did not know what normal was as I knew nothing else but life during war. On his return from the war, my dad took me with him to Silksworth to visit with his mother, as she had never met me and naturally, I was excited to meet my nan for the first time.

One day I borrowed my cousin's bicycle and I was trying to learn to cycle around my nan's home, when I had quite a tumble with the bike, breaking my wrist. My dad was really furious at me for ruining our holiday, as he had to take me to the hospital once again to get mended. It seemed he regarded me as a clutz, and not as tough as he wanted a son of his to be.

Though times were really difficult, my mum ensured Marie and myself were well looked after. We did not have a lot but we were healthy and we had enough to survive. For that, I will be ever grateful to my parents. After the war, my dad joined the Croydon Milk Depot, while my mum started work in Paynes chocolate factory. At the end of work every day, the chocolates that were rejected by the inspection team because it did not pass the factory standards and could not be officially sold, were packaged in small bags and sold at a cheap price to the staff working in the factory.

As my mum had promised, she bought Marie and me chocolates once a week after the war. Marie kept her share for herself, but I was finally able to have a surfeit of chocolates to satisfy the cravings of my sweet tooth. I also kept aside enough to share with my mates from the foster homes on either side of our home, and we all enjoyed our daily sweet treats. And before you ask, no - we did not share any with John Wilkinson, as he still never shared his own private stash with us.

Post-war, everyone did their best to get on with life. During my growing years, my parents took us by train to Herne Bay a few times a year, to visit my nonno and nonna as well as my aunt Concetta and uncle Ark. But more importantly, to give us a fun time at the beach. It was great being spoilt by all the adults, and I always looked forward to those trips.

My cousins Tony any Terry were young teenage lads at that time, and naturally they did not want to be bothered by a kid, or spending their time entertaining me. As such, I had no friends of my age in Herne Bay, but I did have a very special friend in a lovely dog called Jip. My aunt and uncle informed me Jip was really a stray, who always hung around in the alleyway behind their house. As I made a real fuss of Jip, he was my constant shadow everytime I visited Herne Bay, and my only friend.

A very nice elderly retired man called Sandy was a lodger in my aunt's home, and he used the shed in my aunt's rear garden to make and store the fishing tackle he made. With no friends of my own, I always tagged along with Sandy who taught me the art of fishing, and he is without a doubt responsible for me being a first rate angler today. He took me on his fishing trips and even let Jip and me hang around with him while he was working in the shed. When he took me fishing on the lake, our furry friend Jip always joined us. He would get into the small canoe with us and actually sit very still opposite me. My nonna's dog Monty, named after General Montgomery, also stayed by my side whenever I was at my nonna's home. However, Monty only responded to my nonna when called, as he probably only recognised her European accent.

It is said the youngest child is the pampered and spoilt child. But in some respects, though I was the youngest, I always ended up with the short straw by default. From the time I was old enough to understand that money does not grow on trees, I had to help my mum with chores around the home. As I grew older, I even helped my mum to dry the clothes by turning the handle of the mangle, while she fed the clothes through the rollers, which certainly is no mean feat for a child. Marie was supposed to help my mum, but she always managed to get out of doing her chores by going out with her friends.

In those days all of us had our baths on the same day. Like most middle class houses in the 1940s, while the house we lived in had a separate toilet, there was no bathroom. We had a large oval galvanised tub hanging on the exterior wall by the side of the kitchen exit door to the rear garden. It was brought into the house twice a week, placed by the fire and filled with hot water. My parents had their baths on one day while my sister and I had ours the next day. Marie had her bath first, always taking ever so long, you would think she was the Queen of Sheba. And as you can guess, by the time I got a chance to have my bath, not only was the water tepid, but it also had the queen's soap scum in it.

When I complained to my mum, all she said was that's how it is as 'girls are made of sugar and spice and all things nice, and boys are made of frogs and snails and puppy dog tails'. That was it. I was young and I was expected to follow the house rules, irrelevant of how ridiculous it was. In retrospect, I can now laugh at my mum's explanation to a child. However, in those days I doubt I would have made much headway in bringing up the matter of 'equality' anyway, even if I had known the word or what it meant. But I did make a vow to myself that when I grew up, I would always be first in everything and never again be pushed to the back of the queue in anything, or even share my personal bathroom with the family.

My mum's older sister, my aunt Lena also worked at the chocolate factory with my mum, and she always gave me a handful of chocolates whenever I went to her house to visit with her. My mum regularly made me go and visit with my aunt, and when I returned home with my pockets bulging with chocolates, my mum would ask me innumerable questions about my aunt. I was too young to understand the reasons behind my frequent visits, and some time later my aunt suddenly died.

When I was older, I learned my uncle Cecil was a womaniser and his constant affairs and unfaithfulness over the years, had driven my aunt Lena to despair and eventually mentally affected her. My mum never visited my aunt Lena at their home, as she neither liked nor wanted to see my uncle Cecil, and that was why she regularly sent me to check on my aunt Lena and report back to her.

However, the situation got to a stage where my aunt Lena could not take my uncle's unfaithfulness any longer. One day, she just turned the gas oven on, knelt down and put her head into the oven, breathing in the gas fumes till she passed out and died. She must have felt so alone and at the darkest place in her life from where she saw no positive outcome. I just cannot begin to imagine in what state of mind she was in, to consciously do what she did.

Unfortunately, unlike in our world today, mental health was not given high priority in those days. My mum never did forgive my uncle Cecil for driving my aunt to take her own life, and though they had three grown up children Jean, Josie and Peter who were much older than me, with the exception of Marie, our families had lost its closeness as my uncle remarried not long after.

Out of the blue one day, I went to the milk depot to visit my dad and see where he worked. I was astounded to see him gambling with his colleagues at a table in the canteen.

I observed him for a while without being noticed, and went home to inform my mum of what I had seen. Many years later my mum said she had to support our family on her meagre salary, as my dad only gave her an extremely small housekeeping allowance, and she only realised about his vice when I brought it to her attention. My dad was obviously not a good gambler either, as he kept losing his money and squandered his wages at the card tables.

However, my mum said that it appeared the war also took its toll on my dad as he had started gambling, something he never ever did prior to going to war. Life at home during this immediate post-war period was tense and not a happy time. My mum silently bore the financial burden of the family and overlooked my dad's absence from the home and his lack of financial as well as emotional support. She worked at the factory the whole day and in the home for her family after work.

Like all young children, I just got on with my life - family, home, school and friends as well as learning to enjoy life through the fading memories of war, and by blanking out the situation at home. But as I grew older, I knew I would do everything I could to break out of being at the bottom of the scrap heap, with little or no money at my disposal. While I was never ashamed of my parents, I felt my mum deserved so much more, and I certainly did not want to be the man my dad had become. At the back of my mind, I also hoped I never again witnessed or experienced war, and the associated very dark side of life.

People seem to think they are protecting and shielding children by not explaining to them the reasons for war, disaster and the cause of all the ensuing distruction. However, from my personal experience, I believe avoidance of the issue is detramental to the mind of the child. It causes confusion in the child's mind, especially when peers spread misinformation that is told to them by their elders for the very same reasons.

From the time I was adult enough to understand the reason and causes of the Second World War, I assimilated all the information that came my way, learning the true reasons for the war in the process. The evil that caused the torture and deaths of millions of ordinary innocent people like me was shocking, and it did not seem right that people suffered and died for no fault of theirs.

There will always be power hungry, egotistical and evil persons in this world. I believe there has to be a few bad to make the good stand out. But it is up to each one of us to make the choice to expose and bring to justice our evil compatriots.

Young as I was, how could I complain about the early years of my life, after knowing the reasons for World War II? as my life seemed like Heaven compared to what they would have experienced. Who are we to judge the citizens of our world? We may be a diversity of race, colour and religion, but to me everyone is equal and there is no superior or inferior race, colour or religion. Every individual has the same chance to make something of their life, but it is the opportunities presented to us and the personal choices we make that maps out our chosen path.

Many people who experience personal tragedy, go through life looking for closure. For me, though my experiences of the war is nothing compared to the suffering of the millions who were incarcerated and killed in concentration camps, it inculcated in me an underlying interest in the history of the war.

As there are several visual factual documentaries available, my interest continues to this day not only about the evil persons responsible for the torture and killing of millions of innocent people, but also the heroes who risked their lives to save the Jews and children during the war, as well as the nazi hunters responsible for eventually tracking down the absconding war criminals who thought they had escaped justice.

During my growing-up years, travel within our cities was by trams on rails and trolley buses, both being powered by overhead electric power lines. However, when I entered my teenage years, I cycled seventy miles each way between Croydon and Herne Bay once a week, just to visit with my nonna for a few hours. After my nonno had passed away, my nonna lived on her own. I always looked forward to catching up with her and never regarded the six to seven hours cycling each way as a hardship. This same distance can be travelled by car today in just over an hour each way.

I went to Herne Bay to help my nonna with any difficult jobs she could not do, and which she kept aside for my visits. Yes, my older cousins Tony and Terry were around as they lived in Herne Bay, but my nonna said no one from the family visited her or offered her any help. She just managed as best as she could till I made my weekly visit. These weekly visits were my bonding time with my nonna, who always had a huge cast iron pot of delicious meat sauce simmering on the wood fire stove in the kitchen. As I love all food, after a double or triple helping of spaghetti and this out-of-the-world sauce, I was so stuffed that I had a very tough time cycling the long trip back home to Croydon.

However, once I went to sea, my nonna was on her own

again, and struggling to manage all her household chores, with no family help whatsoever. And at her advancing age, she must have gone through a real hard time.

As a young child, whenever I complained to my mum about doing my chores as well as Marie's, she told me to never ever stop doing little things for others, as sometimes those little deeds of mine, took up the biggest part in the hearts of the people I helped. I will forever cherish my mum's infinite wisdom and I will always be thankful I made time for my nonna during her life, as she passed away on the 9 December 1959 while I was away at sea.

I was shocked to learn from my mum that when my nonna passed away, my aunt Lena's husband - my uncle Cecil and my aunt Counge's husband - my uncle Ark (who were also brothers), went to my nonna's home and cleared it out. My nonna had beautiful ceramic clocks in every room in her home and I developed my love for clocks from her, as I too have a unique clock in every room in my home now. My nonna also had very impressive large but delicate ceramic chests in which she stored her fine linen. Through the years, everyone in our family could not fail to notice these rare items in my nonna's home. But my mum and my aunt Nell never did get even a souvenir from their mum as unfortunately, my uncles appropriated everything when my nonna passed away.

It was during my growing-up years, my uncle Jock first introduced me to cars, and when I fell head over heels in love with cars of all shapes and sizes. My uncle Jock and aunt Nell were successful and financially secure. They had a 1947 model Lanchester which was a real beauty, with the doors opening in reverse to our modern cars. He took me for a spin in it and

I could not stop talking about my experience for days. And so started my initiation into the world of fancy cars, which seemed so far out of my reach at that period in my life. But I developed an unending love for high end cars that has never faded with time, and I give full credit for my passion for cars to uncle Jock.

When I reached my teenage years, I was allowed to go out with my friends. But if we were visiting any place where we had to spend money, like to the cinema or for a snack, I backed out of joining my friends. They did not know it, but I never did get any pocket money from my parents, like my friends received from their parents.

I would never take advantage of my friends generosity to loan me the money, as I knew I would not be able to repay them. I also did not ask my parents for money. My mum would offer me money whenever she could, but I never ever accepted it as I knew how she struggled with the housekeeping expenses. I tried getting an after school job but it was illegal to employ children even on a part time basis, and much as I wanted to earn some pocket money, a job was out of my reach.

Eventually, when I turned fourteen years, I managed to get a job in a nursery selling home grown plants and flowers. It was a part-time outdoor job, moving potted plants from the green houses to the area just outside the shop floor. No one liked to see children working on the shop floor, so my job was just working outside. While I attended school during the week, I worked on Saturday mornings at the nursery.

Unfortunately, the nursery was in Selsdon, South Croydon, and I had to travel to and from the nursery by bus, which naturally cut into my weekly wage, though I still had money left over to go out with my friends. That was when plans for my future became clear to me, as I figured only hard work would bring in enough money to make my world go around.

Despite the odds, I grew up into a normal young lad. I completed my high school education at the Lan Franc School for Boys on Mitcham road in Croydon. As the school did not have a football field, my friends used to kick a ball around in the school's small play ground. I was never interested in football, so I joined the school's amature boxing team and enjoyed expending my energy with several energetic bouts in the ring.

I do believe my early life during the war defines me as the individual I am today. It is responsible for the strong ambitious streak I developed, with a tremendous zeal for wanting to push my boundaries to its limits, to achieve the impossible dream on my horizon. It made me realise that while it is fine to dream, it takes focus, determination and hard work for those dreams to materialise.

It also ingrained in me the fact, my life is just a journey to my final destination. My road will undoubtedly be strewn with a multitude of colourful obstacles in the form of problems I would have to overcome; persons I would encounter over time - some who would be a part of my life; sad and tragic times; as well as many fun and happy hours that will always remain with me. Whatever my future held, I knew I would never ever forget my origins or the dark days of my early start in life.

John and Nicolina Forrest, my parents

Me

With my mum and Marie

Chapter 3

Breaking free on the high seas

I always dreamed of being an engineer, but as I was also intent on simultaneously earning a living, I could not avail of the free-of-charge full-time public university courses. With no other viable options available to me, I made the decision to make my own way in the world, and I planned my own future on completing school.

Just out of high school, I worked as a trainee fitter and welder with Brown and Davis in West Croydon for a short time. Hector the workshop manager took me under his wing and trained me in ark and gas welding, and I definitely learned from the best, as I was the most proficient in all the companies I subsequently worked with around the globe.

At the same time, I also made plans to join the National Sea Training School, which would pave the way for my entry into the merchant navy. I wanted to get away from England and the ghosts of war which still haunted my childhood memories. But I was also eager to broaden my horizons, while at the same time experience the various facets of life that the rest of the world had to offer.

I was acutely aware during my growing years, my dad found me a disappointment, as he always wanted me to be a rough and tough lad who played football. My dad was a serious football fan and regarded lads who played the game, in the league of real men. So when I told my dad I wanted to join the merchant navy, I was not surprised when all he said was 'go my son, it will make a man of you.'

I expected an argument with my parents as I was just fifteen years old. But I received none. It was that simple. There was no fuss or farewell fanfare. My parents were not much into showing their feelings, nor expressing their emotions. Or as I say in jest, what they suffered from was the so called 'British stiff upper lip syndrome'.

It was a bittersweet moment saying goodbye to my parents, knowing I would not see them again for quite a while. For the first time I was in charge of my life. I made my way to the National Sea Training School at Sharpness on the river Severn in Gloucestershire, on my own steam. My school friend Ian Pepper who had also joined a few days ahead of me, was there to greet me at the entrance of the school. We lived on-site and trained intensively with several other young lads for the next three months, on the training ship the T.S. Vindicatrix. It was both extremely interesting and a lot of fun, over and above the hard work we put into our training.

We were trained to excel at all jobs on a ship right from navigation, signalling and reading the compass, handling the boats and the associated ropes鱼work as well as cleaning and working in the mess hall. My dad was absolutely right. Life on board was no piece of cake and it did toughen me up, considering I was still under instruction and had not even started working as yet. I was also entrusted with caring for our chief officer's pet canine. However, as I love all animals, it was a pleasure and not a chore.

Boxing was encouraged, and I spent my free time going a few rounds in the ring to keep up with my personal physical training. As fighting was off limits on the premises, whenever any of the lads got into a fight, they were sent into the ring to settle their disputes and we all enjoyed a bit of light entertainment.

On graduating, we took up jobs directly from the National Sea Training School and went our separate ways, though Ian and I kept in touch. At sixteen years, my newly acquired zest for life had just started and I was on the crest of a wave, looking forward to traversing the high seas into the unknown, travelling the globe and making my dreams into reality.

I was the only seaman from my batch of new merchant navy recruits to join the PandO (Penninsula and Orient Shipping Lines) ocean liner 'SS Himalaya'. She was built in 1949 and was the largest ocean liner built anywhere in the world at that time. My excitement knew no bounds as I embarked on my first trip as a working crew member, and just the beginning of my goal to reach that elusive pot of gold at the end of my rainbow.

We sailed from Tilbury in England enroute to Australia and there was a celebratory atmosphere onboard, while God ensured that calm seas and fair weather was with us. However, not long after leaving Tilbury while we were cruising the Mediterranean on 30 August 1956, tragedy struck.

There was an accident onboard due to a gas leak in one of the domestic refrigeration chambers. This caused a massive onboard explosion sending a huge fireball which ripped right through the working companion way and crew area, leaving four crew members dead and more than a dozen crew with various degrees of injuries and severe burns.

The tragic scenes of the disaster and the aftermath will always be etched in my memory. Acrid smoke lingered in the whole area for a while. There were hand-print burn marks on the blackened bulkheads, and the smell of burning flesh and death is something I will never forget, as it was in the air for a long time after the incident and it seemed to follow us everywhere we went.

I did not know the crew who worked in the refrigeration area. But I knew they were highly qualified personnel and experienced in their jobs. However when fate struck, they were gone literally in a flash, before they had the chance to live the rest of their lives or realise all their dreams. And it could very well have been me.

Being my first trip, this unfortunate tragedy did not bode well with me. But when talking with my crew mates about what had happened, it brought to mind the uncertainities of life, and it made me all the more determined to make a success of myself, and enjoy life to the fullest while achieving it. My resolution made, I never looked back. I enjoyed every minute of my time on the vast expanse of oceans, and mastered all the onboard jobs I was assigned to handle. I made several acquaintances and quite a few friends, as well as learned and excelled in water sports. I maximised the time of my shore trips by enjoying the sights at every port of call, and ofcourse like all merchant navy crew, I got a few mandatory tatoos on my arms for good measure.

After the disastrous accident and unfortunate start to my first trip on the 'SS Himalaya', my life on board was extremely interesting, informative and certainly enjoyable. Since that initial tour of duty, my fascination with ships and boats took on a new meaning, and it was the start of my eternal love affair with the high seas and its hidden enigma below, as well as all sporting activities associated with it.

When travelling the world, my excitement at visiting the various countries was unparalleled. I was utterly in awe of the individualistic architecture particular to each country, and as I love food, without a doubt I thoroughly enjoyed experiencing and partaking in their local cuisines. Though I must admit my adventurous palate appreciated the fare of some countries more than others.

But my fascination really was the very interesting people I met, and interacted with along the way, in some countries. Not only was I taken in by their diverse cultures, but I was floored by their exotic looks, which was enhanced by their colourful regional attire, giving them an air of orginality which was unique to each country, and I loved that.

My travels however did bring to light one glaring fact. I realised that no country in our world is free of prejudicism in some form or the other, and one incident comes to mind. In the late 1950s when we called in to port in Bombay, India, I went sightseeing in the city with fellow ship mates.

A young Indian man approached us and we tried to communicate with him with a lot of hilarious signing and back slapping. At once another Indian man approached us and spoke very rudely to this man, who then slowly turned and walked away with a dejected air. When we objected and went to the first man's defence, the man who intervened stated in broken English that the man was an 'untouchable' and in India, the higher castes do not mix with the lower castes.

We tried to explain that as we were not Indian, we did not

belong to any caste, and we had absolutely no problem mixing with anyone. But by now, quite a raucous crowd had gathered as we seemed to have caused quite a stir, and so we just bade them farewell and left the area post-haste. However neither my ship mates nor I could identify any pertinent differences, physical or otherwise, between all the Indian men around us.

I found such openly acknowledged and accepted discrimination between the citizens of India, under the guise of an invisible 'caste system', shocking and an astounding revelation to me. I understand that while casteism still exists in India today, times have since changed with education playing a major factor, and it is now not as endemic or so stringently followed, though like all countries prejudicism unfortunately exists.

After three tours of duty with the 'SS Himalaya' I joined another PandO sister ship, the ocean liner 'TSS Strathaird' as a crew member. I then moved on to the PandO ocean liner 'SS Strathmore'. With the vast sea faring experience making a credible mark on my bio data, I left PandO behind me and joined the BP Shipping Line, and crewed on their oil tanker 'British Sovereign', before bidding a final adieu to the high seas and the many mysteries that lay beneath, for terra firma on the largest of the British Isles.

In 2014, I went down memory lane and visited Sharpness. Though the National Sea Training School has long since been closed, a monument has been erected in dedication to all the seventy thousand young men who passed through its portals, including the many who sadly died during World War II.

I also enjoyed visiting the onsite pub that exhibits innumerable memorabilia relating to the school and its students. And it certainly was a pleasure meeting and chatting with a few other men who had passed out of the school, and reliving stories of the good old days.

'TS Vindicatrix',
a training ship for young men joining the merchant navy

On my visit in 2014 to the 'TS Vindicatrix' Monument in Sharpness

Chapter 4

The return of a man

Surprisingly by 1960, I was looking forward to finally returning to England as an adult, and an independent life for myself. My parents had mellowed, and once again had a close relationship with each other. They were pleased to have me at home as Marie had got married while I was at sea, had left home and was starting a family of her own. My nonna had also passed away the previous year and I really missed catching up with her.

My dad was now working as a postman with the Royal Mail and back on the rails, so life on the home front was normal, and I enjoyed spending time bonding with my parents. While I always loved and respected my dad and mum, I just wanted much more for myself than the life they had. To me there is a vast difference between existence and living. While I believed they just existed from one day to the next, I wanted to experience and live the best possible life I could.

I lived at home with my parents for a couple of weeks. But much as I loved them, my independence was more important to me. I first stayed as a paying guest with the Fields family for a short while. However as I wanted my privacy, I later rented a flat of my own in a house in West Croydon, which gave me my much needed own personal space.

I also started working at the Croydon car breakers, as the owner's son Barry French, a professional boxer, was a friend of mine. At the same time, I also decided to equip myself with a proper trade in hand. As I was interested in steam engines, I registered with the employment office and did a fireman's course. On completing the course in Horsham, Surrey, I was sent to work at the steam locomotives goods yard. I worked on the steam locomotives and we used to shunt cargo carriages from one location to another in South Norwood. However, having got the practical experience I needed, I left the job in a few months.

I then qualified in plumbing and mechanical services and as I was now licenced, I could work anywhere in the UK. My experience on the steam locomotives was an advantage to my qualifications as I also specialised in steam installation. Subsequently, I worked in various companies to expand my experience portfolio and my final job in the UK, was in 1966 with Burn Brothers (London) Limited as their Labour Supervisor.

On my previous tour of duty when I changed ships in England, I had met and got friendly with Jean, a young woman in Croydon. She worked in a local clothes shop as a window dresser. We corresponded with each other while I was at sea, and immediately on returning to England, I went round to her house to visit with her. However, it seemed she had been stringing me along and she was just another good time girl.

Since I was away at sea, she was also in a relationship with my close mate John Sullivan, as they were together when I went to Jean's house. Though Jean was the one at fault, I took a swing at John. He was not only my mate, but he broke our mates code of never encroaching on a mate's territory, as he knew Jean and I were dating. That was the end of my relationship with Jean. John and Jean too were not a couple for long. John later met and married a lovely lady Maureen, and they had two beautiful daughters. John and I subsequently patched up our differences and we remained friends through time. I am glad I made the effort to travel to the UK to attend John's eightieth birthday in 2019, as he sadly passed away in August, 2020.

It was great catching up with my old mates and joining their social scene as I was now permanently back in town. However, having been at sea for so long, I felt I had outgrown my friends as we were no longer on the same wave length and for some odd reason, I did not have very much in common with them anymore. They were also all couples - some were married and the rest had girlfriends. Though I was initially single after breaking up with Jean, my mates were great, always ensuring I was one of the lads, and I never ever felt left out. Through my mates I did meet and get friendly with a few girls, and from then on I always had a date to all our social gatherings.

After I returned from my first trip on the 'SS Himalaya', and before I went on my next tour of duty, at the age of seventeen I bought my first car - a shiny black second hand vintage Hillman Minx Open Tourer. It was a 32 model and I was extremly proud of it. I rented my cousin Jean's garage a few doors from my parents home for ten Pounds Sterling a month, as they did not have a car and my parents did not have a garage. Further, parking my car on the street in front of the house where I lived was not an option as it would have been stolen in the blink of an eye. As I was the only one within my group of friends with a car, let's just say if my Hillman could speak, it would have quite a few tales to tell.

From then on I had a multitude of cars over the years. Whenever a car in excellent condition and with its original documentation came in to the Croydon car breakers, they would contact me. I would buy the car and enjoy it till the next car came along. A very unusual car I purchased once was a Buick straight 8 hearse in excellent condition. It was large, spacious and a wonderful car to drive, though for a young man like me, it was a very expensive car to run as it only did twelve miles to the gallon.

Whenever my group of friends wanted a change of scenery, we would all get into my Buick, drive to Brighton and spend a day on the beach. All the lads chipped in to fuel my gas guzzler, and as it carried all of us with space to spare, it did not cost each of us a lot, ensuring we had a great lads day out. We always had a great laugh at the reaction of people when I parked my hearse next to them. The expressions on their faces at having a dead people carrier right next to them however, was nothing compared to them seeing a bunch of live and noisy lads roll out of the back of it. To say we enjoyed ourselves at their expense, would be putting it extremely mildly.

One evening my mate Vic Bivand asked me to pick up his girlfriend Georgia, and take her to a party we were attending, as her house was on my way. Her father was a minister of the faith and he answered my knock on the door. He took one look at me, saw the tatoo of a crucifix on my forearm, and asked me what denomination I belonged to. When I answered I was a Catholic, he just slammed the door in my face.

To say I was shocked would be grossly understated. How in Heaven's name could a minister behave in such an appalling manner? The fact he personally did not practice religious tolerance even though he probably preached it from the pulpit, made a complete mockery of his role in the Church and Christianity itself. If this was the way he treated fellow Christians, I dread to think what reception I would have received if I was a non-Christian.

I did not hang around to see if his daughter was coming to the party. I left and made my way on my own and if Vic's girlfriend did attend the party, it was certainly not with me. I explained to my mates about my run-in with the minister that evening, and they just laughed, not at all surprised by the reception I received. I on the other hand was exceptionally surprised when a few years later Vic married the minister's daughter.

My football loving dad never let an opportunity go by without mentioning I was a let down to him, and he wished I was more football oriented like my friends, especially Vic who played for the famed football club Crystal Palace. Several times my dad said to me 'why can't you be more like Vic?' Whenever my friends were either playing football or at football games, I never joined them as football never did sail my boat. So other than the company of my friends, I did not miss anything. Instead, I was working or pursuing my own interests.

I had joined the Amateur Boxing Club in Croydon and earned myself quite a few knockouts, while also being on the receiving end of a few hard-hitting bouts from some excellent sportsmen, which damaged the hearing in my right ear. However, my dad did not regard boxing as the combat sport it is. But it was my life and I was not going to change my ways for him or anyone else.

One day with some free time on hand, I accompanied my

childhood friend Freddie Walker, to the boxing club in Tooting. Unlike me, Freddie was not only a much larger man but he was also more of a 'no holds barred' tough street fighter than an amature boxer like me. At the club I was first given a bout with one of the club's regular boxers. On completing my three rounds, Freddie went up against another club boxer in his weight category.

But during the bout, Freddy boxed the club's boxer in the face and expecting a second punch in the face, the boxer hunched his head and body and put his arms up to protect his face. However, Freddy simultaneously brought his knee up instead. His opponent got quite a shock from the unexpected ferocious knee attack to his face, which should never have happened in the boxing ring.

However with Freddie and his street fighter mentality, we always expected the unexpected. The boxer was bleeding profusely, and the next thing we knew was that we were literally being thrown out of the club. It was the only time I went to a boxing club with Freddie, who had always been a real character. Many a time he used to be seen sashaying down the street to the shops at the end of our road, tottering in his sister's high heel shoes and giving all the neighbours a lot to laugh about. He later got married and I lost touch with him, though I subsequently heard he very sadly never survived a road accident he was involved in.

My mates were great lads, and though we have all travelled through the ages miles apart, I have kept in touch with them. However compared to them, I was more impelled to get ahead and succeed in my life's goal, while they were extremely happy with their lot. My work prevented me from spending as much time with them as they would have liked and it was unfortunate that my dad never did figure out how driven his only son was to succeed in life, till it was too late and he was on his death bed.

In 1961 I met Phyllis, who worked as a pump attendant at a fuel station in Croydon, where I regularly filled fuel in my car. While I knew nothing about her, she was a petite, attractive, flirty and outgoing woman the same age as me, and we chatted everytime I went to the station to fill up my car. We got friendly and started dating.

At that age, I guess like most young men I too was only interested in outward appearances and not the internal beauty aspects of women. Phyllis dressed to attract the opposite sex and they certainly were attracted to her. However, my ego was coasting on a 'high' as I had the woman other men desired. I was too young to even contemplate entering into a serious relationship. As such, despite the fact I was extremely attracted to her and in love with her, I was only looking for a girlfriend. Nevertheless, I have always been a person to wear my heart on my sleeve, and not long after we met, she moved in with me and we were in an exclusive relationship, or so I thought.

It seemed to me Phyllis was in some sort of a relationship with the son of the owner of the fuel station she worked at, as I had seen them together many times. However, she suddenly left her job at the fuel station and took a job with a rival fuel station in Croydon. While she did not say anything to me, I can only suspect it had something to do with the son of her now ex-boss and I must admit, I did wonder where I fitted into this grand scheme of things.

Chapter 5

Warm hearth – cold heart

Within a year, I found that at the age of twenty-two, I had to step up to the bar and be a Dad myself, as Phyllis got pregnant pretty early in our relationship. Initially I was not sure how to take the news of the arrival of a child. Phyllis was my girlfriend but children were not on the cards or even talked about. I was brought up to believe children should only be welcomed into happy marriages and I was not ready for marriage. Even though I was in love with her, I was not sure if Phyllis and I were marriage material together, atleast that was what my gut told me. I felt Phyllis had trapped me into a relationship I was too young and definitely not ready for, as we were a couple for hardly two minutes.

My life changed overnight as I did not plan either on having a child, or getting married at such a young age. But our daughter Sharon, a bonny wee lass arrived in October 1962, and the moment I saw her I was enthralled and she was loved and wanted. While I pushed myself even harder on the work front as I now had her as my responsibility, I pulled my weight in the home as well to care for her. The saying that it takes a whole village to bring up a child is not far wrong, especially when you are young and inexperienced yourself. The only problem was we were on our own, and we did not have a village to help us. As both Phyllis nor myself were religious, we also did not get Sharon christened.

Now that I had a child, I thought it was only correct I did right by her. So Phyllis and I got married in 1963 in a civil ceremony. It was not the normal wedding everyone expects to have. It was a spur-of-the-moment wedding and not planned. I did not see any point in having a big affair as we were not only living together but we also had a child. However, the main reason was that I was the only earning member of our small family. As I did not believe in living beyond my means, I did not have any extra money to splurge, even if Phyllis did want all the frills of a fancy big wedding. As such, we just went to the registry office and exchanged vows, with my mate John Munt as a witness. There was no bridal attire, no wedding guests or feast and absolutely no fuss. Not even my parents or the rest of my mates knew I got married, till I informed them of the fact after Phyllis and I had tied the knot.

Unfortunately, my parents neither liked nor got along with my new wife. Though Phyllis looked like every young woman in the 1960s, my parents said she was frivolous, not house proud and more importantly, not a suitable wife for me, with their words 'why did you have to marry her?' constantly ringing in my ears.

Phyllis was dusky complexioned and of Anglo-Indian heritage. My parents were not prejudiced in any way but like all parents, they just wanted what they thought was best for me, and in their eyes Phyllis was not the best wife for me. Being a forthright person, my mum's own words actually were 'she even dresses like a tramp'. Phyllis in her own flamboyant and 'couldn't care less' attitude, contributed to the acrimony.

Eventually, to avoid any discord at home, I kept my parents and my wife apart, even though I regularly visited my parents alone, and finally a modicum of peace reigned in my life.

However, within a short span of time, my parents' views resonated with me as there was an incident which saw me getting treatment in the emergency department. This was followed by an operation to stitch the cut tendons in my right wrist and forearm, leaving me with scars I carry around till today as an unwelcome reminder.

Not long after we were married, Phyllis said she wanted to go to a new club called Utopia in South Croydon to meet her friends, and I said I would take her there. As usual, Phyllis had no problem finding someone to babysit Sharon. I was neither a club person nor a drinker and as such, I was not familiar with the night life in Croydon, as I never ever visited clubs with my friends. With her directions, we got to the club and to my amazement, I found that her friends were all unsavoury males.

Some time later while we danced on the central dance floor, someone tapped me on the shoulder and wanted to cut in and dance with Phyllis. I told him she was my wife and he could not dance with her. One thing led to another, and suddenly all I knew was that the bouncers who were also friends of Phyllis, got hold of me and strong-armed me away from her.

According to me, these men did not give my wife the respect I thought she deserved, and I stood up for her and her honour. But they thought differently, as they unceremoniously threw me down the stairs of the club with such force, I went flying right through the club's frontage floor-to-ceiling glass windows and onto the street below. An ambulance was called by some curious but kind passersby to take me to the emergency department as I was badly injured.

What was both surprising and extremely unsettling, was the fact that Phyllis did not stand by me against her friends in the club. She let them manhandle me without a word. She did not come out to check on what happened to me and how badly I was injured, despite the chaos on the street and the siren blaring when the ambulance arrived. To rub salt in an already open wound, she further did not bother to accompany me to the hospital, but preferred to turn a blind eye and remain up in the club with her unpleasant friends, who had just attacked and injured her husband. Her behaviour sent alarm bells clanging loudly in me and I wondered what I had got myself into.

I only saw Phyllis early the next morning when she returned home, way long after I was stitched up and sent home from the hospital. But she never explained herself or her whereabouts till that unearthly hour of the day. Nor did she bother to ask me how I was or about the seriousness of my injuries, even though she saw my hand right up to my elbow set in a cast. I found it strange, my wife chose to remain at the club with those men rather than be with me. In my view, it was certainly not the behaviour of a newly married woman supposedly in love with her husband.

A few days later when I was in town I bumped into an acquaintance I knew just by sight and who also happened to be at the club on that fateful day. He did not know I was married to Phyllis and I found it hard to digest what he told me. He informed me that after I was taken away in the ambulance, Phyllis was intimate with quite a few men at the club. He painted a vivid picture of Phyllis as a common hooker.

This man seemed to know so much about her personally, and

about what had transpired at the club, that I got the distinct impression he was one of the men who had his way with her that day. It became clear to me now about their lack of respect extended to her at the club. They were treating her not as a respectable married woman dancing with her husband, or even a woman friend, but as a well known hooker dancing with her customer.

Whether her intimacy with these men was consensual or not I would not know as she never brought up the subject. She also never indicated in any way that she had suffered any trauma from being molested or raped either, as if she did exhibit any signs, I would have taken immediate action with the authorities. She was unaware I now knew what had taken place at the club Utopia after I was literally thrown out. Nor did it seem to even bother her about what the men did to her, and I got the apparent notion she was accustomed to intimate relationships with those loathsome pieces of garbage.

I on the other hand, could not get my head around it and our marriage started cracking up even before it had time to mature, with unanswered serious questions fogging my brain. Who had I actually married? What did I know about her previous life? Was she a professional 'woman of the night' outside her day job, as all the evidence now pointed to? What was I going to do about my new wife and her scarlet ways?

That was the first and last time I visited a club with Phyllis, though I am sure she continued to frequent these night spots as several times when I returned home from work, I found Sharon was left with a babysitter. Why would a married woman continue to frequent night spots around town without her husband? Or was I just blind to the obvious?

On these occasions when Phyllis eventually returned home long after the witching hour, she never volunteered any information as to her whereabouts, but I always did catch a tell tale whiff of cigarettes and alcohol enveloping her. If I asked, she just said she was out with friends. No apologies for coming home at such a late hour or even enquiring after Sharon and whether she was OK. We were just married but already living two very separate lives under one roof.

Doubts about her past were now beginning to haunt me, and it brought to the forefront of my mind how little I actually did know about her, as she was a very secretive person. She also continued to dress in seductive clothes to attract men, though she was now married to me. I never ever spoke to her about her attire, even though I personally did not think it was appropriate, as I just left it to her judgement. But she obviously did not care what I thought anyway, as she continued to dress to please herself. She definitely did not purport to my mum's 'good girl' image as my mum obviously saw the tramp in her that I was too blind to see.

I worked long hours and never refused any overtime work I could get. But the accident at the club Utopia put me out of commission as my hand and forearm was in a cast, and I could not work in my day job for a few weeks till my arm was back to normal. However, with a family to support, I could not let a day go by without earning a wage. So I disguised my injury with long sleeves and took on a temporary graveyard shift job instead, at a large bakery in Wimbledon, loading and unloading crates of bread onto the delivery trucks all night long.

I would do anything to ensure my daughter wanted for nothing, but unfortunately, this entailed I worked extremely long hours and in the process, it curtailed my time with my family. Phyllis was thus free to meet up with her men friends without me finding out. I continued working in Croydon, always moving up the ladder to a larger company and a better paid job as it was paramount I was able to provide the best life for my family.

However, life has a knack of throwing curve balls and in early 1964, not even a year into my marriage to Phyllis, I realised that from all accounts, it seemed my parents were on the right track with regard to my wife. They saw what my rose tinted glasses prevented me from seeing.

To my utter consternation, I found out not only did I have a high maintenance wife, with a secret life involving intimate liaisons with a large male population of Croydon, but she also had a special boyfriend Malcolm Townsend, whom I never knew about till now.

If this news was not shocking enough, she further informed me she had a child with him and they had given the child up for adoption just prior to her marrying me, and the child was now in the social services foster care system. But what was totally mind blowing, was the fact they were still continuing their clandestine relationship right through our marriage, and I had no idea of any of this till now.

This news following the episode in the club Utopia, caused a major upheaval in our marriage, and my home and safe haven was now hell to live in. Needless to say, at the age of twenty-three, I had a very hard time processing all this information and how to handle the situation. What did all these men who drew her to them like a magnet have that I did not have? Was I not enough for my wife that she had to constantly satisfy her desires outside our home? A plethora of questions needed answers and I did not have them.

The lifetime of happiness I expected when I married Phyllis, turned out to be just a very short trip on the ferris wheel, with highs and lows and an abrupt stop on reaching its lowest point. My parents too had ups and downs after World War II, but they loved and stuck by each other through it all. My marriage on the other hand was a sham as how can you have a marriage - happy or otherwise, with more than two people in it? I now realised the cause of the depths of despair my aunt Lena went through because of her philandering husband. Obviously Phyllis was no different because she just paid lip service when she said our marriage vows as unlike me, she had no intention of honouring them.

Sharon was my priority but not even for my innocent little girl could I continue to live with her mother any more. Her mother had not only used me, but she abused my trust. She cared only for herself with absolutely no love, respect or regard for me or Sharon either. If she did love me, she would never persistently commit adultery as she had been doing.

I cannot call whatever we had, either a relationship or marriage, as a relationship is a connection between two or more people but what we had was only one sided. I had no idea where I was going and what I would achieve by leaving. All I knew was that I had to figure it out for myself and I had to do it far away from my cheating wife. Telling my parents was not an option as they would no doubt just say 'We told you so!'

So in March 1964, I resigned from my job with Rawlinsons in Thortonheath, Croydon. At the time I worked with them as a charge-hand on the construction of the Middlesex hospital.

I had even bought a motorbike for the journeys to and from work, so I could spend more time at home with my wife and daughter and less time on travelling to and from work. It seemed futile now as 'home is where the heart is' but, there was no heart in my home.

I informed my parents I was going away on a solo road trip. If they found it out of character for me to leave my young family behind and go on a trip alone, they kept their thoughts to themselves, and just told me to have a safe trip and to keep in touch.

My mind made up, I hugged my daughter goodbye, knowing she would be the only one I would miss. I packed a bag, filled up the fuel tank of my motorbike and with a map in hand, I left the house with just enough money for me to manage for a short while. I left the rest of the money in my bank account for Sharon's maintenance, which I was sure Phyllis would depleat pretty fast. I got on my motorbike and rode off without ever looking back, leaving my darling daughter, adulterous wife, disastrous marriage and the UK behind me.

Chapter 6

Gaziantep – Turkey (Europe)

Far away from England, meant across the pond as the English say. So started my solo road trip across Europe. My journey from England ferried me across the English Channel to France on the European continent. As I had no definite itinerary and had never been to central Europe before, I just used my direction map and decided to travel through the central and southern European countries.

My logic was based on the fact that as it was in March, nothern Europe would still be very much colder and not conducive for my open air premium lodgings. I was travelling with just a small amount of money, and I had no options but to sleep rough under the stars by the roadside, wherever I was heading. To tide me over, I had already decided I would work my way through Europe to supplement my existing funds, depending on the length of my trip.

From France I rode blindly right across Europe through the north of Italy, into Slovenia, Croatia, Yugoslavia (now known as Serbia and Montenegro), Bulgaria and into Turkey. I had a sleeping bag and I just roughed it out on the roads at night, under a blanket of stars. There were no proper roads as a majority of the highways through Europe, were not really of the motorway standards we know today. Their condition was good but not excellent, and left a lot to be desired when riding on a motorbike never really meant for long journeys, as it certainly did not help my rear in the least.

While I stopped at fuel stations to fill up the fuel tank and use the washroom facilities, I would stop at any small wayside eatery for a bite, when hunger pangs forced me to give in to my grumbling tummy. English was a totally foreign language in all the countries, and though communication was mostly by gestures and faltering signing, the folk were friendly and I did not have a problem understanding the people enroute, nor being understood.

Other than getting thoroughly soaking wet, I had a tough time riding through Yugoslavia in a ferocious rain storm. I was forced to stop at a small house by the side of a road in a little village. A man and a woman came to the door and from my very bad sign language, they managed to figure out my predicament and very graciously invited me into their home. They put a mattress on the floor of their main living area and also gave me a couple of blankets. I was ever so grateful for a good night's proper sleep on a thin but comfortable mattress.

The next morning they even shared their simple breakfast with me. I don't think they realised what their genuine hospitality meant to me. They were poor but they still welcomed a total stranger without a second thought, into their very own palace. I did not have a lot money with me, but they seemed extremely thankful for the three Pounds Sterling I gave them (equivalent to around fifty-three Pounds Sterling today).

I loved the old world charm and unspoilt beauty of the countries, as I travelled through Europe. The changes in the stunning scenery, complemented the striking buildings and historic monuments I saw in the various countries enroute. It was definitely meant to be recorded but as I never had a camera, my photographic memory had to work overtime, absorbing every infinitesimal detail. However, much as I would have liked to spend time checking out all these marvellous countries, I did not give in to my inner wish.

A sightseeing trip I was definitely not undertaking. Instead, I was on a journey of forced introspection and as I had no travel plan nor deadlines, I had a lot of time to think about my situation while riding through Europe. Unfortunately since I was travelling alone, I had no one to talk with, bounce my views against, or vent my anger and confusion to. My mind as such, was working overtime at full throttle, and though I was covering miles of ground and increasing the distance between me and England, I was no nearer to finding a solution to my marital predicament.

Riding aimlessly into the wind, I entered Turkey and continued riding further through the country. However, God had probably decided that 'enough is enough' and He had other plans for me. I met with an extremely serious road accident just shy of the border with Syria. My motorbike was a total write-off and I was found lying unconscious and critically injured on the road.

No one knew when and how the accident happened, or for how long I was lying unconscious on the road. Nor was anyone aware as to who alerted the police and medical services about the accident. It was a long shot anyone would claim responsibility for my accident, as I understand they were long gone from the scene of the crime when the police arrived. However the police later informed me, based on the condition of my motorbike which was lying in their custody, I was definitely involved in a high speed head-on collision with a large four wheeled vehicle.

As the accident happened on the highway far from any town, the Turkish medical services did what they could for me medically, at the site of the accident. They then transported my unconscious and literally stone cold body to the nearest hospital, which was the American Missionary hospital in Gaziantep.

Till today, I have absolutely no recollection of how the accident happened. All I know is the medical team at the hospital said many a time that they did not expect me to survive the night, leave alone make a complete recovery. I later learned every professional in the hospital was on code blue alert, as I was brought into the hospital not just unconscious, but also with a practically non existent pulse which they struggled to regularise. In addition, my alarmingly grave condition was a cause of acute concern as it was compounded not only by multiple broken bones, but also the extensive internal injuries I suffered as well.

The medical professionals said though their team worked darn hard, and did their very best to keep me alive, there were many tense moments when they genuinely believed their work was in vain, and they were losing me. They said that while they put their skills to good use to try and save me from going to the netherworld, it was nothing short of a miracle I had survived the crash, as medically I was literally knocking at death's door.

I went through a very long and slow recovery process, and I was in the hospital for very many months. In the wake of eventually coming out of the induced coma and regaining consciousness, I found I had responded positively to the surgeries as well as treatment, and due to the excellent medical professionals, I was going to live not just another day, but many more years to come.

It felt like I had visited the afterlife and come back to earth. I now knew I would never again ever take my life for granted. I was just given a second lease on life and I would do my utmost to make every moment of my life count for something, and live my life as best as I possibly could. After the extremely hard work put in by the phenomenal medical team, it would certainly be exceptionally crass of me if I did not make the dedication to their profession count for something.

Having been a patient in the hospital for way over six months, I got to know the staff very well and made good friends in very unusual circumstances. When I was nearly recovered and the time was nearing for me to leave the hospital, I was presented with such a large bill that short of begging, stealing or breaking into a bank, there was absolutely no way I could afford to pay it. On discussing my quandary with the hospital management, I offered to work for them to settle my debt. As they required someone to handle their local maintenance crew, I accepted their job offer as a maintenance engineer.

Being a missionary hospital, they naturally did not have any accommodation to give me. As my complete salary for the next many months was going towards settling my hospital bill, I also did not have any money to even rent accommodation in the town near to the hospital. My motorbike was beyond repairing and I never did claim it back from the police station.

However, as it turned out I did not need transport anyway. The hospital very kindly allowed me to continue living and working at the hospital, because I was still under treatment and in recovery. So I continued to sleep in my hospital bed during the night, while working with and training the local crew on all their maintenance jobs during the day. The Mission also provided me with all my meals, and I have never been so appreciative of hospital food.

The maintenance jobs were varied but constant, keeping me and the small team of Turkish tradesmen I was instructing, very busy. I repaid my hospital medical bill within eight months, from my salary. However, they wanted me to continue working with them. Since I was not yet ready to go back to England, as I felt there was nothing left for me back home, I continued to stay in the hospital and worked with the American Mission in Gaziantep.

Gaziantep or Antep as the city was locally known, was a Turkish gem when I lived on its soil. The centrally located fortress with its innumerable watchtowers was an imposing beauty in art, which could be seen from afar. I loved the traditional old houses with their central inner courtyards, which was the main communal area for the house members. The bazaars had a colourful vibrancy, with an open invitation to spend time, and experience its haphazard and cacophonous surroundings. And last but certainly not the least, I thoroughly embraced the hamams or Turkish baths as it was a real exhilarating novelty for me, and it helped revive not just my broken body but my weakened spirit too.

By August 1965 I had got my thoughts together, with time and distance being instrumental in healing me mentally and emotionally. I then decided the time had come for me to face my future and whatever life had in store for me back home. So I resigned my job with the American Mission hospital. Since

I had no motorbike or vehicle to get me back to England by road, the hospital very kindly paid for my air ticket to England. I was now regarded as a part of their team and while I was sad to leave, they were equally unhappy at my impending departure, after our long and close association.

These good folk had not only worked ever so hard to bring me back to life and make me whole again, but they also empathized and helped me when I could not pay my hospital bill, or return home to England. Thus with a heavy but thankful heart, I bade farewell to the wonderful family I was now very close with. Averse though I was, I returned to England and to my still fractured family after seventeen months away, with great trepidation.

Chapter 7

A new life through a magnifying glass

On arrival in England, my first stop was to visit my parents. Not having heard from me for over a year and a half, I convinced myself I needed to immediately put their minds at rest. Or, was I just delaying going home and dealing with the inevitable? Whatever my actual reasons, my dad and mum were very well and extremely pleased to see me.

It was absolutely not surprising to learn that during my long absence, my parents had not heard anything from Phyllis nor seen Sharon at all. We fast tracked on the news and events while I was away, though I still did not apprise them on the situation between Phyllis and me. They would have been ever so pleased to know their views of my wife were absolutely spot-on. The news I had finally come to my senses, and would be starting divorce proceedings against Phyllis without delay, would also certainly give them peace of mind.

Time and distance did not remove from my mind all the evidence that pointed to Phyllis' secret life, which was more akin to a red light district. We could have had a good life together, but she threw it all away because of her addiction, and constant desire for sampling an array of the two-legged lupine variety. My views may sound harsh but firstly, I had a very long time to review everything in my mind a hundred times over during my time in Turkey, and my views remain unchanged. And secondly, I did not think I should settle for second rate as I believed I definitely deserved much better.

We all know that any person who is molested, gang raped or sexually assualted, most definitely suffers physical trauma. But I personally am of the opinion, the associated mental trauma that effects the victim is much worse. It goes to the extent of requiring professional help to assist them in finding a way to continue to move on with their lives, despite the fact their horrendous experience will never be erased from their memory.

Phyllis expressed no sign of any form of distress or trauma at what those men did to her at the club Utopia. She did not know I was later aware of what had happened, or that I was searching for the signs she never displayed. I had to finally accept that her behaviour and attitude pointed without deviation, in just one direction. She believed that variety was the spice of life, and marriage or not, she was certainly not a woman capable of being in a monogamous relationship.

While my decision regarding my marriage was made, I was not sure how my parents would take the news I was also filing for sole custody of Sharon. I was disturbed that if I did not assume entire responsibility for Sharon, Phyllis would give her up for adoption like she did with her eldest daughter, just to liberate herself and get on with her life, without carrying around any unwanted and inconvenient baggage.

On my part, to be the sole carer for a toddler at twenty-four years was not ideal and would certainly not be easy. But having grown up with friends living in foster care, I was determined it was a place my child would never experience. Like the many single Dads out there, I had unquestionably no doubt I would manage my work and home responsibilities more than adequately, if not perfectly.

There was absolutely no communication between Phyllis and me since I left the UK in March 1964 and now in August 1965, I was no closer to knowing what my reaction would be when I actually reached my home.

As I entered the flat, a mini tornado on legs hurtled herself at me. Hugging an excited Sharon, at once I knew I had made the right decision, and whatever happened, she was one person I would never let go. I thought she would have forgotten me after so long, but Sharon not only knew who I was, she was chatting away at nineteen to the dozen. You can just imagine my jaw dropping shock at discovering from her garbled conversation, she now had a little brother and she was eager to introduce me to him.

It seemed while I was away, our family had just got bigger. Not only did I have a second child, but my son Tony was born in December 1964, while I was in Turkey, and he was now eight months old.

I went through a complexity of emotions when I saw him. The split second of sheer joy and happiness at the birth of my son, was overshadowed and followed by an aeon of brain churning scepticism as to whether he was my biological child. Knowing what I did about Phyllis, I could not prevent myself from constantly but surreptitiously looking at Tony, and searching for some family resemblance to me.

In the seventeen months I was away from the UK, Phyllis must have had a 'free for all'. Considering she was neither faithful to me, nor our marriage vows when I was in the country, she had carte blanche while I was away and it was a fifty-fifty chance that Tony's paternal origin could go any which way.

Infact, I even started wondering about the paternity of our daughter Sharon. It was absolutely heartbreaking to even think these two beautiful children might not be biologically mine. Unfortunately, in those days DNA testing was unheard of, and there was absolutely no way to even clear my doubts and settle my tumultous mind from unnecessarily overworking itself.

Now that Tony too figured in the equation, my decision to divorce Phyllis had just nose dived. I felt like I had broken from my moorings, and was swimming against the currents in a stormy sea of very troubled waters. Divorcing Phyllis was the easy part. My issue was the fact there was no way I could bring up two little humans on my own, while working a full day at the same time to support them. Unfortunately, while I was willing to embrace toddler day care for Sharon who was nearly three years old, I did not believe in baby day care for Tony who was just eight months old.

Was I scared? Sure I was, to the very depths of my being. But I gave myself a pep talk that since I was alone, I had to stand tall and strong and depend on only 'Me'. I had to let go of my fears, and put myself out there to face whatever was being thrown at me. I initially did with apprehensive bravado, which much to my surprise, quietly and without so much as a whimper, turned to an abundance of self-confidence in my ability to handle any impediments that blocked my road ahead.

Phyllis and I were currently like strangers living under one roof to care for two little children. Our communication was practically non-existent and when we did converse, it was stilted. I was experiencing a massive tug-of-war between my head and my heart and eventually, my head won as I had to be practical.

Reaching my decision definitely did not come easily to me, as my life had spun out of control in the last few years. At the age of twenty-one I was footloose and fancy free; at twenty-two I was a Dad; at twenty-three I got married; at twenty-four my marriage was in tatters; and now at twenty-five and despite the terrifying odds, I had decided to step up to the finish line.

I was determined to put the jigsaw of my shattered marriage and life back together again, as well as be the best possible Dad to two little innocent children who may or may not be mine. I was not sure if I was up to the task, but as I was brought up to always uphold my responsibilities, I was going to give it a darn good try.

I now knew beyond the shadow of a doubt, Phyllis was not the right wife for me. She was the first pretty woman who threw herself at me since I returned from the high seas. But then, she unfortunately did not turn just my head. She was a woman who dressed in such a way so as to get it to work to her advantage to draw in the men, which would not have been such a bad thing for her if she was single. However, she was far from being single, as she was not just my wife but also a mother to three young children, and yet she continued to dress provocatively for the attention of other men.

Unknown to me, not only did she have a secret life, but she was also not single when we got together. She kept the knowledge she had a boyfriend and a child away from me. But as the man she fancied could not give her the life she wanted, she married me and kept her lover close too, thus giving her the best of both worlds by sitting on the fence, and going which ever way the gate opened.

Naturally, I felt I had been deceived and taken on one heck

of a joyride. It was totally soul destroying at the young age of twenty-three, to learn the woman who I emotionally invested in and married, and who I thought was committed to me in return, actually never loved me for 'Me'. All she wanted was the respectability of a marriage, which would allow her to covertly continue with her clandestine lifestyle, as she loved and thought of no one but herself and her excessive needs.

But for me, love cannot be turned off like a faucet, and I loved my children. Phyllis may not be the right wife for me, and she may be a lying and adulterous woman, but with my decision made, I now had the responsibility to continue to financially care for her as the mother of my children, even though I no longer trusted her. I just may have it in me to put all this behind me and hopefully forget it with time, but I knew I never would ever forgive her for what she did to destroy the idealistic young man in me.

I was born tough on the inside and not one to throw in the towel just because the road ahead was arduous. So for the sake of the children, I had a long talk with Phyllis and gave her an ultimatum. I informed her I was not going to divorce her at the moment, and I had decided to take her back solely for the sake of the children, along with what was left of our marriage which she had so cruelly ripped apart. I would work to put our family back to some semblance of normalcy for Sharon and Tony, as no child should ever be brought up in a disfunctional marriage.

I further made it crystal clear that if she ever strayed from our marriage again, I would have absolutely no misgivings about divorcing her without a second thought. I also informed her that since the children were born within the period of our relationship, and because we were still legally married, though my doubts on their parentage will stay with me forever, I decided not to dispute their paternity as they were the innocent parties in this family debacle.

As far as the world is concerned, they are my children, they bear my name and I will love and care for them. However regardless of the facts, I do believe all children have a right to know who their biological father is. As such, I told her it was a decision she would have to make at some point, as even though I may or may not be their father, there was no disputing the fact that she definitely was their mother.

Even though I was taking her back, what we had was dead as I could not trust her any more. In my book, without trust in a relationship you have nothing, and for me Phyllis switched off the light in our marriage when she wilfully extinguished the spark. Now what we had was just a matter of convenience.

Like most men, I was inbred with the primal instinct to care for and ensure I am able to provide for my family to the best of my ability, whatever my situation. On returning to the UK and with the growth of my family, I found my responsibilities and financial expectations increased tremendously. Phyllis had given up work when Sharon was born and did not work again.

I got a job with A.N. Coles (Contracting) Ltd on my return from Europe, and I kept moving upwards and onwards to better paid contracts in different companies, as I had to push myself even harder to ensure my children wanted for nothing. I now had to also give Phyllis the materialistic life she craved, just so that she had an incentive to remain in our marriage for the sake of our children. It seemed that love was not on my cards, so I decided I would instead chase the next best thing – Money.

With long hours and hard work, I eventually found myself

solvent again and with a pretty healthy bank balance, I decided to invest in property. I purchased a three storey house at 24, Blyth Hill, Catford. It was divided into five studio flats, with each flat having its own pay-as-you-go electric meter. I completely renovated the building and all the flats on my own during any free time I had, and at times with the help of a great neighbour of West Indian origin, Percy Carter.

Percy helped me to put up the wall paper in the flats as I had absolutely no clue about wall papering. I then converted the ground floor into a self-contained flat for myself with a complete internal kitchen and bathroom, and I rented out all the rest of the flats. When my flat was ready, I moved the family out of our rented flat in South Norwood and into our own property in 24 Blyth Hill. Though many moons have gone by since I sold the building, I still keep in touch with Percy and his lovely wife Joan and even introduced Anne to them on one of our visits to Croydon.

Eventually, it seemed to me the time had come for me to make the decision to move with my family into the next phase of my life, and put distance between Phyllis and her lover or lovers, if I wanted our children to have a stable and as happy a family life as possible. I did not expect my life would be easy, as with the seeds of suspicion now deeply embedded in my mind, every man Phyllis came into contact with was a prime suspect. I also knew that due to my lack of trust in her, I would be consciously looking at my relationship with her through a magnifying glass, searching for minuscule signs she was continuing to defile our marriage agreement.

I regard myself as a highly principled man, and my word is always my bond. If I make a commitment I will never ever default on it. It was no way to live my future tied to a fictitious marriage. But my priority was the upbringing of my children, and sacrificing my personal happiness for their future seemed a small price to pay at that time, to ensure they could look forward with a positive outlook to all their tomorrows. In December 1967, I joined The Drake and Skull Engineering Co. Ltd. in Croydon, and accepted their very promising overseas contract position in Mauritius. And thus started my life traversing the globe as the inveterate 'Rainbow Chaser'.

Chapter 8

The call of the Indian Ocean – Mauritius

December 1967 – April 1969

I fell in love with Mauritius a small British Crown colony, the moment we circled overhead to land on this tiny volcanic island, on the south east coast of Africa in the Indian Ocean. The scene from the air on approaching the island, with its rich and luxuriant green vegetation circled by white sandy beaches and clear turquoise water, was mesmerising.

But on landing in Port Louis in December 1967, it was even better than I expected. My new life was surrounded by a very picturesque landscape of 1960s modern colonial island living, with extensive areas of lush sugarcane fields surrounded by craggy furrowed mountains. Combined with the warm sunny climes and a vast cultural mix of extremely friendly islanders, without a doubt, our welcome to Mauritius was the start of a life I was eagerly looking forward to.

My company put us up in a hotel while I found a house for us to live in. Drake and Skull Engineering was contracted to build the first hospital in Mauritius. The Sir Seewoosagur Ramgoolam national hospital (SSR national hospital) was located in the north western district of Pamplemousses, which means grapefruits in French. With the hospital name more than a mouthful, we just called it the national hospital.

The hospital was being named after the first prime minister of independent Mauritius. At that time however, Mauritius was still under the rule of the British Crown, as the transfer process was not completed. Our company was to hand over the completed hospital in 1969, and on commencing operation, it would be the largest and most modern hospital in Mauritius. My part was supervising the plumbing and mechanical services, with a thirty man strong team of local labour working with me. Infact, the SSR national hospital is till today the largest hospital in Mauritius.

After scouting around the areas surrounding Pamplemousses, I found a very nice house named Peyton Place in Quatra Bornes and we settled in well. I also bought a 1963 Singer Vogue, as a car is absolutely essential for traversing this beautiful island.

The children were enrolled into the local school and were adjusting to the carefree and laidback Mauritian lifestyle with ease. We even had a Mauritian maid to help out around the house, do the cooking and even help with the children. Life was good and we were living the colonial dream.

But our new island life was taking a turn in the wrong direction. Mauritius was in the process of breaking away from its dependence on the UK and going the independent route. When we arrived in Mauritius in December 1967, the political tension was growing in the country. Not everyone was for Mauritius gaining independence. Nearly half the islanders preferred the country to stay with the Crown, due to the uncertainities of the future and what would happen when the British left.

In January 1968, Mauritius was going through a period of severe socio-political turmoil. There were random clashes between the 'texas' and 'mafia' creoles with the 'istanbul' muslims in the Port Louis area. These clashes intensified into full blown communal riots over a ten days period. Many were killed and scores injured as the riots spread through the island communities.

On 22 January 1968, the British Crown declared a state of emergency, and 150 British troops from the King's Shropshire Light Infantry (KSLI) were shipped in from Singapore, to assist the Mauritian police to quell the violence. They managed to prevent the riots from spreading to the whole country by round the clock continuous patrolling of the streets, and containing the disturbance to within the Port Louis jurisdiction.

Though calm prevailed out of the Port Louis area, tensions were still rife in other parts of the country. Due to the state of emergency, the movement of all residents on the island was curtailed and as businesses were closed, we were restricted to our homes. In a show of support during this period, the Port Louis harbour was also crowded with navy vessels on standby, with the Royal Navy's HMS Carryport and HMS Tartar along with India's Delhi as well as a French and a US war ship all vying for pride of place.

Eventually on 12 March 1968, the British Union Jack was lowered and in its place, Mauritius raised its brand new quadricolour for the first time, and proclaimed an independent Mauritius. There was great jubilation by many islanders on gaining independence, though several others were still fearful of what the future held and did not participate in the celebrations. Life in the country slowly limped back to normal with the British army continuing to remain and assist the Mauritian police.

I learned deep sea diving at the British navy diving facilities which was located away from the port. It was well equipped with all the diving gear as the British naval personnel who practiced there were experienced, and I felt extremely safe learning to dive under their tutelage. Since my only recreational interests were water oriented, whenever I was not working or driving the family around the country to view the superb waterfalls, rivers, gardens, or mountain vistas, I was pursuing my love for diving.

I became quite a proficient diver as I frequently visited the naval diving facilities with a Mauritian friend. Daniel Polizei was my diving partner and he even taught me how to save myself should the need arise, from dangerous and aggressive predators like the shark and barracuda. I not only gained this relevant knowledge from him, but I was now definitely more confident in my new found ability to extricate myself from a deadly situation.

However, once the British left the island, the facilities were converted into a diving club with paying memberships, and open to the general public. I did feel the safety aspect was compromised at that time though, as there were no experienced personnel to teach or be at hand should a novice diver get into trouble. But as I was now a seasoned and experienced diver, I went deep diving in the Indian ocean with my local friends.

Another Mauritian friend and his brother owned a successful boat charter company, taking tourists to the best deep water fishing areas. Whenever they had a spare boat, we lost no time hitting the open water. I spent many enjoyable hours deep water fishing with them, and returning with real prize catches.

My palate was educated when I travelled to various countries while at sea. But I learned to enjoy spicy aromatic food during our time in Mauritius, as our maid prepared a variety of authentic Mauritian cuisine, the likes of which I had never heard of but I thoroughly enjoyed. Many folk eat to live, but I make no bones about the fact I live to eat, and without a doubt I have relished, savoured, enjoyed and appreciated a variety of global cuisine, most people have not even heard of.

The Mauritians are a very friendly, warm and welcoming people and their 'joie de vivre' is extremely infectious. I had a large social scene with a harmonious mix of my British colleagues and their families as well as my local Mauritian friends. As such, socialising was the theme every weekend and more often than not, even during the week, which was a welcome break after a hard day's work.

I made good life long Mauritian friends, I am in contact with till today. We even had our children christened in Mauritius, and the Mauritian police chief Lidd Bosky and his wife who are my close friends, are Godparents to Sharon and Tony.

Our time in Mauritius was coming to an end all too soon. The hospital was completed and handed over on schedule. Drake and Skull Engineering were sending me around the globe to my next contract in the West Indies. So in April 1969, I bid 'au revoir' to the wonderful friends I made, confident in the knowledge I would one day definitely be returning to this idyll I felt so strongly about.

Return to my Utopia

January 1976 – July 1977

My predictions were realised as I did return to Mauritius seven years later. In January 1976, Drake and Skull Engineering sent me on a year and a half contract as their plumbing and mechanical services engineer, to manage and supervise the local labour on two large projects on the island.

Returning to Mauritius was like coming 'home'. I had more wonderful friends here than even in England, and I lost no time in getting together and catching up with them. I was lucky to find and rent a great house on Grand Bay, which not only had a viewing turret, but it was also walking distance from the island's water front.

The children were older now and were enrolled into the local school without delay. As their mother was not working, I left it to her to take care of their needs and run the house. I got back into my diving activities, as well as deep sea fishing with my Mauritian mates, and it seemed as though I had never ever left the island.

I could have very happily lived and worked in Mauritius, and I did plan on becoming a citizen. However, before I could proceed with formalities, Drake and Skull Engineering wanted me to go to their latest project in a place called Dubai, on the eastern coast of the Arabian peninsula, surrounded by the Persian Gulf and the Arabian Sea.

So we left Mauritius in July 1977, positive in the knowledge there would once again be no goodbyes - just 'au revoir', as my soft spot for this enchanting island which had cast its spell on me, had grown to full-blown magical proportions, from which there was no turning back.

With my work mates Colin, our boss - Mervin Bezant, Dave Dunford and Stan Pesea, in Mauritius in the 1960s

Chapter 9

Barbados, St. Lucia, Grenada (West Indies)

May – December 1969

On my second contractual obligation with Drake and Skull Engineering, they sent me to the West Indies to supervise the local labour on the new Holiday Inn hotel project in Grenada. However prior to starting my contract in Grenada, the company required me to first sort out a few projects and train the workers in Barbados and St. Lucia.

In May 1969, I arrived on the island of Barbados sans the family, who were on home turf in England. I did not know what to expect on arrival in the West Indies, though I knew the island had gained independence from the British Empire in 1966, so I was confident I would not experience any communication problems.

I was pleasantly surprised though, as Barbados has charm by the bucketload, coupled with its tropical climate and pristine beaches, with frothy white waves lapping on its shores. If I was even a tad talented, my artistic ability would shine through my colourful canvas.

I went straight to the company to meet John Shira, who was the West Indies general manager for Drake and Skull Engineering. John was a very nice and extremely friendly man, who insisted on personally meeting all company employees sent to the islands. This gave him the chance to not only assess their capabilities, but also to develop a one-on-one relationship with them.

I initially stayed with John and his family at their house, and then I moved in with the site manager for the duration of my stay in Barbados, till I had completed my project. John showed me around the island and even took me to the famed 'Harry's Nightery'.

When my project was completed, John and I flew to St. Lucia which is one of the eastern Caribbean islands, and at that time it was still a British colony. St. Lucia is easily recognisable from the air as on approaching the island, all aircrafts have to circumnavigate the two pointed volcanic mountain peaks on the island known as 'the Pitons', before landing at the island's airport.

While John had a few matters to handle himself, I got on with my projects without delay as I had a lot to do and men to train. I stayed in a hotel and did not have much time to make friends. Though, I did organise my schedule to include visits to all the back street marvels which the regular tourist misses out on, before I left this island with its enormous appeal and fantastic potential.

I then moved to Grenada another island in the West Indies, with the Atlantic Ocean and Caribbean Sea teasing its unspoiled white sandy shores. The island also known as the 'Spice Island' due to its exports of a large variety of spices, had an untouched beauty of mystical proportions. Grenada was still a colony of the British Empire, with Sir Eric Gairy serving as the premier of the island.

I was on a short contract of just seven months, but I arranged for Phyllis and the children to join me and I planned on ensuring we would make the best of what the islands had to offer when I was not working.

I stayed in a hotel while I searched for a place for us to live in and to my good luck, I found a quaint wooden beach house built on concrete stilts. It was conveniently situated just across from the beach in St. Georges, the capital of Grenada and a real beautiful city, located on the south western coast of the island, overlooking the lagoon.

The kids were enrolled into school and I was kept busy at work to meet my company's handover deadline. As the company had given me a car, travelling around the island was easy. And I managed to take the family around this wonderful island of volcanic origin, though all the very impressive volcanic cones surrounding the island have been dormant for a very long time. Being a mountainous island, Mount St. Catherine which is the highest point, was well worth the trek even with the children, just for the view from the top.

We also spent long hours during the weekends, at the beach and the surrounding deep bays, when the weather was good and no hurricane was expected, as unfortunately we arrived on the island just before their hurricane season started. Our visits to the smaller Grenadine islands of Petite Martinique and Carriacou with its stunning sandy beaches, were little gems of these bejewelled islands.

With my work taking up much of my day, and the rest of the time apportioned to my family, I did not get any free time to imbibe in my passion for diving and water sports. It was a real shame as I kept receiving open invitations from the island's welcoming azure waters, which were practically lapping on my doorstep.

As usual I worked long after office hours. By the time I returned home late in the evening, I could not fail to notice the water pressure in the whole area had dropped to an extremely low level. With all the town's residents utilising copious amounts of water, the trickle of water making its way through the pipes, was insufficient for me to even have a shower.

However, as our house was located alongside the coastal road, the open beach was just the other side of the road from our house. As such, every night when the beach was empty of people, I would walk across and have my shower under the open beach shower closest to my house.

One night, as I was stripping off at the shower, I heard a man shout 'whooh, whooh' to get my attention and stop me in my tracks. As normally there was no one on the beach at night, I turned around and saw a couple sitting a little distance away. I waved at them and carried on with my shower. After my shower, when I was properly dressed again, I approached them, introduced myself and chatted for a while.

A wonderful couple - Chuck and Emma Moore, were on vacation in Grenada from the USA. And that was the start of a beautiful friendship. I entertained and showed them around the island, visiting the places that as tourists they would never see. Before they left Grenada, they invited us to visit with them for Christmas as my contract was ending before Christmas anyway.

And so when we left the beautiful islands of the West Indies in December 1969, we made our first trip to the USA.

With Sharon and Tony in Grenada, West Indies

Chapter 10

Fremont, California (USA)

December 1969 – June 1970

When I completed my contract in the West Indies in December 1969, I moved with the family to Fremont, on the southeast side of California's San Francisco Bay Area. It was our first trip to the USA and we were invited to stay with our new friends Chuck and Emma Moore.

As Christmas was just around the corner, the Moore family insisted we live with them and join them, their family and friends, in all the seasonal celebrations for our first Christmas in America. So though we initially stayed with them for the festive period, at the same time I found and rented an apartment not far from their home, so we could move into our own place, as I did not want to inconvenience the Moores' any further.

I was informed Fremont was just like any other American residential area, and as I had yet to get a car, Chuck and Emma showed us around the place. We even went with them to buy a fresh Christmas tree for their home, from a large pop-up tree lot in town. I had never seen an open air Christmas tree shop spring up before Christmas, selling all types of trees arriving from Christmas tree farms. The children thoroughly enjoyed the experience as there was a festive air in town with activities for children as well as decorations, goodies and fairy lights to tempt the Christmas shoppers of all ages.

Being a businessman, every year Chuck received tickets to the Dodge Cars Christmas gala. Emma said the Dodge party was an annual highlight of the pre-Christmas season and it was looked forward to by all the residents of the town. I have no idea how Chuck managed to get extra tickets, but they invited us to accompany their family. It seemed that everyone in town was invited, as the event was packed to the rafters.

We found a table to seat all of us and while we lads went to get in the drinks, the ladies made their way to check out the buffet tables and the delicacies on offer. When all at our table had decided what interested them from the extensive buffet, Chuck left the table saying he was getting me something special, and not to bother with the general buffet.

I was dumbstruck at what he returned with and placed in front of me. It was the largest steak I had ever seen, resting on a massive oval platter that could hold nothing else. As such, all the vegetable side dishes were served separately. I must admit, till today I have never seen nor had a single serving steak that large any where else in the world, and though it took me quite a while, I did it absolute justice and enjoyed every moment of my experience. Needless to say I was a very satisfied man that day, as my eyes and taste buds were completely enthralled by the beauty in front of me. It totally eclipsed all the side dishes, and eye catching as they were, none of them did stand a chance for my undivided attention.

One of Emma's friends was selling their Dodge Charger, and since I needed a car I bought it. A cheap second-hand run-around was just what I needed. It would do us just fine till I found a job in my line of work, if we were going to make the USA our home.

Chuck had his own company and with a team of skilled workmen, his company manufactured both large industrial refuse bins for factories and businesses, as well as smaller residential garbage bins and metal housing cages. In early January when Chuck's factory re-opened after the Christmas break, he hired me as a welder in his factory to fabricate the refuse bins, till I found a job in my field. Within a week he was paying me the normal workmen rates, as he could find absolutely no fault with my work.

The children were also enrolled into day school and our lives were back on an even keel. I continued working with Chuck for a couple more weeks, and then I moved as I found a job to suit my qualifications. I joined 4 Star Plumbing and Heating as a journeyman plumber, gas and mechanical services specialist and I also specialised in installing Honeywell control systems.

I had a company van with all the tools and spare parts required for various jobs and I got to know the whole area extremely well as I had to drive to the customers' premises to sort out their problems. I enjoyed my work as much as I did meeting all the clients, who kept calling the company and asking specifically for me to handle their call-outs. I was not sure how to take this, but the company personnel laughed, saying it was probably because they liked my British accent!

Unfortunately, I did not work long as Drake and Skull Engineering needed my expertise on a large project in Addis Ababa, Ethiopia. So to the disappointment of my company and clients, I resigned from my job in May 1970, to move to the African continent. We bid a fond farewell to Chuck and Emma and I told them I was sure we would be gracing their shores again in the not too distant future.

Since I had always wanted to drive on the famous 'Route 66', we drove from Fremont first to San Francisco and then on to visit the Grand Canyon. We next changed course and drove all the way up the west coast to Vancouver in Canada. We checked out the city and then took the gondola up to Grouse Mountain, the peak of Vancouver.

A friend had informed me that Canada was a good place to live and bring up a family and infact, Vancouver was the warmest place in Canada. However after visiting Vancouver, I decided if that was the warmest place they had on offer, they could keep it, as there was no way I was going to live in any country resembling the climatic conditions of a freezer. I sold my car and not long after, we flew out of Vancouver by the now defunct Trans World Airlines (TWA), to England.

Tulsa, Oklahoma (USA)

May 1972 – January 1973

I was not wrong, as my words to Chuck and Emma came to pass. After we left Uganda we went back to England, but I very soon decided that living and working in America would make a great change. So we crossed the big pond and returned to the USA in May 1972.

We arrived in the Big Apple and I had absolutely no idea where we were going to live, or what I was going to do to look after my family. So we took a Greyhound bus going on the 'Route 66', up to Oklahoma City. At a rest stop enroute, we met a couple in a restaurant who were from Tulsa, and their very positive reviews about the city, was what guided me to take a chance on Tulsa. I thus decided to break our journey in Tulsa, which was the stop just before Oklahoma City.

It was late at night when the bus reached Tulsa in Oklahoma. I was lucky to find a reasonable roadside motel for us for the night. The next day, I surfaced bright and early, while the family were still catching up on their sleep. On leaving the motel, I found that Tulsa seemed a real nice place to live and maybe, I just might find a job as well.

I had three big tasks to accomplish that day, if we were to make Tulsa our home base. But I was not alone, as someone up there was showering me with tons of luck. Before it was even time for breakfast, I had not only rented us a two bedroom apartment and bought a second hand American car, but I had also secured myself a job with Quality Plumbing, Heating and Airconditioning Company, handling plumbing and mechanical services in houses and apartments.

I was actually astonished at what I had accomplished, as where else in the world can a person secure a job, rent an apartment and buy a car all in a few hours in a new country, before he even sat down to have breakfast? I have travelled the world and I honestly do not think I could have achieved what I did in any country other than in the United States of America.

Extremely pleased with myself, I went to the motel, picked up the family, and moved into our apartment. As I was by then falling asleep on my feet, I crashed and woke up early the next day to start work at my new job, while Phyllis sorted out the groceries and found a school nearby for the children.

As I was qualified at what I did, the work was not a problem, though I found out that licenced specialists earned more. So I applied to the American Plumbers Association and they sent me the course study material. I worked during the day and studied during the evenings. In next to no time, I had prepared myself and travelled to Oklahoma City to appear for the examinations. I passed with flying colours and received my American Plumbing and Mechanical Services Licence.

As I was now registered, my job opportunities increased since my licence enabled me to work anywhere in the USA. Once licenced I automatically advanced up the ladder in the company, and I worked alongside a great guy Melvin Chapman.

We worked on Saturday morning, and as the company closed at mid-day for the rest of the weekend, Melvin and the lads from the company spent a few hours on Saturday afternoon at the rodeo. Never having been to a rodeo, I joined them on a Saturday soon after joining the company. From then on, I was a part of their Saturday ritual and I thoroughly enjoyed our weekly and entertaining lads day out, before we went home to our respective families and reality.

I however left Quality Plumbing in November 1972, as I wanted to expand my experience in American plumbing and mechanical services, and I worked for myself for a couple of months. But my genuine intentions did not come to fruition, and I did not get the chance to start my own company as I had planned, because I was offered a job in Zambia and I was by now ready to go back to the African continent.

So in January, we finally left Tulsa and drove first to Niagara falls, to see for ourselves if it lived up to its proclaimed splendour. To our bad luck, our car broke down enroute in London, Ohio but to our good luck, a very helpful small repair shop in the area sorted the problem without much of a dent to my not so deep pockets, and we were on our way before long. Niagara was breathtaking, and neither did it disappoint us, nor fall short of our high expectations. From there we drove straight to New York, where I found a buyer for my car, before we flew out to England and our home.

Though I loved America and did plan to return, my life has since been extremely busy and preoccupied in other parts of the globe. However, I have promised Anne we would travel the length and breadth of the country to visit our innumerable family and friends. I would like to show her the wonders of the country through my eyes and to see a fresh perspective myself, through hers.

With 4 Star Plumbing in Fremont, USA

Chapter 11

Addis Ababa – Ethiopia (East Africa)

June – December 1970

In June 1970 I flew with my family to Addis Ababa on a three year contract with Drake and Skull Engineering, to supervise and rectify a local contractor's substandard workmanship on the new Hilton hotel in the capital, and to hand over the contract on completion.

The company gave me a car, and I found and rented a part of a villa from a military colonel. Our residence was from the main entrance of the villa with stairs leading to our living area on the top floor of the villa. The colonel had his living quarters on the ground floor with a separate entrance from the rear.

Phyllis handled the shopping, household chores and looking after the children, since as usual I had to work long hours. I had my work cut out for me, with practically re-doing the complete job throughout the hotel, to set it right and bring it up to International standards.

During the short time we were in Ethiopia, I took the family away from the city of Addis Ababa at the weekends. I had heard about a scenic mountainous area, in the Ethiopian highlands just north of the city of Addis Ababa. Thus, I decided to take the family up to Mount Entoto one weekend, which is about three thousand two hundred meters above sea level. The mountain was also referred to as 'the lung of Addis Ababa' due to it being covered with a dense forrest of eucalyptus trees, which was used as building materials and also the main source of firewood for the residents of the city in those days.

We left home for Entoto after I returned from work on a Saturday evening, as we were spending the night up on the mount at one of the little guest houses there. Initially I was pelting up the mountain roads, as it was only about an eighteen kilometers drive up to the mount. However, I soon realised I could have caused an accident and killed not only myself but my whole family as well. The blind and steep hairpin bend winding roads up to the point, was not much more than a stony track. But, there was also no sign of even a barrier, to prevent us from going over the sheer drop and down the side of the mountain. As such, from then on it took me about an hour of careful driving in the dark to reach the mount.

Mount Entoto is steeped in local history from the time Emperor Menelik II who founded Addis Ababa, had built his palace there. While his palace is nothing but a collection of rustic and simplistic thatched roof huts, its history is indeed interesting. The locals still consider Mount Entoto to be a sacred place and there are several monasteries and churches in the area. But the aerial view of the city of Addis Ababa was certainly worth the nerve-wracking drive up to the mount.

When we went to Ethiopia, the laws of the land at that time were extremely stringent. One of the first rules I was informed of by my company on our arrival, was that photography was not allowed in any part of the country. It was a criminal offence for a foreigner to take photographs of either the people or any sights within the country, and that is why I do not have any photographs of the short and unsettling period of our life in the country.

However, though the state of the hotel's workmanship was without a doubt totally unsatisfactory, and in a real bad way that it required several thousands of man hours to set it right, to me it was nothing short of a hardship posting.

Since living in Ethopia, my views of the country went from terrible to horrifying. I did not think anyone in their right mind would volunteer to take on an employment contract in the country, leave alone with their young family in tow. If I had known better or done my research before I signed the contract, I would not have done it either.

The Ethiopian men who worked for me were hard workers and I never had a problem with them. I trained them on the job and they followed my instructions well. But they did not trust each other to refrain from reporting them to the authorities for even a minor misdemeanour. So each one just did their assigned work and kept to themselves. It was an extremely sad way to exist. I say exist, because I could not call their way of staying alive, as a form of living life as we understand it. But as I was a foreigner there was nothing I could do to help any of them.

The strict laws of the land were for all the citizens of the country and not just for the foreigners. If anyone committed a crime, however minor, they were unceremoniously hung up by a noose at the site of their crime and left there for a couple of days, after which their bodies were removed and buried by their families. We were not on the outside, watching an old 'wild west' western movie. We were actually experiencing first hand the very disturbing state of our modern age living.

As we are not used to people being treated in such a barbaric and inhumane way, these frequent macabre sights were extremely shocking and utterly disturbing, and it was one of the reasons why I forced myself to complete my contract as quickly as possible. I definitely could not have subjected my family to life there, nor could I have continued to live in the country for the duration of my three year contract, without either getting involved in helping the people in some way, or getting killed myself in the process.

Even before I commenced my rectification work on the Hilton hotel, I knew I had to leave the country without delay. So I surveyed the complete job and accordingly pushed my men to their very limit, and I actually managed to complete the project in six months. We were thus able to leave Ethiopia in December 1970 and without ever looking back, I moved onto my next contract in Uganda.

Once when I was travelling on my own with Ethiopian Airlines, the flight was without incident or so I thought. On arrival at our destination, we had to exit the aircraft through the first class cabin. It was only then, we economy class passengers found out there were highjackers on board.

They were fortunately overpowered by the onboard airline security who killed them by slitting their throats. The dead terrorists were then put in a sitting position in the first class seats and covered with blankets. However, there was a large amount of blood on the floor of the aisle and we unfortunately had to step on it to exit the aircraft. The next day the local newspaper screamed the headlines 'Ethiopia's answer to terrorism'.

My life in Ethiopia may have been over in the blink of an eye, but my experience there is a part of my life story I will never ever forget, and it is one country I know with certainty, I will never return to.

Chapter 12

Kampala – Uganda (East Africa)

February 1971 - April 1972

After moving from Ethiopia, we were looking forward to a peaceful existence in Uganda. However, the stars were not aligned in my favour as unknown to me, I was walking freely into a quagmire of pure unadultrated evil, with my family in tow. I had already signed a three year contract with Haden (East Africa) Ltd., to supervise the local labour on three of the twelve new rural hospitals being built around the country.

Unfortunately, the timing of my contract in Uganda was inopportune. Between the short time I signed my contract and our arrival in Uganda, the country was suddenly thrown into utter turmoil. We arrived in Uganda in early February 1971, to utter chaos in the country. The military general Idi Amin had just a week earlier at the end of January, seized power of the country in a coup d'etat from the elected Ugandian government president Milton Obote, who was away in Singapore for the Commonwealth Heads of State meeting.

A few days before we landed in Uganda, Idi Amin self-proclaimed himself as president-for-life of Uganda, which was now known as the 'second republic of Uganda'. He also named himself as the commander-in-chief of the armed forces, army chief of staff as well as the chief of the air force.

Overnight he showed his true colours to the people of Uganda and to the whole world. He turned out to be not a leader for his people and country, but a self-serving dictator to his very core. He rode rough shod over everyone and everything if it did not conform with his views, agenda or twisted way of thinking. While the people tried to go about their daily life with as much normalcy as they could muster, there was always an underlying tension and we were informed to lay low, avoid confrontation and to be on our guard at all times.

We moved into a company villa in a small compound in Kiyinda-Mityana, which was a district about an hour and a half drive away from the capital Kampala. A few other villas occupied by foreign company staff completed the residents of the compound. While I had a company car, I bought Phyllis a second-hand car as her run-around, and the children were enrolled into the local school near by. Our life in Uganda had started out so far on a very weak and shaky note.

The Uganda company manager Alf Benham and his wife Maureen, were good and welcoming friends to have both as neighbours in our compound, as well as friendly faces in a strange country fraught with danger, and we have remained in contact over the years since.

I was in charge of three hospital sites in the rural areas of Nakaseke, Kiryandongo and Itoso. Daily travel to and from these sites was arduous in those days as the country roads, if you could call it that, were far from being regarded as in a good condition. It took a toll not only on our vehicles, but its occupants as well, who were discourteously relegated to a minor matter of collateral damage.

I also worked with Mowlems Construction Company Ltd., in charge of and supervising the steam installation and plumbing on four of their twenty-three rural hospitals. Sometimes if my work at the Itoso site over-ran, I was forced to stay over at Dave Bird's residence, rather than drive back through the dark of the night on unlit and extremely dangerous roads, which were terrorised by Idi Amin's thugs. Dave was the Itoso site manager of Mowlem Construction Company, and he had his villa in Itoso, which was run like a well oiled machine by his local houseboy.

Over the weekends, I would take the family for drives through the country or to the national parks, where we could interact with nature and the free roaming animals. It was marvellous observing the excitement of the children at seeing the massive elephants and wild animals just strolling across the road in front of our cars. But I always ensured we returned home before dark, as it was unsafe for anyone to be driving around on the lonely country roads at night. The danger as usual was not the dark and unlit roads, but Idi Amin's henchmen who instilled terror in the people of Uganda. They raped, pillaged and killed at will without a conscience, just because Idi Amin encouraged them by turning a blind eye. This gave them free rein to do whatever they wanted without any repercussions.

Uganda also has the distinction of being one of the six African countries to lie on the Equator, though most of the country lies to the north of the Equator. Driving the seventy plus kilometres from Kampala to Kayabwe just to stand on the spot where the imaginary Equator line runs, was a well worth drive.

With a large western community like us in Uganda for one reason - to help develop the infrastructure of the country, we were all living and working in and around Kampala. As such, socialising was the constant theme over the weekends to unwind, with private parties and formal functions held quite often, which kept us sane as it cleared our minds and lightened our moods for a while.

In December 1971, the Uganda Inspectorate Ministry of Education offered me the position of practical examiner for their ministry's examinations in 'plumbing in tropical countries'. From then on I was even more busy, with very little free time to call my own.

But despite our fairly comfortable life, there was also a dark side to living in Uganda, and our every day in the country was turning out to be far worse than what we first expected. After being witness to certain situations in Ethiopia and now in Uganda, it made me skeptical about the tenets of religion and even the existence of God. My faith in mankind was being put to the test and my trust in people was already practically non-existent.

In my view, God would never allow innocent people to be treated so brutally. Yet, it seemed that in Uganda, some people out of totally misguided loyalty to Idi Amin, blindly took a leaf out of his book of evil and followed in his extremely vicious and torturous ways.

Houses were regularly broken into by his followers, people were attacked and women raped. Even children were not spared. To say I was scared for my family would be an understatement. Every night I went to bed with a panga (an African machete) by the side of my pillow. If I ever had to use it in self-defence of my family, to kill someone who attacked us in our house, I would never have hesitated, irrespective of the consequences.

Once when I was driving through Kampala from one job to another, I saw a hungry young boy of about five or six years, steal a single fruit from a roadside fruit vendor's handcart and run. From the confines of my vehicle, I laughed in encouragement as I saw his little impish face. However, my mirth changed to shock and horror as the drivers of a row of taxis parked not far from the vendor's cart, caught the child before he could get away. They poured petrol over the young lad and lit him on fire.

To say that this was an extremely savage and primitive act, would belittle their actions. As I had children of the same age, it was ever so distressing to see this little child on flames, screaming and running till he dropped. I shouted from my car to stop it and help the child but no one took any notice of me. Not one person prevented it happening or went to the aid of the child. Passersby just pretended they were blind and hurried on their way, for fear of getting involved and on the wrong side of Idi Amin's law.

I did understand everyone was just trying to stay alive and survive. But this is not supposed to happen to the hungry and definitely not to innocent children. However, I was witness to it happening in front of me and unfortunately being a foreigner, I could not intervene. Certain incidents like this have caused an indelible stain on my memory which can never be erased and in the process, it changed my mindset on humanity. It is from this time I even began questioning God and though I am not agnostic, I stopped believing in either His power or His mysterous ways, till I met and married Anne in 1996.

There was a Catholic Carmelite sisters monastery very close to our residential compound. Every Sunday we saw long queues of local people belonging to the working and disadvantaged class outside the gates of the convent. These were poor folk but obviously with great faith. They queued outside the convent to give alms, so that the nuns would pray for a place for them in Heaven in return. These poor people could not afford to look after themselves. But without a thought, they gave the nuns what little they had - be it a few coins or even a handful of raw rice meant for their daily sustenance.

They were already living in hell on earth, and starvation was just a minor matter which did not bother them, as long as God took them into his eternal care in Heaven. I learned of this as our local maid made her pilgrimage to the convent every Sunday with her little offering. She depended on us for her food and wages, as she had to support and care for her entire family. But come Sunday, she never missed giving her charitable contribution to the nuns for her little spot in Heaven.

Though I am a Catholic, I was never religious and now witnessing this weekly occurance, I totally turned away from God and my religion. I had infact criticised the nuns for taking from the poor, as I could not understand how they could with a clear conscience, receive so much from these folk who literally had absolutely nothing. Was it right to use God's name to accept and live off the donations these people could ill afford to give in the first place?

Had I known when I was in Uganda what I know now, that this is a cloistered convent, and what a cloistered convent actually is, maybe I too would have queued with the faithful every Sunday, and just maybe a bit of their faith would have rubbed off onto me. But I was lacking of the facts at that time and actually, I only found out some time ago when mentioning this story to Anne. She checked out the monastery and found that it is a cloistered order and infact, they celebrated fifty years of religious service in Uganda in 2017, as they had started the monastery in 1967.

Anne further explained to me that cloistered nuns take a vow never to ever leave their monastery. They are deeply religious and devote their time in prayer for the church, the people, the country and the world. And more importantly, they really do depend on the generosity of the faithful. I could have helped them so much when I was in Uganda, but I never did as I was blind and ignorant of the commitment to their cause, and too busy between my work and keeping my family safe. Another situation to darken the colours of my rainbow.

Life in Uganda was getting worse every day. Idi Amin said Uganda was only for the Ugandians, and directed all the Asian community to be expelled from the country. People were leaving with just a carry on bag and nothing else. Their homes and all the rest of their possessions were being left behind. He also instructed that the seven thousand plus British nationals still in the country, were to be marked and watched.

On hearing about this, I first telephoned the British embassy, and I was absolutely shocked to learn the embassy staff had given a local Ugandian man a British passport, and put him in charge of the embassy. When I informed him I wanted to speak to a British passport holder, he confirmed he now had a British passport. He further informed me that all the staff from England had already returned to the UK.

I was totally flabbergasted to learn the embassy staff had fled the country, without sparing a thought for the thousands of British citizens still living and working in the country. With no British embassy to rely on for either information or a speedy getaway, it dawned on me that in situations like this when one is in dire straits, it is every man for himself as it felt like God and Country had let me down.

This was my cue to make hasty but discreet plans to get my family and myself out of this 'hell hole' and to safety. We could not talk to or tell anyone anything, as we now could not trust anyone since we were all under surveillance. Phyllis and I discussed and planned out our strategy. She stitched valuables and all the money we had into the lining of our heavy jackets. We packed our clothes, as well as enough food and water to last the four of us for the duration of the dangerous trip ahead. I ensured my company car was fighting fit for the journey and all fueled up, with extra cans of fuel as well. Phyllis' car and everything else had to remain behind, and the house left as though we were still in residence.

We packed the car under the cover of darkness, and the next day when our maid came in to work, we just informed her we were going to Kampala, and the four of us left on our covert journey on a sunny day in April 1972. We had not informed the children of our plans, as we did not want them frightened or privy to information which could endanger all our lives, should we get stopped by security and are questioned. It is common knowledge children have a knack of not only speaking out of turn, but also divulging unsolicited information to strangers. So I thought it was best we kept them in the dark about our furtive plans.

Though the Tanzania border was probably a bit closer to us,

I had decided it was safer going to Kenya. And as we had to go through Kampala, if anyone was watching us, they would think we were driving to the city. We had a long drive ahead of us and while the children interspersed playing between squabbling as usual in the back seat, Phyllis and I were caught up in our own thoughts and the unexpected dangers which lay ahead.

As we were driving on the road to Busia on the border with Kenya, we noticed a car ahead of us on the side of the road engulfed in flames. From the car's rear number plate, I recognised it as belonging to Tony Longhurst, a fellow British citizen and workmate who worked with Mowlems Construction Company Ltd.

I told the children to sit quiet and low in the car and while I did not stop, I slowed down as we passed. The image I saw will haunt me forever. The hands of the driver were tied to the top of the steering wheel. There was no one else in the car and as such, I have no idea whether his family was with him or not. I also could not say with certainty that the driver on fire was Tony, as the whole car was in flames and even though I knew him well, I could not identify him from the condition of the flaming corpse. However, it definitely was his car.

As we reached Uganda's Busia border with Kenya, there was a short queue of cars ahead of us. We quickly noticed utter chaos, as Idi Amin's heavily armed security personnel were going from one car to the next, yelling at its occupants. They were forceably dragging screaming women out of the cars, and beating the objecting men and crying and shrieking children with the butt of their guns.

I knew when they reached our car, they would do the same with Phyllis, the children and me. These security men were pure evil. We had heard they just raped women all over the country before killing them. Was that what happened to Tony's wife? Would the children and I also end up with the same fate as Tony? Was I sealing the destiny of Phyllis and the children at this final stage of our escape, within sight of the Kenyan border and our ultimate freedom?

Seeing the tragedy unfolding in front of me, all I knew in a split second, was our end was upon us. However, there was no way I was going to allow these immoral disciples of satan, to take me and my family without a darn good fight, or die trying. Without pausing to think or to even discuss it with Phyllis, I just ordered Phyllis and the children to keep quiet and to lie low and still in their seats with their heads bent to their knees, to avoid the breaking glass from the gunfire that was sure to target us. All vehicles were manual in those days, and our car doors were already locked, the windows rolled up and the car engine still running, as we were waiting in the queue.

Without wasting time in thought or hatching a plan, I just caught the bull by the horns. The next thing I knew was I had swerved around the car in front of me, on the opposite side to where the border security with a licence to kill, were creating chaos. Hunched low over the steering wheel and with my pedal to the metal, I blindly bombed it straight past the six or seven cars in front of us in the queue. I drove right through the Uganda Busia open border, across the stretch of 'no man's land' and just as we were entering Kenya's border, Idi Amin's Ugandian guns started firing at us in earnest.

The Kenyan Border Control kept a twenty-four hours watch on the Ugandian border. When they saw us speeding towards them, they immediately raised their border control barrier for us to drive straight through. They were as surprised as we were, that we had made it across safely. They said they had not had anyone enter Kenya from the Busia border, for a very long while. This was due to the fact, anyone trying to leave Uganda was being killed, as Idi Amin did not want the outside world to know what was actually happening in Uganda.

We relaxed for an hour or so at the Kenya border control, while I caught my breath and got my heart to start beating normally. Suddenly the realisation hit me! in revenge for what I had done, the Uganda border security would without a doubt conduct a blood bath, and kill all the innocent people who try to leave Uganda through the Busia border like we did.

But the Kenyan Border control personnel reassured me I should not think any more about our escape, as the Uganda security were killing innocent people for a long while anyway. So, I was not responsible for any of their wicked actions. They were just glad I had the guts to take the chance I did, and lived to tell the tale.

Maybe I did live to tell the tale, but at the rate I was going, I was running out of my nine lives. However, I was pleased our ordeal was over and my family was safe. The thought of what could have happened to us if I had not acted so swiftly, is beyond belief. I would certainly not be here now writing my 'life story'. Instead, just like all the other victims, Phyllis, my two children and myself would be nothing but just a row of unidentified statistics on the butcher of Uganda's murderous register of evil.

I drove straight to the Haden (East Africa) Ltd. office in Nairobi and met with George Searl who was the manager of the Kenya office, and brought him up-do-date on our escape from Uganda. The company put us up in a hotel in Nairobi and organised our flight back to the UK. The next day I returned my car to the company, and I signed off on my contract with them. We then left for the airport and straight home to the UK and safety.

While we had made friends and there were good times initially, the several dark incidents and our getaway mission from Uganda will unfortunately always cast a gloomy shadow on my memories of the country.

From my personal experience, I find it is not until a person is subjected to torture and abuse or even confined in invisible chains, that they recognise the importance of a democracy, free speech and the value of their freedom. And the one thing I will never ever relinquish is 'my freedom'.

With Sharon and Tony at the Equator in Uganda

Chapter 13

Kitwe – Zambia (East Africa)

March 1973 – August 1975

After our earth shattering escapade from Uganda, we went home to England for a while, before moving to the USA. However, in November 1972, I was offered the position of mechanical foreman with the Amalgamated Construction Company Limited, for their Kitwe site in Zambia.

So it was back to the African continent for me, with my family in tow. We settled in quite well in our villa in Kitwe. Life was tranquil and there were no untoward incidents to blot out our sun and darken our horizon. There was an extensive western population and our social life was extremely hectic, with a lot of enjoyment thrown in for good measure.

When I was not working, I spent most of my free time taking the family on trips around the neighbouring countries, visiting the Democratic Republic of Congo, Tanzania, Rhodesia (which is now known as Zimbabwe), and Mozambique. The Victoria Falls on the Zambezi river was a favourite spot of mine, while the children as usual enjoyed the safari trips through the national parks.

I also visited Cape Town on a business trip and took in a

few places of interest like 'table mountain'. As South Africa was under apartheid rule at the time, there were rules in the country even we as visitors had to follow. When I travelled on the train, I could not travel in any carriage I wanted. I was sold a ticket for the carriages only for the whites, and I could only travel in those carriages, which were pretty good.

I however learned from some local people, in contrast to the carriages for the white people which had upholstered, padded and comfortable seats, the carriages for the blacks had just ordinary wooden slats for seats. The same racial segregation was prevalent in various aspects of society like the local bus service and even restaurants. Everywhere I went, there were signs saying 'White Only' or 'Black Entrance' etc.

The Black Pimpernel as Nelson Mandela was then known as, was incarcerated on Robben Island at the time of my visit to South Africa. It was extremely hard for me to fathom the minds of the white people who were the architects of apartheid, as the country was predominantly a black country, and yet the minority white community ruled them with a racially motivated iron fist. I must admit, I rejoiced when apartheid was relegated to the annals of history, and Nelson Mandela took over the leadership of his country and the people he loved.

The children were happy in their school in Kitwe, and Sharon even made her 'first holy communion' when we lived in Zambia. They had their own group of friends, who were the children of friends in our social circle as well as my work associates.

I worked with AMCCO and did very well till July 1974, when I was offered a senior managerial position with the Anglo American Corporation (Central Africa) Ltd., in Kitwe.

However, I did not accept their offer as I had by then, decided to start my own company.

Power Construction (1968) Ltd. located in Chingola, was a well established company owned and managed by G. F. Cooper a fellow British national. As he wanted to expand his Company's presence in Zambia without any additional expense, he asked me if I was interested in opening my own company in Kitwe.

Never one to let an opportunity slip through my fingers, I accepted and opened my own company in Kitwe, using the same name - Power Construction (1968) Ltd., and I never regretted my decision. My company concentrated on the fabrication, manufacture and installation of cable trays, to house the electrical cables going right down into and through the copper mines.

In addition to running the company, I trained and at times worked alongside my team of local tradesmen. I also frequently accompanied them into the mines, to ensure the installation of the cable trays were carried out to international standards. My company's business increased alongside my credibility and reputation, and our life in Zambia was moving forward in the right direction.

Much as I would have liked to continue working and living in Zambia, Phyllis said the family wanted a change. So to appease them, I closed down the company and we bid a Bantu 'Shalapo' or 'Goodbye' to Zambia in August 1975, making our way to the other side of the world and to our new life literally 'down under'.

With my staff down the copper mines in Zambia

Chapter 14

A cockney Down Under (Australia)

Townsville – Queensland (Australia) 1975 – 1976

I had left Zambia in August 1975 and as I was not returning to the African continent, I had accepted a job as a foreman plumber with Brian Dunn and Sons in Brisbane. I was to start work in October 1975, to supervise their local labour, working at the Australian Institute for Marine Science in Turtle Bay, located on the north eastern coast of Queensland.

With not much time to spare, I moved my family to Queensland, and we stayed in a hotel for a few days while I found and purchased a house in Townsville, as it was not far from Turtle Bay. I also purchased a car and while the family settled in, the children made friends and adjusted well at school.

I on the other hand got on with the job I was contracted to do, with the team of skilled tradesmen under my supervision, in order to get the contract completed in record time. Every morning I picked up my men, to take them to Turtle Bay in my car. One day during the first week on the job, as I was driving to the site after picking up the men, they suddenly shouted and asked me to stop the car. I pulled up on the side of the road and they excitedly jumped out. I did not know what was happening, and was absolutely astounded to see them pick up snakes slithering on the hot sand by the side of the road.

All these tradesmen wore ordinary rubber beach flipflops to work. I was surprised there was no regulatory safety gear or footwear requirement on jobs, in those days in a country like Australia. And I was worried this extra curricular activity they obviously enjoyed, would get these men bitten by the cold blooded reptiles.

But I soon found out it was not just an extra curricular activity for them, nor had I any reason to be perturbed, as this was a sport they were professionals in. To my amazement, as they caught each snake, they just swung it above their heads and cracked it like a whip to break its neck area. They laughed heartily at the look of consternation on my face, when they opened the boot of my car and threw the reptiles in, assuring me the reptiles would not be making an appearance on the seat next to me, as they were no longer alive.

The next stop the men directed me to enroute was the laboratory, where a specialist took the venom from each of the reptiles into separate vials, labelling the vials with the date and the type of reptile, before paying the men for their catch and sale of the day. And this activity was my lads' very own resourceful method for making their 'schooner' money, or for a pint of beer, as I call it.

Over time I got accustomed to the mens' unusual activity, as it happened many times during my time at Turtle Bay. However, I did ensure the men cleaned out the boot of my car, as I had no wish to come across any uninvited guests either staring back at me or scaring the family at the most inopportune moment.

I have always loved travelling the world, visiting various countries and interacting with its people. Our time in Australia was no different, as I made friends in the unlikeliest of places. I enjoyed my free time as I took the family on long drives around Queensland. We drove down south right up to the Gold Coast and north through Cairns and Cooktown, as far as we could go.

In January 1976, I was offered a job in Mauritius and the family and I left Australia, after I put the house in the hands of a local real estate agent to sell, and to our good luck, it sold without a problem. We left Townsville and instead of flying directly out to Mauritius, I decided to drive across Australia first, to see a bit more of the country, after which I would be in a better position to make a decision on whether I wanted to retire 'down under'.

So we drove to Brisbane, from where we went through the northern towns of New South Wales, and across Australia into the north of South Australia. Onroute we got stuck during a heavy rain storm at a floodway area, which is quite common in Australia. I misjudged the distance between the actual floodways, thinking we could make it through the floodways before the whole area flooded and hence, I took a chance by driving through. Unfortunately by the time we reached the top of the first floodway, the water was rising all around us. The peak of the floodway we were on, actually became a little island in the middle of a lake, cut off from land due to flooding all around it.

I could neither drive further nor reverse, and we had to stay perched where we were, and wait for the water to go down. After quite a while though the water level receded, I knew I would still have to drive through the lower water level, and the car would most certainly float. So I got the children to collect as many rocks and stones as they could find, to weigh the car down. We stacked the rocks inside the boot as well as on the floor of the car to keep the car as steady and stable as possible, till I got us through the floodway.

I had a real tough time driving the car in the flood waters, towards the railway tracks and to the train station, quite a distance away on the otherside of the floodway. Frequently I was forced to exit the car and swim around it, to get its wheels out of the mud, which I could not see due to the flood water. I had to do this on my own as neither Phyllis nor the children would get out as they saw snakes gliding around in the water, and it made my job that much more harder. Eventually, I managed to reach the station after many hours of intermittent driving and pushing the car myself.

I booked us and the car on the train and we travelled further through the desert. The train terminated at the end of the line after crossing all the flood areas. Our train journey was however not easy on us. There was a putrid smell on board, which for some odd reason seemed to be emanating from every other passenger on the train. It was the most sickening and unfortunately, the worst train journey I have ever been on. We were all really green by the time the train reached the end of the line.

On arriving at our destination, we eagerly disembarked along with all the passengers from the train, and wallowed in the fresh air to clear our systems, before we continued to drive the rest of the way to Perth. It was a very long, extremely hot and uncomfortable last leg of our journey into Perth, as the car's airconditioning system died of heatstroke. I managed to sell my car in the city before we booked and boarded our flight to Mauritius.

I had made up my mind by the end of our road trip, I would most certainly return to Australia when I retired, as while it is no Utopia, I liked the country and its climes. More importantly, I was enamoured by the carefree lifestyle and the laid back attitude of the people, even though they did speak with a strange accent and called everyone 'mate'. But then, while I was used to various languages and accents, the Aussies probably thought my London accent was strange too.

Duncraig – Perth (Western Australia) – 1980

And so it came about that in March, 1980, my family and I again returned 'down under', but this time to Perth in Western Australia. When I was in the merchant navy, on every trip from the UK, our first port of call on the Australian continent was always Perth. While I had also traversed the length and breadth of the country, I decided Perth would be a good start to a new life in Australia.

I bought a house in Duncraig and we all settled in without a problem. We were now veterans at adjusting to different environments in all the countries we lived in, getting involved in the local communities and meeting and making new friends along the way. Hence our new life in Perth was not an issue with us.

I found a job extremely easily, joining Karlovsky Plumbers Pty. Ltd. in Joondanna, as their construction manager. My work on a new continent was as good as it could get at that time in my life. But sadly it did not last long, as the owner of Belhasa Anthony Pools, in Dubai, contacted me with an enticing proposition to set up and manage their latest large new venture. They wanted me to take over as general manager and start a general maintenance company for them in Dubai. Naturally, I could not turn down the very lucrative offer, which would take me back to my desert dream.

So once again I left Australia, this time for Dubai in September 1980, to take up my position in Belhasa Anthony Pools, while the family followed shortly. Regrettably, we never went back to Australia as a family. In 1983 when Phyllis and I divorced, I sold the house in Australia to finance the purchase of a house for her in the UK.

Duncraig – Perth (Western Australia) – 1991

My decision to retire in Australia was still a plan at the back of my mind. And in 1991, I returned to Australia and purchased a property in Duncraig, Perth. Lovely as the house was, it was not fantastic. So I hired a local company to carry out modifications based on my designs, to bring the property up to my expectations.

In the rear garden I also built a swimming pool with a rockery and waterfall at one end which flowed into the pool, as well as a covered bar-be-que and bar cabana, which was half on terra firma and half over a corner of the pool, so that anyone in the pool could swim right under and into the bar for a quick thirst quencher.

I never did get to live in the house though, as my life and flourishing business was in Dubai. On one of my trips to Australia to check on the ongoing work on the property, I was jumped on and surrounded by a group of five or six immigration officers on arrival in Perth, who accused me of misusing the system.

According to them, since I had applied to settle in Australia when I retired, I was expected to live and work in the country and not leave the country with immediate effect. This was over and above the fact I not only owned a property in the country, and currently had contractors working on enhancing the property, but I was even paying taxes in the country.

I explained to them my company was in Dubai, and I had employees who depended on me for their very livelihood. I informed them I could unfortunately not leave Dubai currently, as it takes time to get all my men sorted with new jobs, before I could even think of closing the company, and moving permanently to Australia.

They said I could have another year to move to the country. However, by then they had pushed all my buttons too far with their totally illogical reasoning. I informed them that this was the final trip I would be making and they could keep their residency, as there was a very big world out there, and I would now certainly not be taking up formal residency in their country.

When Anne and I married, though she thought the modifications I carried out certainly transformed the house into a stunning property, she felt Australia was too far out of the way to live. Life 'down under' was just not for her. I must say though I initially had reservations, I sold the property and I have never regretted my decision to abandon my plans to retire in Australia.

Chapter 15

The draw of the desert – Dubai (United Arab Emirates)

1977 – 2009

In August 1977, I took on an overseas contract with Crown House Engineering Limited, UK and worked as a plumbing and mechanical supervising engineer on the construction of the Al Ghurair Development in Dubai, which was at that time, one of the largest construction projects in the Middle East.

Just like Qatar and Bahrain, the seven Trucial Sheikhdoms of Abu Dhabi, Ajman, Dubai, Sharjah, Fujairah, Umm Al Quwain and Ras Al Khaimah were all informal British protectorates under the terms of a treaty which expired on 1 December 1971.

On 2 December 1971, the Trucial States as the UAE was then known as, declared independence from the British and became the United Arab Emirates. Ras Al Khaimah remained a separate Sheikhdom but joined the UAE a few months later on the 10 February 1972.

By the time 1977 rolled in and the UAE welcomed me, they were forging ahead to make a name for themselves on the global spectrum. With the vision of its leaders, a desert of sand dunes was being transformed into a vast oasis of ultra modern living.

This naturally encouraged a plethora of people like me from around the globe, to bring in with us the best ideas, technical know-how, expertise and workmanship to help create the UAE dream for a sustainable future in an arid desert land.

As far as the eye could see, the horizon was marred by construction cranes on building sites spread over the desert, all working to produce the most modern architecture in this 'new world'. The UAE was a very rich young country booming with development at every turn and changing the skyline daily as more modern construction took shape, defeating the theory 'the shifting sands of the desert can hold no weight'. It was a marvel laying credence to the fact, God would not have made deserts, if he thought man could not make it into God's country. I soon grew to love this 'promised land' and after my initial contract ended, I decided to return to my oasis in the desert, the place I now called 'home'.

A few of the other personnel on our construction site, were folk I had worked with previously on contracts around the globe, and we worked well together. We even socialised together at times. However, with a large expatriate community all there for the same reason, socialising was wide, varied and very much more than just a pastime.

I found our family a villa in the neighbouring Emirate of Sharjah, where our villa was one among many in a large compound, occupied by the expatriate community. Everyone was friendly and while we worked hard during the day, we made new friends and socialised all evening long.

During the 1970s, there were fledgling English language schools in the Emirates, but they did not cater for the senior students. The schools were at that time adding grades every few years, going from junior to middle and high, at the end of which they would be able to accept children in all grades. As such, parents with children in the middle and senior grades, sent their children to boarding schools out of the UAE, and we too followed by sending our children to private boarding schools in the UK.

The Emiratis are very friendly and welcoming people. While they were not proficient in speaking English in the 1970s, they were quick learners. Their attempt at speaking English, was more than adequate for us to have extremely productive communication. We westerners were not as good or quick at learning Arabic, which compared to English, is a much more difficult language to master. Today, the Emiratis are a very educated and learned people, and while Arabic is the national language, being such a cosmopolitan country, almost everyone speaks English as a commonly understood language.

Dubai was the most modern of the Emirates, and residents from the other Emirates used to occasionally drive over to Dubai on a shopping expedition. While each individual Emirate was being developed, there were single lane roads connecting the Emirates. But no one drove through the desert at night or after a sandstorm, for fear of getting lost. Sand was not only in the air reducing visibility, but it also covered the roads, making it difficult to see in which direction the road ahead went.

In 1979 when the Sheikh Rashid Tower was built, it was the first tallest structure in Dubai and as it could be seen from a distance, it was used as a road marker, when driving from Abu Dhabi. This building is now known as the Dubai World Trade Centre, and has since lost its stature as the tallest building either in Dubai or the Emirates.

The Al Ghurair Development also included a shopping mall which when completed, would be the first of its kind in the UAE. In those days, there were souks or markets housing several small individual suppliers, selling everything from food to clothes and house hold items. There were also a couple of newly opened supermarkets catering to the requirements of all the residents.

Unlike today, we never carried shopping bags to the supermarket, and nor did they supply shopping bags either. However at the checkout counter, they packed our shopping into the empty cardboard cartons the supermarket items had originally been transported in. We took these cardboard cartons back to the drop off area, when we next visited the supermarket. Merchants and traders from the sub-continent, were slowly moving into the fray and opening shops as well. Life then was extremely simple but according to me, very much happier.

As is a well known fact, where there are expatriates, a surfeit of alcohol is not far behind. While alcohol has never been one of my vices, as I am just the occasional social drinker, most of the western expatriate community, used to imbibe like it was going out of fashion. The Emirates is quite liberal and a very tolerant country. As such, the expatriates did not miss their daily tipple, since there were two companies that operated in the country, supplying alcoholic beverages to the hotels and the non-Islamic community, on the presentation of a liquor licence. These two companies infact, not only operate but are doing very well even today, during our worldwide economic downturn.

Every country has their own customs and traditions, and the Emirates is no different. I believe not only should we treat other people the way we want to be treated, it is imperative we respect and wholeheartedly accept, the religious beliefs, social customs and traditions of the people of any country.

If we go to another country, it is we who should integrate into their society. We cannot expect them to make concessions for us, as it is their country and we are just guests there. That is the only way one can easily unite with the local community, and gain acceptance into their society. After all, are we all not just God's people with different views?

In August 1978, when my work at the Al Gurhair Development was completed, my company sent me to Egypt on a six months contract, to sort out and set right some problems on a job, so as to meet its handover deadline.

I returned to Dubai in February 1979 and decided to take the family on a vacation to the UK, prior to taking on my next contract in March, with a local Dubai company. But instead of flying, I thought it would be a very unusual, interesting and educative experience for the whole family, if we drove from the UAE to the UK.

Though the children who were now teenagers, were not interested, they had no options but to change their attitude towards the trip, if they wanted to go on vacation. As we were doing the journey in my new compact four seater, two door Datsun 280ZX, we could not carry too many clothes or personal items with us, as the boot space was limited and the teenage children were occupying the rear seat.

The roads were basic by today's standards, but pretty darn good in some areas, for the 1970s. We stayed in available hotels, when we stopped in various countries enroute, to take in the places of interest, absorb their cultures, sample new cuisine and educate our palate, in addition to interacting with the local people of these exotic countries. To say this journey was a real multifaceted cultural experience for me, would not be far wrong.

It was an extremely long but definitely not tedious journey, taking us right through the golden sands of the deserts of Saudi Arabia, to the archaeological delights of Jordan, from where we entered into the old world charm of Damascus in Syria. We then continued through the splendour of Turkey to Izmir, where we boarded the ferry to Athens in Greece, with its world renowned Grecian architectural ruins taking us back in time.

We again proceeded by ferry to Italy, and drove right through the length of the country, stopping at several places of interest enroute like Bologna, Rome, Venice and Lake Garda, just to name a few. Since my first trip through northern Italy in 1964, my fascination with the romance of Italy's historic monuments, Roman architecture and subsequently, its exceptional operatic arias, has never waned, and I knew I would one day return to the land of my ancestors. The last leg of our journey took us through the very scenic countryside of France enroute to Calais. We then embarked the ferry, crossing the English Channel to Dover in the UK, and our home at Tyndale Park in Herne Bay.

On returning to Dubai in March 1979, I joined the Fikree Pipe Company as their general manager, to set up and manage a large workshop and maintenance company. I worked till January 1980 when the company was a profitable up and running venture, and I moved to Perth in Australia. However, I returned to Dubai in October 1980, and joined Belhasa Anthony Pools as their general manager, to set up their large maintenance company. In July 1981, I joined Chicago

Maintenance Company, as the general manager of their Dubai operations.

During that period, I felt the time had arrived for me to start my own company. I realised all my work with various companies, gave me the vast experience that would stand me in good stead. I further knew from my personal experience, no one ever made money by working for someone else. My decision made, I resigned my position as general manager and started the process of opening my own company.

Quality General Maintenance Company Ltd., was thus born in January 1982 in Dubai. As I was looking to move our residence from Sharjah to Dubai, I was lucky enough to find a villa in Jumeira in Dubai and we moved home as well.

I initially started the company, with just three men and a second hand Datsun estate car. The first client on my company's books was Ed Abernathy, an American with a commanding presence, a booming voice and a great sense of humour, who had recently started his own company in the oilfield sector. Ed was extremely pleased with our work, and gave me the annual contract for his entire company's general maintenance work. He also became a very close friend of mine, and though distance now separates us, we still keep in touch with each other.

Within no time, I had made a name for myself as well as my company, and I expanded my staff of three men to a full fledged labour force. I have however never been blinded to the fact, that without folk like Ed and another friend Mike O'Kell, I would not have achieved my initial success. I will always remember, and appreciate their faith in my abilities, as well as for remaining a staunch patron of my business.

I had a general manager to handle the day-to-day operations

and the labour force, while I concentrated on bringing in the business, as well as overseeing the technical aspects and training the workmen. I had always worked long hours and overtime, when working for various companies. But running my own company was a game changer. While my staff and labour force followed the company timings and rules, it was different for me. I worked all hours as I had to catch up on paperwork after regular working hours.

Not only did my reputation swell, but I earned a couple of monikers 'Dave the Plumber' and 'Easy Plumber'. I was known as the plumber who never found a job that could not be done, and done well. My company's credibility and customer base grew, and I can honestly say I never lost a customer due to shoddy workmanship, giving strength and credence to my company statement 'there is no substitute for quality'. My customers remained loyal to me and my company, and I ensured we never ever let them down.

My greatest asset was my workforce, who were a qualified group of great men, most of whom I trained myself, to ensure my company's high standards of workmanship were maintained, and they never disappointed me. I believed that 'boss' or not, I could not expect my men to carry out a job, which I could not do myself. As such, very often I worked alongside my men, incase they had a problem or the job had a time frame.

A few months after Anne and I were married, an extremely large under water metal diving cage fabricated by my company, had to be delivered to a client located in Jebel Ali. As all my drivers were busy on other jobs, it was left to me to deliver the cage to the client. On my way to Jebel Ali, I realised I had to stop at the bank before it closed. So I drove by Jumeira and parked the large truck with the cage atop, just outside the bank. I completed my bank work in ten minutes, and was on my way to the client's premises.

A few days later, Anne asked me if I had recently gone to the bank in a truck. When I confirmed that I had, she laughed heartily and for the life of me, I could not understand her cause for such hilarity. Anne then said while chatting with her sister-in-law, a funny story came to light. A friend of Anne's sister-in-law had seen me getting into the truck at the bank and drive off, and immediately called her and said 'I did not know Anne married a truck driver?'

Well, the person may have been a total snob, but she was not far wrong, as I have never regarded any job as too menial for me to tackle. I believe in dignity of labour and I have worn very many hats over the years, and that of a truck driver was actually nearly at the top of the list. I guess my all encompassing attitude to my work, was partly why not only my workers but also my clients, treated me with the greatest of respect.

In order to give our customers the best possible service, they knew we were available twenty-four hours a day, seven days a week, for any general maintenance problems they may have. On the other hand, our workforce were informed at the time they were hired, that in my company we were on call twenty-four hours a day, and they would naturally be entitled to overtime if they went on a call after office hours. If they did not like my company policy, they did not have to take the job.

While job call-outs after working hours was few and very far between, it was something even I handled myself, to save my workmen from going out at night. All my foremen were given their own company vehicles, in which they carried their tools and essential spare parts at all times, so they were always ready to handle any job.

Customers called me if they had an emergency out of office hours, and if I could handle it with my limited tools, I sorted the call-out myself. But if additional material or tools were required, I contacted the concerned foreman to sort out the problem with his team. All my foremen were initially given pagers and with the advent of mobile phones, contact and communication was much easier.

My company also worked on a Friday morning, which was part of the weekend in the United Arab Emirates. I closed the company before noon, when many of my men had to go to the mosque for their Friday prayers. My view is that a general maintenance company cannot follow regular weekly office schedules.

The customer is our priority, and when a customer has an emergency, it has to be sorted out without delay. If a company's policy is not flexible and accommodating, they lose not only customers but also revenue and most importantly credibility. At this time, I was also contacted by the Dubai municipality and appointed to sort out the country's mechanical services standards, to conform with international regulations and thus I set up the first 'International Plumbing Code' for Dubai.

During the Iraq-Iran war which started in 1980 and went on till 1988, there were jobs which had to be done in Iran but being a war zone, it is understandable there were no takers for the jobs. Eventually, one of these jobs landed on my desk through a businessman Quinten Cope, who said my name came up when he was asking around the business circuit in Dubai, as to who could handle and pull off a hardship job in a war zone. As far as I was concerned, war zone or not, if the price was right, I would get the project done.

The job was to move a base camp in Iran, from a site close to the Iraq border to another location a bit inland, and away from the line of fire. So I got a good small team of six of my best workers, who were brave enough to accompany me, along with a couple of mates in the trade, Roy Sands and Brownie, who I hired to handle the electrical and heavy lifting jobs.

On arrival in Iran, we were transported by the client from the airport to the camp, passing through remote villages across the country enroute to the site. As the area was a war zone, large stretches of land were mine fields. However, their method of clearing the mine fields in those days without modern equipment and protective gear, was one I will never ever comprehend.

Poor families in the surrounding villages were paid and their young innocent children were taken away and made to run through the mine fields, blowing up the mines in the process. Many children were maimed and many others were killed by this process of clearing the mine fields. We saw the results of this extremely tragic modus operandi through the villages we passed, as we could not fail to notice many of the children were no longer able bodied.

To me it was the conscious destruction of innocent lives who were the future of Iran, and that in my personal opinion is an unpardonable act. When I asked if they had no other recourse to clear the mine fields, I was informed their country was at war, and it was not what they wanted to do but what they had to do.

I was however there to do a job and my thoughts switched to the project I had on hand. My priority was to get the job carried out on schedule, and to keep my personnel safe. At my prior instructions, the camp to be moved was already vacated and ready for us to commence relocation. After our inspections, we planned the logistics of the decommissioning which was to start the next day, and we put our plan into action.

Working in a war zone so close to the border, meant we had to take into account the artillery coming in from Iraq. As we were surrounded by hills, we could not see the incoming missiles. On reflection, I thought it would be a good 'advance missile warning system' to have one of my men stationed at the top of the hill, to wave a white flag on sighting approaching missiles. This way, we could get on with our work, keeping an occasional eye on him, and the moment he signalled, we would all run for cover. There were no mobile phones or convenient modes of communication in those days, and I thought this was a good idea to save our skins.

Unfortunately the first day, my lad proved to be more mouse than man. He went to the top of the hill with great bravado, and the rest of us got on with our work, confident in the knowledge our lad had our backs. However within a short while, we were caught off guard at the camp by the sudden shriek of a low wizzing missile above us, followed by the subsequent bang nearby. Looking up the hill we noticed that our 'advance missile warning system' was missing from his post. A few minutes later a frantically waving white flag appeared to be moving as if by wind power, as we could not make out my lad from the distance we were at.

A good tradesman he might be, but my lad definitely wouldn't earn a medal for valour. Instead of first sending us a warning signal, he kept ducking for cover himself whenever he saw a missile shooting in our direction, leaving us at the camp desperately scrambling to safety on hearing the missiles. Needless to say, when he came down the hill at the end of the first day, he received quite a vociferous reception from his colleagues, who did not mince their words when speaking their minds, and he was demoted to a mundane camp job instead. To our good luck during our time there, our camp was spared any artillery damage, though the area around us was bombarded with constant shelling.

With the assistance of the locally hired team with their lifting equipment and low loaders, coupled with the expertise of my team, and despite my absolutely louzy 'advance missile warning system', we managed to pull off the job. We decommissioned, relocated as well as re-commissioned the base camp in record time. My lads could not wait to return to the safety of Dubai, and I was sure they would not accompany me on any further war zone or hardship contracts.

My company had grown tremendously and in addition to moving to larger premises within the Al Jadaf dry docks, I also took Derek deWilde on as a partner in 1994, as I could not handle the increasing workload on my own. I knew taking on a partner would have positive and negative connotations for me as well as for the company. Unfortunately, over the years this move would prove I was not far wrong.

He was a British electrical engineer employed by the Hilton hotel, and was recommended to meet with me by mutual friends. I am well aware a business partner should be selected on the basis of not only his technical expertise in the concerned line of business, but also for his contribution to, and participation in the various aspects of managing a thriving business. Like choosing a marriage partner, outward appearances may sometimes be deceptive. And with my past dismal track record in wives, the odds were no doubt stacked against me in my choice of a business partner.

I chose to go with Derek as my business partner because he had a sense of humour and he made me laugh. Yea I know! that very statement should have relegated me to the psychiatric hospital. Instead, I was the managing director of a very successful company and a respected member of the community, who obviously seemed to have lost all his marbles. But I was always a workaholic with no private life to speak of, and I guess Derek's sense of humour was just what I needed at that stage in my life.

Derek did not have the capital to invest in my company for a fifty percent share. In hindsight, what I should have done was to take him on as a full fifty percent partner only after he invested his full fifty percent share of the capital. However, I not only took him on as a full fifty percent partner right from the start, but I also paid him fifty percent of the company's monthly profits instead of twenty-five percent, as he was able to invest only twenty-five percent of his share of the capital. No. I was not blind in this instance. I was just extremely busy and it was sheer oversight on my part.

However, the fact he took advantage of my lapse and kept quiet about the excess monthly payments, should have sent loud bells jangling in my brain, bringing to the forefront his lack of forthrightness and honesty. Oh! I have no excuse, but I was totally preoccupied with my excessive work and I took my eye off the ball. By the time realisation hit me, it was too late and I let it slide. However, Derek kept taking the fifty percent extra profits and repaid it into the company towards his balance investment, and probably rubbed his hands in glee all the way to the bank. But this proved to me early into our partnership that Derek was not as straight as I expected him to be. Having the ability to make me laugh was one thing but I would have to be alert where he was concerned.

As in every business, payments from debtors require constant follow-up. But the company still has to continue functioning, and staff and workmen paid on schedule. I always said that the day I could not pay my workforce on time, was the day I would close down the company. The people who worked for me were the very lifeline that kept my company in business. I may have been the brains but they were the veins which kept the various divisions of my company in fine fettle, and I always ensured they were well looked after.

As such, whenever the company was low on funds to pay the monthly emoluments, I would transfer the amount required by the company from my personal account, and the company would repay me when the monthly debtors cleared their dues. Even though Derek was now an equal fifty percent partner, when it came to loaning the company money, he always excused himself saying he had already transferred his complete salary to the UK and he had no residual money in Dubai to loan the company any funds.

Derek was basically a good guy and always ready for a laugh, but he was a follower and not the leader I needed to help me run the company. I even overlooked his regular disappearances from the company during office hours, and though I knew where he was, I never said anything to him. We got on well generally and even socialised together, though he was the type of person who joined friends for drinks at the pub but always forgot his wallet at home, when the time came for him to pay for a round of drinks. I know this for a fact, as over the years I paid for his round of drinks as well as mine several times, and received neither a 'thank you' nor any offer of repayment.

When Anne and I married in 1996, I asked her to join me in the company. She put her business management qualifications to good use by managing the company, basically keeping an eye on my investment and checking on any irregularities. Shortly after she joined us, the partners were required to each put in fifty thousand Dirhams to cover monthly overheads. Running true to form, Derek said he was not able to put in his half and I put in the full amount of one hundred thousand Dirhams.

Anne immediately instructed the finance department to draw up a loan repayment agreement from the company and got both of us partners to sign it. The agreement stated that as Derek and myself were equal partners, we each own fifty percent of the company. As such, we are not only entitled to fifty percent of the profits, but are also responsible equally for the daily running costs of the company and are expected to loan the company equal amounts whenever required.

However, if one partner defaults in paying in his equal loan amount, then the other partner will pay both loan amounts and the company will compensate him by paying him bank loan interest rates for the duration of the loan. Obviously the prospect of making interest on the loan was uppermost on my partner's mind. Some months later when the partners had to put in a loan amount, he was the first to put in his half.

When the company payments came in, Anne informed the finance department to repay both the partners only the loan amount. Derek immediately questioned the non-receipt of the interest amount and was informed by the finance department that the interest is only given to the partner who has to carry the complete financial burden of the company and not when both the partners share their financial responsibilities equally.

Needless to say, as my partner did not want me to earn any interest on the loan amounts, he made sure that whenever the company required any further loans, he put in his half of the amount. From the time Anne joined my company, the combination of her managerial skills and my technical expertise made us a team to be reckoned with.

Since Derek became a partner, he handled the office staff, signed cheques, checked salary statements and oversaw the daily administration of the company, while I continued to bring in the new clients and handle the tradesmen and technical aspects of the business. Over time, I noticed a trend set in. Every year when Derek went on vacation to the UK for the whole month of August, I took over the supervision of all the financial records of the company as well as Derek's jobs. During this one month, the company made a very much higher profit than the rest of the eleven months, when Derek was checking all the company finances.

When I mentioned it to Anne, she said she would look into it as the company's international auditors annual report would shed some light on the issue. But Anne surprisingly found discrepancies in the auditors reports as well, and started a covert check into the financial affairs of the company, going back a few years.

What Anne uncovered was a steady siphoning of company funds by our head accountant Khurram Iqbal, a few months after Derek joined the company. The accountant observed my partner was extremely lax at checking the accounts. He realised

Derek only checked that the statement's grand total and the cheque amount were the same, and blindly signed the accounts and the cheques on that basis. Derek never checked each individual statement amount or physically totalled the statements, as he should have done.

In actual fact the accountant maintained two sets of salary payment statements, and increased up to twenty thousand Dirhams a month on the statement my partner signed. When the accountant withdrew the cheque amount from the bank, he pocketed the twenty thousand Dirhams and destroyed the statement, bringing out the correct salary statement for the company records. This day light robbery was going on since Derek became a partner. However, every year during the month of August when my partner went on his annual vacation, I thoroughly checked the financial records, and that was the only month the accountant knew he could not push his luck.

As the accountant had embezzled over one million Dirhams from the company through various means, Anne proceeded with involving the CID, Police and eventually Interpol as he skipped the country and returned to his native Pakistan. We subsequently found out he had overdrawn credit cards with several international banks and as Anne was fed up with the banks calling her about this skip case, she informed the banks to directly contact Interpol to connect the cases.

Our international auditors were taken to task and sacked and Anne hired another audit company. I could also no longer trust Derek's slipshod management ways as he was solely responsible for leaving the gate wide open for our accountant to have easy access to our company funds without any form of restraint. As such, Anne instituted a company policy requiring the signatures of both the partners to authorise financial records and even sign cheques. But unfortunately, it was the case of 'too little, too late' as the ship had already sailed away, with all the loot.

At this time, I also expanded my business and opened companies in heavy engineering related to the oilfield sector. Anne worked with me and this was an extremely lucrative venture for us. Though we worked long and odd hours due to global time differences, we reaped rich rewards.

I took on a turnkey job in Cheleken, Turkmenistan, with a crew of men from Dubai, to commission an offshore oil rig eighty man camp in the Caspian Sea. Unfortunately, the job took a bit longer to commission as due to the choppy seas, the supply vessel could not get too close to the rig. As such, my crew were extremely frightened of precisely timing their jump from the ship to the rig with the swell of the sea. I explained that the wrong timing or hesitancy, would land them in the sea between the rig and the ship, and in grave danger. So, I gave them the option to exclude themselves from jumping onto the rig if they were not comfortable, as their safety was my priority.

Eventually, my plumbing foreman Nasser and I were the only ones who did the twice daily jump on to and off the rig. And as we both worked well together, we managed to complete the commissioning and handover of the camp to our Clients without delay, before returning to Dubai with the rest of my crew, who mainly enjoyed a vacation by the Caspian Sea.

I also went into partnership with Chris Green, a British man I had seen around but did not know well. He worked for an oil company owned by my close friends. He was leaving the company and wanted to open an oilfield heavy engineering company in Oman, but did not have the capital to start the company. I had the finances but did not know Oman. I was warned by a few friends not to go into partnership with him, and Anne too asked me to heed the warning of my friends, as we did not know him. However, I wanted to branch out of the UAE and it seemed the right time to do so.

While Chris was neither a partner nor involved in any way with my Dubai companies, I went into partnership with him and financed the start-up of the totally separate and independent company in Oman. I decided not to leave Dubai, and while Chris would run the Oman company, I would co-manage the company from Dubai, with visits to the Oman company as and when required.

He started the Oman company with a 'Bang', in large premises. He produced a company brochure indicating both of us as partners in the Oman oilfield heavy engineering company and had business cards made for both of us as managing directors. He rented a palatial mansion for him and his wife Karen as their residence, to keep up with his new image as managing director. He even organised a large party with around a hundred oilfield personnel and their spouses in attendance, to launch and promote the Oman company. Considering it was my money he was playing around with, Anne and I drove to Oman from Dubai for the weekend to attend the launch party.

However, Anne is good at what she does, and in due course she soon uncovered numerous discrepancies and scamming schemes, while going through the Oman company accounts. Like when he purchased a pickup for the Oman company with a credit card. A few months later, the same pickup was purchased again by the company, but with cash this time. Considering the company had only one pickup on its list of assets, this was a blatant scam and he was questioned about it. But he quickly got out of it by saying it was an accounting error, though the company first paid the local automobile dealer for the purchase of the pickup, and Chris was later paid cash for the same pickup again.

We also discovered that while I personally funded the start-up of the Oman company, which was to be registered in both our names as fifty percent partners, Chris deceived me, as he opened the company with my investment, but legally registered the company only in his name.

To prevent me from filing legal charges against him for taking my money and ripping me off, he used my money and filed charges against me in Dubai first. His charges were that he was a partner in my Dubai company, and unless I paid him one hundred thousand Dirhams to withdraw his case against me in Dubai, he would ensure I would go to jail for transferring funds from my Dubai company account into my personal account.

Chris knew how I operated as I am an open book. So he knew I transferred funds from my personal account to my Dubai company account, when the company was low on funds, and that the company transferred the funds back to my account, when the company debtors settled their bills.

I am not sure if the laws have changed now, but many foreign UAE business owners may not be aware of the UAE law, stating that it is illegal to transfer funds from a company account to any company personnel's personal account. Irrelevant of the facts, as firstly in my case, it is my Dubai company in partnership only with Derek and secondly, the funds were legally my funds as I transferred it from my personal account, and it was being returned to me by my company. But as per the UAE law it is a criminal offence.

My Dubai local solicitors advised me to pay the money to Chris and avoid going to jail. I refused pointblank as at that time, he already owed me over a million US Dollars and secondly, it was a matter of principle. I am a person who has always been very straight in my personal and business dealings. No one can ever say that I either took advantage of them financially, or misrepresented myself for gain. I will also never ever give in to the threaths of terrorists and conmen, what ever the consequences.

And finally, Anne agreed with me as she said Chris could not be trusted, as even if I did pay him the money, there was no guarantee he would keep his word. However, as we had the truth on our side, we could prove it with a bit of time. Anne was not happy with my solicitors and was looking for another local solicitor to sort out my legal issues, as in the UAE only local solicitors can represent anyone in the UAE courts. So meanwhile, Anne and I discussed the matter and I decided that vacationing in jail it was for me, till Anne sorted out my legal affairs.

Chris thought he had outsmarted me and had me over a barrel, as I would give him the money to avoid going to jail. But he did not reckon on the fact that since he already owed me over three million Dirhams, it did not matter to me how good a card shark he was, as there was no way I was giving him even a penny more of my money. So I decided to go the whole hog and let him put my money where his mouth is, to try and prove his case in the Dubai Courts, that he was a partner in my Dubai company. I was looking forward to enjoy his downfall from the confines of my barred premises.

One sunny day, I informed Derek about what I had planned

to do, and we decided to keep it under the radar for the sake of the business, with Anne managing the company along with him in my absence. Other than Derek, Anne and myself, no one knew about my situation. Later that day, Anne drove me to the Dubai courts, and she was with me while I handed myself in, before being subsequently transferred to the Al Wasl central jail.

My time in jail was the start of what cleared my name, and any record against me in the Dubai courts. During the first couple of days there, the police in charge who knew of my case, recommended I appoint a particular solicitor who was not only a tough legal expert in the field with a very good track record, but a woman as well.

I conveyed the details to Anne who visited me regularly, and she had a meeting with this high profile local lady solicitor. Anne was happy to hire her services and from then on she worked very closely with the solicitor. I was within no time released on a one million Dirhams bail, which Anne paid when she picked me up from the jail, pending clearing of my name and proving my innocence in the matter.

While I continued my daily work and managing the company with Derek, Anne concentrated on my case with the solicitor and they were making extremely positive headway as Anne had facts and figures not only for my Dubai company but also for the Oman company. If I did not have Anne in my corner, I would have had a very tough time sorting through the legalities alongside running the business. As with all legal matters, documentation had to be translated into Arabic for the courts and all the legal procedures had to run its course.

Chris never realised he had no leg to stand on, against the truth and facts from my side. He had hedged all his bets on me giving him the one hundred thousand Dirhams before the case went to court. He tried every trick in the book to get more money out of me, by using my money which he still owes me, to fight me and file the false cases in all the Dubai courts against me.

However, the truth always wins and the prosecution and all the courts right from the 'Court of First Instance', the 'Court of Appeals' and the highest body, the 'Court of Cassation', found in my favour, based on the naked truth and undisputed facts from my side. They certified that I was innocent of all criminal and civil charges and any record against me was expunged.

Based on my innocence, the Dubai courts ordered Chris to pay all the court charges for lying under oath and filing a false case against me, by claiming he was a partner in my Dubai company, and that I had cheated him by transferring our joint company funds to my personal account.

As he still owes me over a million US Dollars for my fifty percent share of the Oman company, I then wanted to chase it through the Oman courts. But living in the UAE, the legal logistics proved to be very complicated and I kept the matter in abeyance. My mum always said 'what goes around, comes around' and I have absolutely no doubt he will get his comeuppance one way or the other.

At that time, the best way to bring him down was to make what he had done public knowledge within the business and oilfield community. Since the news was common knowledge as it had appeared in the newspapers, this was no great feat on my part.

However we understand through the business circuit, that a short while later, Chris and his wife Karen divorced. She was trying to get a good divorce settlement from him, but he had no intention of giving in to her demands. As such, he misled her by informing her to get her payout from me, saying I had pilfered all his money. This ofcourse was a misnomer, as he had taken a gamble on me, and lost my money, paying for his very expensive lawyers and court costs in Oman and Dubai, to fight me and con me out of more money.

What I learned during my short time in jail however, was an eye opener. Fellow inmates were friendly and respectful towards me. While many spoke English, there were many more who did not. But they still offered me help and assistance, as they were there long before me and would probably be there long after I left. All the police also treated the inmates well, and I noticed there was an easy comaraderie between the police and the inmates, which made the inmates tenure there, I guess much more bearable.

There were people in jail right from bounced cheques to other more serious offences. But as most of them did not have the funds to clear the bounced cheques or their names, since being in jail prevented them from working to pay it off, I helped a few genuine persons with money to clear their dues and get out of jail, knowing they would not be able to repay me.

There were other people I met who had stories to tell, which would make very interesting and extremely shocking fodder for a book in itself. But most importantly, while many were incarcerated for justified offences and felonies, there were several like me who were wrongly imprisoned as unfortunately, jurisprudence the world over is just another flawed and broken tool.

But unlike me, these people did not have the resources to get them out of their predicament and I was not in a position to help everyone financially. Though, I did visit a few of them and took them whatever personal items they required.

Yes, there are conmen all over the globe. But in countries like the Middle East, fly-by-night cowboys without a bean to their name, but wanting to see their name on billboards, are plentiful. And then, there are folk like me who attract these undesirable characters like a magnet. Many folk knew I was one of the few people in Dubai who would help anyone financially. I guess I was blind and used big time, or maybe it was that huge neon sign on my forehead saying 'blind mug'.

Another British man Tony Caden had messed up with the company he was working with and I did not know what the exact reason was. All I knew was that he was not only out of a job but he could not stay in the country as he also lost his employment visa. I have helped several people to start up their own companies and someone in the business community informed him about me.

Tony approached me and asked me if I would help him to start up his own company. I very candidly told him he obviously did something unethical and terrible, for his company to sack him. I would not under any circumstances tolerate him repeating his grave mistakes and taking me for a ride, if I decided to help him. He assured me there would be no irregular dealings to tarnish either my name or the reputation of my company, and based on his word, I did help him.

A few months later he informed me his father was on a visit to Dubai during the Dubai annual Shopping Festival. Tony visited me at the office one day and asked me if I could loan him thirty thousand Dirhams. He said his father had a heart attack and was being treated in the Dubai Hospital, and he needed money to settle the hospital bill before his father could be released from the hospital.

As his need seemed genuine, I told him I would organise the money in a few days. However, Tony called me the next day and said his father was released from the hospital, and he did not need the money, as he did not have to pay any bill. Since his father was a visitor to Dubai during the shopping festival, the office of the Ruler of Dubai had settled the full hospital bill. This I did believe, as despite the global populace in Dubai, the Ruler of Dubai is well known for his philanthropic nature across the community divide, even though I truly don't think he receives either the acknowledgement, or due credit for his humanitarian efforts.

Tony did not like Anne either, as she put a spoke in his con and quick getaway. During the Iraq war, his company was handling a large deal on some machinery. But as he did not have the money, he asked me for a loan of twenty-five thousand Dirhams. He bought the machinery and unfortunately, it was lying in my workshop for a very long time as his deal fell through.

By this time Tony was starting his own company and he approached me to sign the papers to transfer his visa from my company, to his own separate new company. One day to Tony's bad luck, Anne walked in when he was in my office. At a glance she immediately noticed I was about to sign his visa transfer documents. Angrily and without ceremony she took the papers off me, checked I had not signed it, and returned it back to Tony.

She informed him that when he repaid the loan back to us in full and retrieved his machinery from our workshop, his employment visa would be transferred without a problem. Anne's arrival at the opportune moment saved me from being conned out of the twenty-five thousand Dirhams loan, I had totally forgotten about.

Tony would have disappeared, with me holding the baby and also out of pocket. On the other hand, Tony could not open his own company until he was off my company visa. As such, he had no options but to do as Anne demanded, and I then signed his visa transfer and he was off our company.

Some time later when on his new company, Tony Caden was signing an agreement with the Iranian national oil company. But before they would sign on the dotted line, they required Tony to prove he had one million Dirhams in his bank. As he naturally did not have a bean to his name, he asked me to loan him the money for a week. I informed him I did not have the money on me and I would have to transfer it from out of the country, at which he said he would cover all the costs of the exchange rates up and down, as well as the international bank transfer charges.

As you will understand, Anne is certainly justified in her dislike of Tony due to his handling of past dealings, and she advised me in the form of a long lecture against giving him any money. She also informed me in no uncertain terms to stop trusting the wrong people, and not to look in her direction when things blew up in my face, and I needed someone to pick up the pieces. But my way of looking at it was that if the boot was on the other foot and I needed financial help, just maybe he would be there for me. At the end of the day, it was just money. So, I loaned Tony a million Dirhams and he secured his agreement.

But Tony never kept his word, as he did not repay me the money as promised in a week. I was forced to not only look in Anne's direction, but also beg her on bended knees to pick up the pieces. It took her over two months of continuous follow-up directly with his bank, to finally get the one million Dirhams back.

But he has not paid me either the international bank charges, or the to and fro exchange rates as agreed. He knows where to find me to repay me the money he owes me, as I met him at his home in Dubai in 2015 to get my money back. But obviously his word is not his bond as till date, he has not bothered to repay me. It is shocking that after all I have done for him, he still ripped me off.

With Anne's business acumen guiding me into diversification, I spread my wings and I now had the Q.G.M. Group of companies in fields as varied as marine and land based general maintenance, small construction, marine survey and offshore services, oilfield engineering, general and specialised security, just to name a few. Naturally, with the growth of our group of companies, our staff and labour force increased a hundred fold, and Anne and I were working extremely long hours to keep the wheels of all the companies greased and in motion.

I initially held an annual party for all our staff and their families and it was a great family get-together. I always hosted it at hotels but I later hosted the parties at my villa. Further, as a 'thank you' for my clients loyalty to our company, I also had annual greeting cards custom designed with a different humorous theme on some aspect of our company, running through the design for good measure. To our surprise, the cards were greatly received and appreciated by all our clients and business associates, and it was the talk of the town every year.

When I decided to sell my share of the company and retire, Derek said he would not be able to manage the company on his own, and nor did he have the funds to buy me out. So we agreed to sell the complete company, and our international auditors began their audit and due deligence. We found a buyer for the company, and Derek and I agreed on the sale price which was being paid in three stage payments.

Anne informed me that before Derek became a partner, in order to regularise the company assets, I should have sold all the assets which were personally owned by me, to the company. But it really did not even strike me at that time. Now at the time of selling the company, I still personally owned about seventy-five percent of the company assets, which I had allowed the company to use without any charge, and which was documented in the annual audit reports.

When the initial tranche payment for the sale of the company came in, Anne informed our finance department to first pay me in full for the complete value of the company assets I owned, before dividing the balance amount equally between Derek and me. She said once this payment was out of the way, the balance two stage payments could also then be divided equally between the two partners.

However, Derek would not have it. He insisted that the full sale price had to be divided equally between the two partners, irrelevant of the fact I owned the subject company assets. But Anne is not someone to either be bullied, or to back down when she is correct. She informed Derek that if he did not agree with either the payment decision, or the fact I personally owned the concerned company assets, he should not have signed off the company's audit reports every year. He tried his luck, though he knew there were no discrepancies, since the payment being made to me was correct and legal. As such, the sale of the company went ahead without further hurdles.

What was extremely surprising though, was the fact once Derek received his fifty percent of the sale of the company, he took his money and scarpered. He proved he was just another user and no friend. He never ever kept in touch and even when I contacted him, he never replied. And that was the last I saw of the partner who grabbed unearned company profits, lost me over a million Dirhams and whose dead weight I continued to carry till the very end.

Not only were Anne and myself successful on the business front, but we were also extremely happy and enjoyed our life in Dubai to its fullest. But in 2009 Anne and I decided the time had come for me to sell the rest of my businesses and finally hang up my boss' hat. We were now ready to move onto the next chapter of our lives, and join the exclusive club of the 'retired gentry'. We did not know where we would go as yet, but we knew our little Utopia was somewhere out there in our world and we would definitely find it.

Yes, I will always cherish the wonderful, colourful relationship I had with Dubai for over a period of thirty years, despite the spectrum being marred by a few shady characters I encountered enroute during my life there. However, while I can hold my head up high, they will eventually have to account for all their cons and misdeeds, when being turned away at the 'pearly gates'.

I still visit the Emirates regularly, and we just may live on its sunny shores once again in the not too distant future. Having been given the honour of calling this wonderful country my home for very many long years, I will always retain more than a soft spot for the Emirates, and I will never stop wishing only the very best for this spectacular desert oasis. And without a doubt, I will forever treasure the longlasting friendships I made with my Emirati friends, during my yesteryears in their little corner of 'Heaven' in the desert.

With staff at a QGM Reunion in Dubai with Nasser, Prasanth, Hassan, Jain and Baba in 2015

EASY PLUMBER

Easy Plumber

Chapter 16

The land of the pharaohs – Cairo (Egypt)

1978

When my contract with the Al Ghurair development in Dubai ended in August 1978, the company sent me to Cairo in Egypt, to supervise and sort out problems on a project which was in its final stages, before being handed over to the client at the year end.

My family accompanied me and we rented a house in Cairo belonging to a colonel in the Egyptian army. I really enjoyed the bustling vibrancy of the city around us. The charm of Cairo over forty years ago was like no other, with its narrow streets and market stalls or souks deliberately encroaching onto the roads, selling everything under the sun, and teaming with local people shopping all day long. Like the UAE, Egypt was in the process of developing, and construction sites in Cairo was the view in every direction you looked.

Driving on the roads was always chaotic, as pedestrians as well as traders pushing heavily laden hand carts, interspersed with the traffic without caution. I was informed that if a driver even touched one of them with their vehicle, the vehicle would suddenly be surrounded and the driver hassled for money, by a mob of people who seemed as if they were waiting for just such an incident to happen, as they just keep coming out of the wood work.

I could not get over the fascination of being in such a country steeped in ancient history, with the River Nile coursing through its very veins, and ofcourse the wonders of the world at Giza on my doorstep. The old city transported me back in time with my imagination running riot, wondering what it would have been like to live in that bygone era, or about the people who walked these very same routes.

When I was in Egypt, I realised I prefer the old world charm to the chrome and glass monstrosities of our modern age living. However, as life moves forward, our population increases and so does innovation and technology, which changes the very essence of every developing country. Unfortunately being just miniture cogs in the wheels of advancement, we have no options but to accept change with dignity and finesse, moving with the times, even though it may not appeal to us.

Chapter 17

A woman of substance – La Puttana to La Buttana

In the early 1990s, I moved my company from Bur Dubai to the Al Jadaf dry docks, as my company had grown and I required larger premises. Another reason was that I had bought a 1963 Dutch harbour tug originally named the 'Argus', and I was converting her into a top of the line survey and pleasure vessel in the dry docks.

I renamed the vessel 'La Puttana' an Italian word meaning 'the whore', as I always intended she would sell her services to the highest bidder for hard cash. However, in 1996 when I married Anne, my friends said I should change the name as it was not appropriate. So I just changed the 'P' to 'B' and she was named 'La Buttana'. She was now called 'the bitch', as all the women in my life till that time, definitely fell into that category. However, Anne just laughed and said whatever her name, she certainly had no problem sharing me with her.

With my company located in the dry docks, whenever any of my men were free, they went across the yard to work on my vesssel. All my tradesmen were trained by me personally, and their workmanship was nothing short of exemplary. They knew my high standards and never ever let me down. The complete vessel was being built of solid steel meant to withstand the fury of the high seas, and my welders had spent long hours getting the job right, before the rest of the work on the vessel could commence.

Based on my instructions, my men re-built and modified the complete vessel to my specifications, right from the hull to the mast. As the engine room in the original tug was miniscule, the first job I had carried out was to cut the vessel down the centre horizontally into two halves. I lengthened the vessel by approximately fourteen feet with a brand new extended keel, increasing its total length to just shy of twenty metres. This extension enabled me to get all the engines, generators and equipment I wanted, into the new engine room. It was no small feat as I had to maintain the vessel's centre of gravity and stability. Subsequently, I widened the vessel by one metre each, on the Port and Starboard side by fitting sponson tanks, which increased the stability of the vessel.

As I had always planned to use the vessel for work and pleasure, I fitted a crane on the top deck to lift the engine room equipment through the vessel's hatches, for major maintenance work if called for. Further, it served to lift my Harley Davidson on and off the ship, when at Port.

With my youthful seafaring experience behind me, I knew exactly what I wanted my vessel to be equipped with. Besides the main bridge with all the state of the art steering, radar and navigation technology, there was a fly bridge on the top deck as well as an aft steering station on the vessel.

The vessel was driven by two main engines and in addition to the main propeller, I fixed four dedicated thrusters, out of which two were hydraulic fixed pod thrusters which also acted as a second main engine. The bow and stern truster could be operated either manually, or by joystick control from all three steering stations, making it a very manoeuvrable vessel, that could literally do pirouettes in tight places. With such a vast amount of equipment, there was a fully equipped onboard workshop to handle its maintenance.

For fire fighting, I installed a pump which could pump eight hundred and fifty gallons of water a minute, with a fifty metre throw, through all the four water cannons on the vessel. Additionally, there were four generators providing auxilliary power supply. To move with the times, I had (ROV) remote operating vehicle technology installed. An onboard desalination plant, produced eight hundred and fifty gallons of fresh water a day, more water than the resident twelve persons could use in a day.

Though the vessel was only licensed to carry a maximum of thirty-three persons, passenger safety was of high priority for me. I had life jackets and safety equipment for nearly double the passengers, as well as two inflatable twenty-five man life rafts, and a fully equipped eight persons, inboard jet engine Nautica Rib 14 Jet tender boat, with ship to shore communication.

People always asked me why I did not just buy a million Pounds Sterling vessel, as my 'La Buttana' was like a bucket with a permanent hole in it. However, my answer never satisfied them and it did not matter to me. I had finally completed and put the vessel in the water for its sea trials in 2001, after working on it for ten long years in the dry docks and to me, it was nothing short of a labour of love and an absolute personal achievement.

Anyone can buy a vessel as it is only money. But not many can design and personally construct their top of the line, custom built survey and pleasure vessel from the hull up, and enjoy every moment of it taking shape, and attaining fulfilment of a life long dream. I was called on several times to talk on the various aspects of building the 'La Buttana', and her special features. However, as Anne was an expert on the 'La Buttana' by now, she gave the talks and I handled the question and answer sessions.

My close friend Derek Petrie who was the chief of the Al Jadaf Drydocks, did mention that several personnel from other shipping companies in the docks were out en masse at the sea trials, to see if the 'La Buttana' would float or sink. Everyone in the docks had seen and knew of the 'La Buttana', as she went through innumerable changes over the ten years in the dry docks.

However, they could not believe I would actually accomplish my personal project to successful fruition, considering they were the professional ship builders and I was just a plumber, albeit with an extensive amount of knowledge and technical expertise. So they had to witness the sea trials of my 'La Buttana' for themselves. Unquestionably it was my proudest moment, when my 'woman of substance' demonstrated her true mettle and gave all the 'doubting Thomases' something to really talk about.

On the work front, the vessel's capabilities encompassed survey, ROV, diving, salvage, towing and firefighting facilities. The vessel even had enough auxilliary power supply to power another ship, a complete oil rig or any other facility. It also doubled up as a supply and a crew change vessel. While on the pleasure side, the vessel had a range of onboard outdoor facilities including diving, fishing, water skiing, target practice shooting and skeet shooting.

The 'La Buttana' had three cabins providing very comfortable ensuite sleeping quarters for twelve persons on long trips, in addition to its saloon and work stations, galley and outdoor barbeque and dining on deck. She was also certified to carry a total of thirty-three persons including four crew, when on pleasure day trips.

My last project before the vessel was launched, was to affix a life size fibreglass figurehead of my 'La Buttana' on the bowsprit of the vessel. I designed and had the drawings done of a sexy woman with long flowing hair holding up the bowsprit. We found a lady who was a sculptor and she laughed when I asked her if she could sculpt the 'La Buttana' based on the actress Sandra Bullock's figure.

She said it was a big ask, and she would have to sculpt it to a figure more akin to her own. The end result she came up with after it was painted and completed, was rather more voluptuous but nevertheless absolutely fantastic, and my 'La Buttana' was finally completed. Without a doubt, she drew a lot of attention to the 'La Buttana', as people were drawn to the vessel the moment they saw her.

On the 11 January 2004, the 'La Buttana' was officially launched at the Al Jadaf dry docks by my close friend Mrs. Dolly Lamprell, and the onboard launch party was attended by my genuine band of merry friends and business well wishers, who were all extremely thrilled for me and my 'woman of substance'.

A very memorable job the 'La Buttana' undertook was in 2004, when the vessel was hired by a company in Scotland to do a two weeks offshore job. The company sent its six member team of highly specialised experts, to remove the 'well head' from the decommissioned SEDCO oil rig located in the Arabian Sea.

My crew were onboard and always ready for any eventuality. However as I did not have an onboard chef, I asked Anne if she would join our crew as 'galley slave' for the duration of the job, catering three meals a day for a full ship of twelve persons, and round the clock open bar and snacks for our clients.

Anne was hesitant, but I tempted her with the perk of sharing the owner and captain's cabin. She laughed and said 'now how can I refuse such an enticing offer'. As she is an expert on the culinary front, I knew she would handle the galley with aplomb. Actually it was the first time in the United Arab Emirates and probably the last, that a working vessel had a woman chef as part of the crew.

While the rest of the crew and myself got the ship fuelled, its various checks carried out and ready for the trip, Anne had her own checklists and she got all the cabins ready, before ordering the food, drinking water and beverages. It was the first time she was accompanying me on an offshore job on the 'La Buttana'. While we worked well together in the company, we had never crewed together and I was very happy indeed to have her onboard.

She was doing all the cooking onboard and was kept busy prepping and preparing, though she had help with the washing up from the galley's integrated dishwasher. With a ship full of down and dirty working men, the onboard self-service launderette washer and dryer was also in constant use, and the clients were never inconvenienced in any way.

Our client's team were a great group of very friendly lads, who had absolutely no problem having a woman on the crew.

They loved the vessel and very quickly made it home. They came from all professional backgrounds, including a few ex-Royal Marines and even an ex-Legionaire.

As the client had a penalty clause to their contract if they did not dismantle and handover the 'well head' by a specific date, I regarded it as my job to ensure that I was not responsible for any delays on getting them to the rig on schedule.

However, on the day we left Al Jadaf, from the onshore swell we knew there was a storm fast approaching. The Dubai coast guard subsequently warned us not to leave Dubai. But as I had given my word to my client that fair weather or foul, I would get the team to the rig, I decided we would brave the waves and get to our offshore destination.

By the time we reached the rig it was dusk. The storm was furious, with wild waves over six metres high, and we were naturally unable to moor alongside the rig. We had to anchor at sea some way off the rig, so as to avoid being thrown against the rig and damaging the 'La Buttana' by the prevailing gale force winds. All we could see from the windows and portholes was a wall of water as the vessel rose and dipped with each heavy swell, while at the same time being buffetted by the waves whipped into a real frenzy by the storm.

Our galley slave left a wide selection of cold food, hand pies and salads in the chiller for all on board. But she was not seen as she was confined to her cabin with sea sickness. While our clients were also tucked up in their warm beds at night, I was on constant watch, with my crew taking turns to watchstand with me, till the storm subsided.

The next day calm reigned, and I was extremely proud and pleased as punch, that my 'La Buttana' had passed her 'perfect storm' moment with flying colours. She had braved the high seas and defied the elements, to prove she could handle anything Mother Nature threw at her. Everyone onboard was bright eyed and bushy tailed, including our galley slave.

However, the supply vessel that was to collect the 'well head', could not make it because of the storm and would not reach the rig for a week. Hence we returned to Dubai at a leisurely pace, enjoying the sunny weather and the party mode on the vessel, with everyone enjoying the open bar and brunch.

We were returning to the rig in a few days, and I was not sure if Anne would grace us with her presence, after her first experience at sea on the 'La Buttana'. But she is obviously not a woman to give up easily, as she just reorganised her checklist and made preparations for the return trip.

This time, the journey and our client's job was on schedule and as planned. We moored alongside the rig and after a week or so, the supply vessel moored alongside us. While our clients worked on the rig during the day, Anne and our crew got on with all the onboard jobs. When the clients returned onboard at the end of their day on the rig, everyone cleaned up and then relaxed and had fun before dinner was served. They went diving and swimming, jetted around over the calm blue waters in the tender boat and even spent happy hours trying to reel in the best catch.

All the clients respected Anne's position on the vessel and they always removed their dirty boots and overalls on deck at the entrance of the ship, so the interior of the vessel was always kept clean. Anne excelled in the galley and we were treated to cuisine from a different country each evening, while she also catered separate vegetarian meals for our captain from India, who was a strict vegetarian.

The La Buttana, resplendent at Jebel Ali hotel marina in Dubai

Aerial view of the La Buttana moored alongside the SEDCO 708 oil rig

Rolls Royce Phantom - playing wedding car chauffeur for my friends Tim and Nikki

Lamborghini Diablo (Hard Top) rear wheel drive

With my Rolls Royce Silver Spur

Lamborghini Diablo VT front wheel drive

With my Ferrari 328GT (T Top)

My De Tomaso Pantera and Bugatti EB110

My De Tomaso Pantera

My GMC Sierra Z 71

Bugatti EB110

Lamborghini Diablo VT Roadster

Maserati Ghibli

With Mum and Dad

My last picture with Mum in 2007

With Anne and my cousins - the Roberts family

Friday 26 April 1996 - The day we met in Dubai

Our bridal party at St. Mary's Church in Dubai

At our wedding reception on 12 June 1996, in Dubai

With my band of five merry best men -Tim, Ed, John, Brian and Derek

Little Miss Mischief - Coral

Coral's first day of school

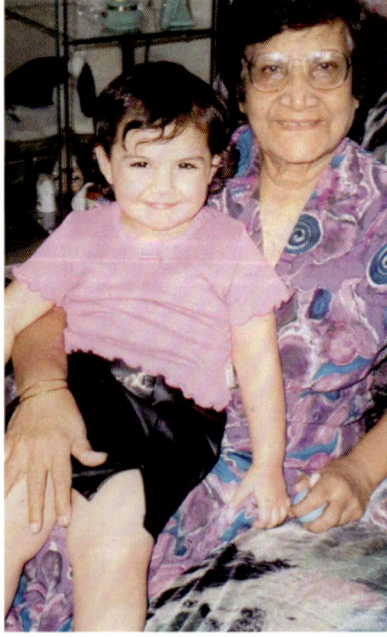

Coral at two years, with Nana

Family on the La Buttana

Anne even found the time to prepare a cake and a celebration for one of the client's team whose birthday fell during this period. Needless to say, our clients were indeed extremely happy not only with the 'La Buttana' and her facilities, but also with our first class service extended to their team. And from my side, I would most decidedly prefer to have Anne as my first mate on any future trips on the high seas.

The 'La Buttana' for the first time subsequently left the Al Jadaf dry docks and the only home she knew in Dubai, and cruised her way in style through the Dubai creek and out to sea again, this time making her way to her new mooring at the Jebel Ali hotel marina.

The resort was pleased to have my vessel with its onboard fire fighting facilities on site at the marina. Just a couple of weeks earlier, a yacht in the marina caught fire and the staff had to tow the vessel away from its mooring as it was very close to the Sheikh's yacht. Unfortunately, they could not put the fire out and the yacht could not be salvaged. My crew worked and lived onboard the vessel full time and though I was the official qualified captain, my crew also included a captain, as my time was split between managing my group of companies as well.

When I sold my group of companies, I had planned on working only with my marine company and concentrating on the 'La Buttana'. But life chose another path for me and we decided to split our time between the UK and Dubai, to be closer to my mum who was a nonagenarian, as spending more time with her during the ending years of her life was a priority for me.

And the end result was that the 'La Buttana' was sold to a client who knew the vessel well, was familiar with all her facilities and was extremely satisfied with her capabilities. She made the journey with her new owners to Singapore, and even got a change in identity, in the corner of the globe she now lives in.

As my friends said, she was a large bucket with a hole in it and yes, she never batted an eyelid about draining my bank balance. But in return, she gave me very many long hours of pure unadulterated joy, when I was working and spending time with her. To me she was my 'woman of substance' and she will always hold a special place in my heart – the one 'bitch' I would most certainly love to see some time, some place, some where again in the near future, before I finally kick my bucket.

La Buttana was transformed from the Argus, a Dutch Harbour Tug

La Buttana being lengthened in Al Jadaf Dry Docks

A view of the La Buttana's main bridge

Dolly Lamprell launching the La Buttana

Guests at the Launch of the La Buttana

Some of the Client's Specialist Team on the SEDCO oil rig

Chapter 18

My high octane pleasurable toys

Everyone has something that gives them an adrenaline rush. For me it is my 'boys toys' as Anne calls them. As a child I did not have toys to play with, but I never missed what I never had in the first place. When I reached adulthood, and completed my stint on the high seas, I had dreams of having my own custom made ship and my dreams eventually became reality.

Unfortunately, not many folk can achieve their dreams at a young age. I was one of them. I was not born with a silver spoon, never received any financial handouts from my parents as they could not afford it, and nothing ever fell off the back of a lorry and dropped at my feet. If I wanted something, I had to plan, work hard and go after it. As they say - 'life's a bitch'.

I believe everyone has the choice to live their lives the way they want to, within their means. I reached that time in my life, when the children were independent adults and I was single again. I suddenly had the means to pamper myself, without a thought for anyone else. I took the chance and I did not disappoint the young hearted lad in me, as I felt the time had finally arrived for me to put 'ME' first.

I have never cared what people either think or say about me. My life has taught me there will always be two groups of people around me. One group who are genuinely happy for me and my life's achievements, and the other group who are the users and who say what they think I want to hear but are disparaging behind my back.

Over the years, I have lost friends who felt they could not keep up with my lifestyle, and dropped out of my life. It is very unfortunate, but I cannot change their views, and I definitely am not going to apologise for working hard to achieve my success. I accept people for who they are, and not for what they are or have. If they cannot reciprocate the same way, then they are not genuine friends in the first instance.

People around me however, have viewed my high-end toys very differently. My elder two children saw it as a waste of money, squandered on pricey inanimate trinkets solely for my personal pleasure.

Business associates thought I was crazy to use my luxury wheels to work. When I sometimes drove my Lamborghini to my company in the Al Jadaf dry docks, people said it was not a car one took into the dry docks, where all around ships were being worked on right from sand and water blasting to welding. They even thought I was insane to use my Rolls Royce Silver Spur as my daily work car.

As I was single again, my toys also drew in an array of women who filled up my invisible little black book, which to be totally honest, I seldom used. And then there is Anne, who regards my toys as just that – my 'boys toys'. As long as the wheels take her from A to B, she is not really bothered about its dash from zero to sixty miles per hour in under three seconds, its luxurious interior or even its sleek, curvaceous body.

However, while Anne does not get any form of a buzz from

my toys, she has always encouraged me to pander to my whims and purchase any toy I fancy, as she often says 'you deserve to spend your hard earned money any which way you want. Life is short, so go for it if you want it'. And though she will never ever admit it, I know she too secretly enjoys driving my high end wheels.

But however people view my toys, for me they are an expression of self-satisfaction with my life. Despite working all hours God gave me over the years, happiness eluded me and I just survived in order to ensure my family had everything. Now I am living my life to the beat of my own drum, and I am enjoying every minute of it. This is 'ME!'

My boy's toys – 'Cars'

I love any vehicle with a high powered engine beneath its bonnet. But I also have a real soft spot for the vintage Classics.

In January 1994, I won the first 'Dubai Classic Car Cruise' with my 1928 Rolls Royce. I loved the car, and I used to have fun with it. I once played chauffeur and used it as the bridal car for the wedding of my close friends Tim and Nikki Lamprell. (Tim graciously returned the favour when Anne and I married, and played the bridal car chauffeur in his brother Steve's Rolls Royce).

On another occasion, my friend Ed Abernathy who owned an oilfield company, was in a fix as his American associate was arriving in Dubai. As Ed was stuck in meetings and could not get to the airport in time to pick him up, he asked me if I would do him a favour. I not only stepped in, but I decided to give Ed's visiting American guest the royal treatment, and played chauffeur again. I picked him up in the car, complete with a champagne bar in the rear.

To my amazement, the visitor was no gentleman. He spoke very rudely and even left his luggage for me to handle. I guess I should not be surprised at how prejudiced some folk are when treating people in the service industry, as I was now at the receiving end. If he had given me a handsome tip it may have softened the blow! But like his luggage, I guess his wallet was securely locked.

Nonetheless, his unwarranted snobbishness was about to hit him right between the eyes. Ed was hosting a cocktail party at his home that evening to welcome his associate and I was invited. We were all at the bar having a drink when his associate noticed me and said to Ed. 'I see you have your chauffeur with us here this evening'. Ed laughed and said I was not his chauffeur. He explained I was his business associate, with my own company, and I had just stepped in as he could not make it to the airport in time. Without a doubt, the look on the guy's face was a picture for the records, though he never did apologise for his rudeness, incorrect assumption or his prejudicism. Unfortunately, there are very many folk like him who let down their countrymen.

I subsequenty sold the car to a buyer from Bahrain. But I understand the car now has a pride of place in the classic car museum in Sharjah, and I look forward to a bonding session with my old 'classic' on my next trip to the United Arab Emirates.

My next classic was a 1983 Rolls Royce Silver Spur, I had purchased from Mr. Al Habtoor who had started and owned Al Habtoor Motors in Dubai. The car being his personal pride, was cared for extremely well and used sparingly. I put my company logo stickers on the sides of my Rolls Royce, making it undeniably a truly successful 'plumber's car', and I used it as my daily work car.

Well needless to say, some folk thought I was treating the Rolls Royce image with disdain. However, the fact everyone in Dubai knew of 'Dave the plumber' and his Rolls Royce, was a sign I had finally made it to the top. But ofcourse, Rolls Royce took all the credit.

I later shipped my Rolls Royce to the UK, so I could use it when on vacation, and for my parents to experience a little bit of luxury. I had a sunroof fitted into the car at Rolls Royce in the UK, which actually enhanced the look of the Silver Spur.

After Anne and I married, I shipped the Rolls Royce back to Dubai, and continued to enjoy her classic beauty, till a like minded person convinced me to sell her so he could give her a good home with him.

At the same time, I also had a De Tomaso Pantera, which started my love affair with the hot and sleek bodied Italian beauties. To me, no other country in the world other than Italy, has managed to seduce the global car enthusiasts, with its high powered engineering, luxurious interiors and superb titillating exteriors.

A few months later in November 1994, I could not resist buying the Bugatti EB110, which was designed by BBurago and just released throughout the Middle East. I had the privilege of receiving a congratulatory letter from the managing director of Bugatti Italy, on being the first person in the Middle East to buy a Bugatti.

But my love affair with the car did not last long. As my

EB110 was the only Bugatti produced in its company colours – 'Bugatti blue', it was a much sought after toy. Shortly after I purchased it, an anonomous buyer from Panama sent his representative to Dubai, to buy the car from me at any cost. I did sell it and I have regretted it ever since.

I purchased a Ferarri 328 GT (T Top) from Al Tayer motors. But within a few months, I was made an offer from a private party to sell my car to them. As I wanted to go in for the higher V12 model, I sold it and went to Al Tayer motors to buy the new Ferrari I was upgrading to.

However, the sales manager refused to sell me the car, as I had sold the one I had recently purchased from them. I informed him that he firstly fell short on his job, which was to put his employer first, and sell his company's products. Secondly, he had absolutely no right to tell any customer what they could or could not do with their own possessions and finally, he had not heard the end of this incident.

Undeterred, I went directly to German Cars, now known as Al Jaziri motors and owned by Bader Al Jaziri, and purchased the Lamborghini Diablo (Hard Top) Rear Wheel Drive. Though, I did telephone Saeed Al Tayer, the managing director of Al Tayer motors, and explained to him as to why I purchased a Lamborghini, and not the Ferrari I actually initially wanted from his company. As I understand it, the inept sales manager was subsequently on the look out for a new job, and rightly so.

The Lamborghini Diablo VT Front Wheel Drive followed a short while later, as I absolutely loved the Lamborghini and I could not stop myself from upgrading my set of luxury wheels.

I then purchased the BMW L7 on a whim, just to teach the British sales manager of BMW in Dubai, that prejudicism holds no place in our world, and no person should be judged on the clothes they wear or the vehicles they drive.

I received a call from my friend Statis, who was and still is the managing director of BMW and Rolls Royce, informing me of the arrival of five new BMW L7 Limousines. The four coloured ones had been sent to the palaces of the Sheikhs of the various Emirates. Only a white one was left in his showroom, and he invited me to go and test it out that day.

Unfortunately, that very day both Anne's Cadillac and my Mercedes 320CE had gone in for their annual service. I was also in my work overalls as I was helping some of my men on a project in the workshop. Anyway, Anne and I went to the BMW showroom in the one company vehicle that was free, a Datsun 1300cc, four cylinder pickup which was the first pickup I had purchased when I started the company. I had recently changed its engine to a Nissan Patrol six cylinder engine which performed as expected. Drivers on the Sheikh Zayed highway were left mystified to see an old battered pickup overtake them and put all their fancy cars to shame.

Other than boxing and weightlifting, exercise has never been high on my list of priorities and I have never been known to enjoy walking. As is usual with me, since there was no parking available in the BMW parking area, I parked my pickup right outside the main entrance of the showroom, to avoid parking further afield and walking.

As Anne and I entered the showroom, Statis saw us from his first floor office and called down to us to first check out the car which held a pride of place on a swivel podium, before we went up to visit with him in his office. As we were walking across to check out the Limousine, Statis spoke to his sales manager Roy who was on the showroom floor, to extend to us all assistance.

As we were still within earshot of their conversation, we were totally taken aback by Roy's response. He turned to Statis and asked in a stage whisper if Statis was sure as I was not dressed to be in a BMW showroom, leave alone buy a BMW high-end car. Roy further said I was not going to buy the car as I had come in an old pickup, I had the nerve to park in front of the showroom entrance.

Statis sounded angry when he replied if anyone could buy the Limousine, it would be Dave Forrest, and asked him to do as he was instructed. To Roy's chagrin, I not only purchased the limousine and left the showroom within half an hour, but before I left I did drop a not too subtle hint to him, that people should never judge a book by its cover as they just might find themselves totally embarrassed.

Anyone owning a limousine expects to luxuriate with the wet bar at hand while enjoying a movie from the comfort of the plush rear seating, when being chauffeured around. Unfortunately, Anne point-blank refused to don a chauffeur outfit and drive me around town, and she also sniggered at my idea of hiring a woman chauffeur with something that sounded like 'fat chance of it happening' and thus, the limousine did not live in my care for long.

A couple of weeks later, Allan Nicolson a friend and business associate came in from Singapore. I took him to German cars as he wanted to purchase a Ferrari. While at the showroom, a young Emirati businessman came in and casually asked as to who owned the limousine parked outside. When he was informed by the staff that it was mine, he asked me if I wanted to sell it. So I jokingly replied 'make me an offer I can't refuse'.

And, he did.

It turned out he recently bought a Lamborghini Diablo VT Roadster, but he was now getting married, and it was not regarded as a married man's car. So we agreed on a deal and he bought my Limousine which was a car more suitable for his soon to be family image, and I bought his Lamborghini and naturally, paid the difference in cost for the higher priced car.

Coincidentally, a few weeks earlier, I was invited to a function by Bugatti and Lamborghini. At the event, this very same white Lamborghini was exhibited, and I was subsequently sent a photograph of Anne and me along with our guests Derek and Margaret Petrie, admiring the car. It thus seemed kismet I would end up adding this very same Lamborghini to my stable of toys.

To celebrate Allan's Ferrari and my Lamborghini Diablo Roadster, we decided to have a few drinks at my bar. My partner Derek joined in our celebrations, and we were having a real good time. Atleast, that was till Allan suggested we try a drink called 'rusty nails', which is a mix of scotch whisky and Drambuie. However, the combination of rusty nails after imbibing in our own personal choice of mixed poisons during the evening, sent all of us over the edge and we started having one heck of a good time from then on.

Anne did feed us something to bring us down to earth along with our obviously high alochol levels, but all three of us were way over the top by then. So Anne decided it was time for us to break up our 'boys with new toys day out', as we were giving her a king size headache.

We could not walk the line, leave alone being in a fit state to drive, so Derek left his car at our villa. Anne managed to get the three of us into our two door Mercedes 320CE without killing us, and told us to 'shut up', as we were still in high spirits and straining our vocal chords on maximum volume. She put the car hood down to let a lot of fresh air hit us and clear our foggy brains as she drove.

We reached Derek's house and as he was getting out, Allan who was riding shotgun with Anne, just had time to say 'I'm gonna be sick', before Anne reached over, opened his door and pushed him out saying 'Not in my wheels, you're not'. For some reason, Derek and I found that ever so hilarious and we could not stop laughing. Allan was back in the car within a few minutes feeling much lighter and more clear headed.

We then drove him to the Sheraton hotel in Deira where he was staying, and he even managed to walk into the hotel with not much of a drunken sway, though the silly grin on his flushed face gave him away. Yes, we did have a wild evening we vowed never to repeat, that is till we bought our next set of sporty wheels. In all the years Anne and I have been married, that was the only time she saw me drunk and I lay the blame squarely on Allan and his rusty nails.

Anne and I enjoyed and used my Diablo Roadster frequently and over many years, even going to work at Al Jadaf dry docks in it. This model had the hydraulic lift that was great when going over speed breakers, unlike my previous two Lamborghinis which suffered, being low slung cars. We even drove to Oman for the launch party of my Oman company, and once let loose on the interstate roads, the Roadster's superior performance definitely demonstrated the fact I made the right decision when I added her to my favourite toys.

However, it did hinder us everytime we went out for formal functions, as Anne had to first strap herself into her seat, and then I handed my dinner jacket to her, as I could not fit comfortably behind the wheel with it on.

Whenever we attended a formal occasion, Anne instructed our office to advise the concerned venue we were visiting their hotel for a function, and requested a parking place for our Lamborghini. Every hotel, including the world's first seven star hotel, the Burj Al Arab, always gave us a pride of place parking right at the hotel's main entrance door, manifesting the fact that money does talk. In contrast, we used to laugh as several times when we visited the same hotels in our highend but mass produced day cars, we had to park in the hotel's carpark.

We did not expect to sell the car for a long while, but when a couple of young royals from the Oman Royal family approached us with interest, and an offer for our Diablo Roadster, it convinced me to sell it to them, as I knew it was going to another great home.

Somewhere down the line, Anne commandeered my Mercedes 320CE Convertible and I bought the Mercedes S-Class W 140, which I sold on in a couple of weeks as it was too sedate for me and just not my usual flamboyant style.

A string of high-end day cars and four wheel drive vehicles also passed through my stables over time. A favourite of mine was the GMC Sierra Z71, which was a beast of a truck. People were always amazed when seeing Anne at the wheel. She was even stopped by the Dubai police a couple of times, but as she was licenced to drive it, they waved her off in awe.

While I will never outgrow my love for high speed luxury,

I have outgrown the low slung sports models. Maserati - the latest love of my life on wheels is an ageless beauty with a contemporary twist, and definitely an Italian classic. It suits my current retired lifestyle just fine and without a doubt, it will be a part of my family for a long time to come.

As a constant reminder to me about my lowly start in life, I have a sticker on my car that makes me chuckle as it boldly proclaims 'life's a bitch'.

As you can see from my love of luxury cars, the Rolls Royce will always be at the top of my list as the car wth a lot of heart. But for body and soul, my Italian beauties will always come first in my life.

Fax N°	Data: 16 novembre 1994	N° Pag. Compresa la Presente: 1
Da: Dario Molaschi		
A: Quality General Maintenance - Dubai		
Att.ne: Mr. David Forrest c.p.c. : Mr. Bader Al Jaziri - German Car		
BUGATTI AUTOMOBILI S.P.A. LARGO E. BUGATTI, 1 - 41011 CAMPOGALLIANO (MO) ITALIA - TEL. 059/899111 - FAX 059/899222		

Dear Mr. Forrest,

Many thanks for your letter of November 8, and congratulations for being the first Bugatti owner in the Middle East.

We do regret the inconveniences at delivery and understand your disappointment. With the exception of the C.D. player, which has to be ordered separately, we are working closely with Mr. Bader Al Jaziri of German Cars to make sure that you shall be totally satisfied of your EB110 in the shortest possible time.

On your next visit to Europe we would like very much to welcome you at the factory and show you our facilities. In the meantime do not hesitate to contact us, we do in fact appreciate customers' opinion.

Wishing you many happy miles with your Bugatti we remain, yours sincerely,

Dario Molaschi

Congratulatory letter on being the first owner of a Bugatti in the Middle East

My boy's toys – 'Motorbikes'

My fascination with motorbikes comes a close second to my love for my luxury sports cars. While all motorbikes give me the thrills, I do have a soft spot for Harley Davidson. I personally feel there is nothing like riding into the wind on a solid Harley Davidson, especially on a long journey, as they are meant for comfort and easy riding.

Over the years I have had the Springer, the Anniversary Chopper model and after Anne and I got married, I bought another Soft Tail Custom.

Like in many countries, Dubai has a Harley Davidson club. However, I never did join the club as after a short ride, all the members spend most of the evening socialising at a pub. As I am not much of a drinker and definitely not a barfly, I preferred to go for a ride on my own and at my own time and convenience. Anne and I regularly enjoyed a leisurely ride to Hatta Fort hotel for brunch on a Friday, after we closed the office for the day, though Anne does prefer the comfort and especially the safety aspect of a car.

My boy's toys –'Boats'

As you know by now, I love all water sports and boats will always have a special place in my life. My friend Mike O'Kell owned a Riva Saint Tropez, and we spent many enjoyable hours on it, and I even water-skied behind it at high speeds, in the Arabian Sea. Before I started building the 'La Buttana', I had six boats right from a Boston Dory, Bayliner and a Glastron to name a few.

Many weekends a few friends would join me on the water, and we would water ski and at other times, we would spend hours just guzzling beer and fishing. Yes, we men are creatures of habit just like they say 'Give a man a fish and he'll eat for a day. Teach him to fish and he'll sit in a boat and drink beer all day'.

One weekend Derek my partner, his wife and three other friends joined me on a fishing trip. While the three women spent their time chatting, imbibing in copious amounts of vino and just sunbathing onboard, we men were trying our hand at baiting the biggest catch of the day.

Derek was not much of an angler and without much ado, he very efficiently got his fishing line caught somewhere onto the hull of the boat. I did suggest the best way was to go overboard to free the line manually. But as he did not want to get wet, he kept trying to get the line free, though it seemed to be caught tightly and refused to be dislodged.

Suddenly Derek just yanked the line, and to the shock and horror of the three women as well as us surprised anglers, he somehow managed to capsize the boat with all six of us in it, and we were left not only treading water but yes, very very wet.

It was lucky we were not too far from the shore when we capsized, as unfortunately, the women were only sun bather show-offs and not strong swimmers. They could not even float on a wave, forget riding it. And we men had a choice of either leaving them to drown, or struggle to drag their vino heavy bodies back to shore, before we returned and sorted the boat out.

Needless to say much as we were tempted, we did do the

right thing and the ladies lived to tell their fabricated versions of the tale. However while the boat could be repaired, a few items did survive Derek's attempt to drown them, but my camera and everything else, could not be salvaged.

My boy's toys – 'Aircraft'

I had sent my son Tony on a trial flight with a close friend of mine who was a private flight instructor. Subsequently when Tony said he wanted to learn flying, I bought the Cessna 150 Aerobat that Tom Brown used to teach his students on, so Tony could learn flying as well as get his flying hours before he applied for his pilot's licence.

I paid to park, secure and maintain the aircraft at Aero Gulf in the Dubai Airport, and after Tony learned flying and moved on, I too did the same so as to put the plane to good use. Flying was an experience I thoroughly enjoyed, though I was not passionate enough about it, to take my casual interest any further. I did not get a 'high' as I do whenever I am on the water. There is absolutely no doubt I prefer the mysteries of the sea to the glory of the heavens.

Since I would not be using the aircraft again, I decided to sell it as if it was left unused, without a doubt it would deteriorate quickly since the humidity and salt sea air would hasten its corrosion. But people were not in a financial position to purchase it and I could not find a buyer.

As such, I passed the word around that I was syndicating the sale of the aircraft. Each joint owner had an equal shareholding, and they had to pay me for purchasing their share of the plane, which would be registered in all their names. To my surprise,

I sold the aircraft within a week. All the shareholders of the plane were able to learn flying, and at the same time indulge in their new found passion whenever they wanted.

As I naturally could not go to the airport to check on the aircraft daily, the person I hired, ensured the aircraft was kept fueled and maintained for my use, as well as secured properly when not in use. However, I understand after I had sold it, the new owners did not collectively agree on the additional maintenance costs, and they never paid to ensure the aircraft was either maintained or thoroughly secured every day.

To my dismay, I learned that some time later during a storm, the aircraft which was not secured well, was at the mercy of the elements and damaged extensively by the strong winds. As the aircraft would never take to the skies again, it had to be placed out of its misery and it ended up gracing a scrap yard.

Once I sold my flying machine, I concentrated on my passion with the high seas, and my core interest with boats including the 'La Buttana'. I continue to enjoy my toys while they are in my life, and I do miss them when they leave my stable. I bounce back quickly though, when they are replaced with the next new model that attracts my attention and takes my fancy.

At the end of the day and irrelevant of age, as they say, 'boys will always be Boys!'

My Cessna Twin seater 150 Aerobat Aeroplane flying over the Jebel ali Hotel Marina, Dubai

Chapter 19

Sharon and Tony – through the years

Sharon and Tony had a very normal upbringing within the parameters of our global lifestyle, if you can call living in several countries around the world from a young age normal. The children had the best education not only in regular schools, but also by travelling the world and integrating into the various communities of all the countries we lived in. In my opinion, travel is an education and exposure without comparison, which broadens a person's horizons, cultivates their inquisitiveness on language and cultural differences and enhances their general outlook.

I had hoped by living around the globe, Sharon and Tony would not only adapt unreservedly with our changing lives, but maybe it would instil in them a sense of unity with the people of the various countries we lived in. Was I asking for too much in expecting them to genuinely respect these people, even though our language and cultures were so diverse? As after all, experiencing their world first hand is without a doubt an exceptional adventure.

Was I wrong in thinking maybe Sharon and Tony would develop a sense of compassion and empathy with their peers, on the realisation of their very noticeable lifestyle differences? Would my children actually appreciate their own personal situation, with an attitude of graciousness in the process? If I can integrate happily and with ease in any country of the world despite the language barriers and cultural contrasts, then anyone can do it.

Though I was a great provider for my family, like most families I left the daily caring of the children to their mother. I guess it was not the wisest choice I made, but it was the best option for me when I took their mother back in 1965. There are always a multitude of reasons for not making certain decisions. But it was just one reason that made up my mind and changed my life. I had committed myself to my children and they were my sole priority. There was no way I could care for the children after working extra long hours, just to provide them with not only the basic necessities, but the little luxuries in addition to the vacations they would crave as they grew older. The children had a good life and never wanted for anything, as whatever they asked for within reason, I gave them.

As children, they were no trouble at all, did well at their schools and even made friends easily. I spent as much time as I could with them around my heavy work schedules, in which ever country we lived in. I also made every effort to document their growing years, as over time I bought all the visual aids as soon as it was out in the market, from cameras to a slide projector and finally a video camera, which was a novelty in those days.

However, when Sharon and Tony became teenagers and entered adulthood, I noticed a gradual change in them, specifically towards me. Unlike our world today, computers, mobile phones or the internet were not even thought of in the 1970s. As such, keeping a teenager out of trouble in any country was down right tough, especially in the countries where security was a serious issue and they could not go out alone. Or maybe, they were really just like most teenagers of their time period, as I was brought up in an era with absolutely nothing and I turned out just fine.

Like other expatriate parents living in the UAE with young teenage children, we were forced to put the children in boarding schools, as in the 1970s, the school education in the UAE was not yet up to high school. Their mother found and enrolled them in two very good private residential schools in the UK. All I had to do was come up with additional money to foot the bills. So it meant longer working schedules for me.

Sharon was in St Lawrence College in Ramsgate and Tony was in St. Edmund's Independent Day and Boarding School in Canterbury. As I was working, their mother insisted I did not have to take any unscheduled leave from my work to accompany them to the UK, as she could handle everything herself, and she got them settled into their respective schools.

Financially I always came up trumps for my family and they wanted for nothing. But the negative side was the simple reality, I was always working and taking on the best overseas contracts and jobs I could get, working long hours and frequently even overtime. It is a common fact that no one can provide a good life for their family without putting in the hours working.

It however cost me a lot personally, as very often I had to sacrifice time with my children. But it was a price I had to pay, to ensure they lived the life they were now accustomed to. I tried to involve them in activities, day trips, and taking them out whenever I could, when they were children. As they grew older, we took family vacations to various countries. I even taught Tony water skiing and much later even bunjee jumped with Sharon. As such, I did miss them now they were not around, though I would never divulge that titbit to them.

After working hard just so my children had the best education, I was absolutely shocked to find one fine day on returning home after work, that both the children had left their high-priced boarding schools in the UK without a second thought, and were back home in Dubai. When I questioned as to why they returned home, their mother said they wrote to her about not liking their boarding school life and wanted to come back home. Without discussing or even mentioning the matter, she made her decision independently and immediately took them out of their boarding schools, before they had even completed one term of the school year, and brought them back to Dubai.

To say I was furious at the disruption of their education would be grossly understated. Sharon and Tony were teenagers and no longer young children. But they and their mother were extremely short sighted, as none of them thought about their future, or how far they could go in our modern world without the proper and best education. This view is from a man who did not have the educational degrees to back him. Yes, I had to prove myself in my initial jobs over the degree holders and as such, I most certainly know what I am talking about.

Secondly, they never gave a thought to the amount of my hard earned money they threw away, by not completing their education in the specially chosen private residential schools, after I not only paid the fees, but also extras for their study material, paraphernalia, uniforms etc. Having been brought up in the school of hard knocks, when my parents had to tighten their war time belts, while I enjoy spending money for our enjoyment and betterment, I do not appreciate money being unnecessarily squandered.

I came to realise, having lived the life they did at home, they were thoroughly spoilt, and not used to discipline. As such, they could not handle the boarding school rules and regulations, and were not willing to even try and adjust to the new life. Their mother on the other hand, instead of keeping their education her priority and insisting they would get used to boarding school life if they gave it a chance, gave in and made all the plans to bring them home herself. In my personal opinion, any parent would want their children to have the best possible education to assist them in their future success, especially considering like me, their mother herself was only high school educated.

All three of them knew if they told me what they were planning, I would insist they continue with their education in the boarding schools. So they sidelined me, and did it without informing me. This was the first time my children made me feel like I did not belong as the head of our family and home, and they wanted me for nothing more than to just bankroll the lifestyle they were now attuned to.

They subsequently had to continue their education at St. Mary's school in Dubai, as we had no other avenues open to us. But eventually on completion of their high school, I was disappointed as both of them were not interested in going to university in the UK. I wanted them to have the best education even I missed out on, but nothing I said could change their minds.

They were adults now and made their own decisions to earn their living in the work environment, though they still lived at home without contributing a penny to the household expenses. I asked their mother to take a nominal amount from each of them and without their knowledge, deposit it into a separate savings bank account solely for them. Paying for their upkeep was to me, a way of teaching them nothing is free in life. However, their mother who always played the good cop and made me the bad cop, never heeded my request.

But I was no longer responsible for them financially. I had done my duty by them. I had given them a good life, brought them up and educated them as far as they themselves wanted to go. As they were now adults, working and independent of their apron strings, my financial responsibilities were completed.

Sharon celebrated her twenty-first birthday with a large party I had organised for her. I presented her with a car gift wrapped in a red ribbon and bow, as her birthday gift. She had a high social life being the gregarious character she was, and this meant alcohol was always a big part of their parties. However, she always said I was too strict and controlling if I deigned to say anything to her.

Drink affects people in different ways and unfortunately, it had an adverse effect on Sharon. But when she sobered up, she was all sweetness, as she never remembered anything that happened when she was inebriated. But once said, she could never take back anything she had said, and she caused a lot of problems with me and several other people too.

Not long after her birthday, she was driving home after a late night party. She told me she lost control and drove the car into the centre reservation of the main road, which was landscaped with a variety of flowers. The car rolled many times over through the centre reservation, getting totally tangled with, and ripping up the underground black plastic garden pipework system, laid out to water the flora and foliage.

How she walked away without a scratch was remarkable. She just left her car where it was, flagged down a passing taxi and came home. She woke me up, told me about the accident and just went to bed without a care in the world, confident in the knowledge I would clean up her mess with the authorities.

But as she was now an adult, I did not interfere and I left it to her to sort out her dilemma with the police. If she expected me to have her car repaired and returned to her, she was in for a surprise, as I never ever collected her car from the police pound either. I strongly believe that no person should get behind the wheel of a car while intoxicated, as they are a death knell to other motorists when driving on the roads.

Tony too had his fair share of young and hot-headed police incidents. Once along with some of his friends in Dubai, he got into a punch-up with a few other lads in the Metropolitan hotel on Sheikh Zayed road, and damaged hotel property in the process. They were all trotted off to the police station and he naturally expected me to go and get him out, as I received a call from the police station. The police also informed me I had to first pay the hotel for all the damage Tony had caused in the hotel.

As I knew the hotel management well, I went straight to the Metropolitan Hotel and paid them for the damage caused by Tony. But I did not go to the police station to get him out. I felt it would do him good to remain in the cooler for a while. However, the hotel probably informed the police I had paid the money, as Tony was released and came home with not so much as even a 'thank you Dad'. For his ungracious attitude,

I then lectured him on his abhorrent behaviour, and informed him it was the first and last time I would be throwing away good money to get him out of trouble.

While I wanted both Sharon and Tony to have dreams and a vision of their successful future, I knew it was up to me to prod them in the right direction, so they could arrive at their own decision as to their chosen path in life.

I would have liked Tony to work in the company I had built up from scratch and maybe take over from me one day. He did try it out for a very short while, but being young, he partied the whole night and just waltzed into the company late the next day, as he was the son of the boss. Unfortunately, this did not sit well with me as boss or not, my company rules were for every individual in the company starting with me. I never ever expected anything from my staff that I could not do myself. I was the first to open the company every morning before 0800 hours and the last to leave after all my men had left at 1800 hours. And as Tony could not keep to my company's timings and rules, I told him it was best he found a job elsewhere if he could not toe the line.

So he got a job with an oil company, and I was very amused as he had to be on time in the morning to make the helicopter from the pick up point to take them offshore. He got himself a few loud bell alarm clocks and it worked, as he managed to keep the job longer than I expected. However, even after working for quite a while, the company did not make him up as a qualified tradesman, along with the requisite salary increase. As such, he left and hung around in Dubai looking for a job. But as he did not find any job he was interested in or qualified for, he decided to return to the UK.

That was when I blundered with regard to Tony. I was rather dubious about his decision to leave the UAE as like Sharon, he did not have any educational or technical qualifications to help him in his quest for a high paying job. Tony was in his mid-twenties by now and I did not want him to go back and end up doing odd jobs just to survive, like his mate John.

John a close friend of Tony's, had also returned to the UK and just like Tony, he did not have any educational or technical qualifications to fall back on. He ended up struggling to live his life, as his businessman father refused to fund him saying, just as he was a self-made man, his son John too should make his way in the world on his own steam.

And this is where I subsequently made a grave mistake with Tony. I respected the code of ethics guiding John's father to take his stance with his son, and I should have done exactly the same with my son Tony. Instead, I gave Tony everything he asked for, which he took but never appreciated. Nor did he ever thank me for my financial help. Sharon and Tony were adults and I should have allowed them to get on with their lives as they had wanted, and let Tony go back to the UK to learn for himself the art of survival through his financial struggles.

But the Dad in me, instead asked my pilot friend Tom Brown who was a flight instructor, to take Tony up in the light aircraft he used to teach people flying, as I wanted to guide Tony towards a career which would hold him in good stead for the future. Tony enjoyed the experience in the air and when I asked him if he would like to do it for a living, he answered in the affirmative.

I then bought the Cessna 150 Aerobat two seater plane Tom Brown hired to train his students. I parked it at a bay I rented at Aero Gulf in the Dubai Airport, and I also hired and paid Tom Brown to give Tony private flying lessons in my plane. I hoped Tony had finally found his calling as I could only lead him out of the rut he was digging himself into.

Now as I was no longer financially responsible for him, it was up to him to think seriously about what he wanted, follow through with his decision, independently organise the finances and student loans to fund his dream, and make his action plan reap rewards for him, well into his own future.

With Tony's career sorted, I turned my attention to Sharon. Eventually, Sharon decided on joining the hospitality industry. So I paid for and enrolled her into the first culinary school in the UK to offer a Cordon Bleu qualification - the Tante Marie culinary academy in Woking, to pursue her Cordon Bleu diploma.

On returning to Dubai after securing her Cordon Bleu accreditation, I asked my neighbour in Jumeira, if he could give Sharon a job in the food and beverage department of the Dubai Marine hotel which he owned, so she could learn her way up the ladder in the hospitality industry. I felt the only way she could make a long term successful career for herself in the hotel industry, would be to start at the bottom and work her way right up to the top. She was in her mid-twenties and the world was still her oyster.

They did offer her a job in food and beverages. Unfortunately, Sharon has never ceased to amaze me. She went to the hotel, only to learn she would be just a member of the food and beverages team and not in management. She was not impressed to find that like all staff, she would have to work and prove herself to the manager before she could even start climbing up the chain of command.

This was not what she wanted. She said she expected to get a managerial position, even though I informed her she had neither the experience nor the qualifications in hotel management. She did not take the job, as she said she could get a much higher salary as a personal assistant in a company. Sharon did get a job in an office, but whether the remuneration was good I have no idea, as she never did tell me anything.

When Tony learned flying on my plane and got the mandatory flying hours, he told me he wanted to go to the USA to do his simulator course and asked me for the money for his course. That was the time I should have been firm with him, and told him to get a student loan like most students all around the world. But I did not and I blindly paid for it. He took advantage of the fact that he did not have to struggle for money to fund his career, as when he passed the simulator course and returned to Dubai, he informed me he wanted to proceed with the rest of the courses like night flying, etc., and I paid another big bill.

But he then said he had to get his airline pilot's licence and the other licences, and it was expensive. He asked me for a further fifty thousand Pounds Sterling, saying he would pay me back when he started working. I took him at his word as if he was anything like me, his word would be his bond and hence, I blindly wrote out a cheque to him.

That was the second major mistake I made with my adult children. Their actions opened my eyes to the fact that they did not know the value of money. They had depended on 'Dad's bank' for so long, they expected to just make withdrawals from it without a second thought. I did not have to directly loan Tony the money. I should have loaned him the money through the bank, with the clause that when he started working, he had to repay the bank loan directly to the bank, on an agreed staggered repayment plan.

But he was my son, and I trusted him to keep his word and pay me back and so, I personally loaned him the money without taking the official bank route. But from the time he received the money, I did not see him nor hear from him at all. I felt Tony did not need me any more, as he got what he wanted out of me. He avoided me like the plague, knowing he promised to pay me back, and that I would ask him when he was going to start repaying his debt.

Once in the early 2000s, when I was working on the deck of the La Buttana at Al Jadaf dry docks, he called me and during our conversation, I asked him on the telephone what his problem was as he seemed to have a chip on his shoulder. His reply utterly shocked me. He said 'we were never a family. I have my own family now and don't need you'. He further said 'You should not have taken me out of boarding school. If I had a better education, I would have been able to get a better job'. And his finale was the scorcher 'what did you do for me? I am where I am today because of my hard work' and 'it was your duty to give me the money'. His attitude and total lack of gratitude for everything I had done for him, was astounding.

I was so enraged, I just threw my mobile phone overboard and it still rests in peace at the bottom of the Dubai creek. Obviously Tony worked hard to become a pilot. He is not the first and definitely not the last. Every student worldwide knows that while the tuition fees are paid, they have to work hard at making sure the tuition fees count for something and is not wasted.

But would my son have become an airline pilot without my financial help? Would he have learned to fly with a private flight instructor, earning his flying hours in my private plane without paying a penny? no – certainly not. He would have had to take a student loan to finance his complete pilot's training, and repaying the loan for the rest of his life.

It was then I knew I had done wrong by loaning my son the money, and when I realised how easy it is for some overindulged children to sometimes lose their principles and values in life. Like his friends' parents did, and millions of students do even today, I should have stood firm and let my son organise his complete training fees on his own.

Then he could hold his head up high and honestly say with conviction, that other than his dad buying a plane to teach him flying, and paying for a private flying instructor as well as all the overheads for the aircraft, 'he is where he is today due to his own hard work, with absolutely no other financial help from his dad'. However as things stand, Tony unfortunately will never ever be able to say that, as it would not be true.

I did not get any hand-outs from my parents as they did not have the financial capacity to do so. My success was not handed to me on a silver platter. It was sheer sweat and toil that got me to where I am today. As such, to have my son very brazenly tell me I did nothing for him, and he is where he is only due to his hard work, is nothing short of disrespectful in my book.

And further, it was not my duty to give him over one hundred thousand Pounds Sterling as he said either, since I had completed my financial responsibilities and done my duty by both my children many years earlier. Both of them were now reaching their thirties, independent and working adults. Since that time around thirty-five years ago when I unfortunately gave him the money, I have not seen him and that was when I lost my son.

He qualified as a commercial airline pilot and started working. I expected him to honour his word to repay his debts, irrelevant of where the money came from. But since he got the money, communication has been negligible between us. He visited Dubai several times subsequently, but never ever contacted me. I used to find out about his visits to Dubai by default, from his mates like Alex who naturally thought he was staying with me and hence telephoned me.

But whenever Tony wanted something, or help in a specific matter over the years, I was the first one he called and I helped him without a problem. Whether it was writing out a job application, sort out his employment status at the Labour department, get my input on the regulations and legalities to assist his wife in starting a real estate company, or even get him a new laptop through one of my companies, I blindly helped him without thinking twice, though I was well aware I was just being used.

Some time in the early 2000s, during a telephone conversation with Tony, I mentioned I was selling a house in the UK. At once he said he would have it as it was conveniently located to the airports. I informed him he could have it at market price, and I never heard from him again. I could not believe my adult son expected me to give him the house for nothing. While I may be impaired by figurative blindness, I have however, never been blighted by stupidity.

I know Tony is never going to pay his debt back to me, so to be fair to Sharon, a few years ago, I sent him a message and told him to pay Sharon ten thousand Pounds Sterling from the final amount of money I had loaned him. I left the payment plan to his own convenience as I was not interested in when or how he did it, but just that as per my wishes, he gave Sharon the amount I stated. They could then regard all the payments I have given to them as gifts, though Tony received more than what I had given to Sharon.

But Tony messaged Sharon and me saying he did not have any money to spare as he had family responsibilities. I wonder what he would have done if I had told him I did not have any money to spare, when he asked me for money to become a pilot, as according to him it was my 'duty' to give it to him.

Both Sharon and Tony got on with their lives while I got on with mine. Sharon married and divorced, while Tony had a child from a relationship and he later got married to someone else and had a few children, I think. I have never met any of Tony's family as for some inexplicable reason he does not want me to meet his family.

I was never either informed nor invited to any of their weddings. They never kept in touch regularly. For some unfathomable reason which I do not know till date, our relationship was strained from the time they entered their late teens and just disintegrated further from there to the point of no return.

Out of the blue and without prior intimation, Tony visited me in Dubai with his first partner and infant son, sometime around the late 1980s or early 1990s. I was at work as I was extremely busy with my growing company. My house boy Baba telephoned and informed me that Tony and his family had arrived. I told Baba I was on my way back to meet them, and instructed him to offer all assistance to them in the meanwhile.

However when I reached home about an hour later, Baba informed me they had left my villa and that Tony mentioned they were checking into a hotel. Tony did not have the decency to call me or even leave me a note by way of explanation, and I was extremely disappointed I did not meet him, his partner nor my eldest grandchild.

Around this time, Sharon informed me about her lapses in paying the mortgage on her flat, and I helped her by regularly giving her the money to keep up with her mortgage payments. However, after I had given Tony the final fifty thousand Pounds Sterling loan, which I now realised he would not repay, I decided to help Sharon too with a similar lumpsum mortgage payment so she would be debt free and secure in her future.

I asked her for her mortgage company details so I could transfer the money directly to them. She refused and said if I did not trust her to pay off her mortgage, she did not want the money. So I held-off and eventually after a couple of years I gave her thirty thousand Pounds Sterling. However, within a short while she had squandered the money, and her collateral damage was she lost the flat for non-settlement of her mortgage payments. She then asked me for help to retain her flat, but I refused to throw good money after bad or give her any more money, and she had to fend for herself as I did not help her financially again.

Being brought up in a mixed marriage home, Sharon and Tony were taught to treat everyone equally and to never discriminate. However, becoming a pilot changed my son overnight. I am certainly proud of him for persevering and becoming a pilot, but according to me, he did not stay true to himself or his heritage and I do not recognise my son in him any more.

It seemed to me he now regarded us - his parents, as way below his status in life, and he distanced himself from his mother as well as from me. Tony's attitude towards me, laid bare the fact he regarded me as just a working class plumber and beneath him now, even though without me or my 'plumber's money' he would not be where he is today. My son forgot two important cardinal rules 'never ever forget where you came from' and 'never ever bite the hand that feeds you'.

Further, Sharon and Tony have problems with me marrying Anne. Sharon subsequently visited Anne and me at our home in 2010. But even though Anne and I have been married for over twenty-six years, Tony has never met Anne. Yet, their uncalled for accusations verbally and in writing against Anne is absolutely astounding.

Eventually in November 2020, I gave them both a final ultimatum and informed them in writing, if they do not accept and respect Anne as my wife, it means they do not accept and respect me as their dad. Sharon made a reconciliatory move and sent us a Christmas wish in a message in 2020. However, Tony ignored my ultimatum and has yet again proved to me without a shadow of a doubt, he is not like me.

When they reached adulthood, while they called me Dad, I have never received the due respect that accompanies the word. I felt and still do feel, that they have never cared for me or about my personal happiness, and they certainly did not want me to find love and get married again, for fear they would lose their inheritance. I have received messages and emails from them that just proves my point.

A few years after Anne and I were married, Sharon who lived in Europe at that time, called me and casually mentioned she and her boyfriend Rai had recently visited the country and stayed with Tony and his family. I was flabbergasted and asked her why she did not come to visit with Anne and me. Her answer shocked me to the core. Sharon said Tony only agreed to her visit and staying with him and his family, on the condition she did not contact or visit me. I later questioned Tony about this and he vehemently denied it. One of them lied to me and they know it.

Having absolutely no contact with Tony even though we lived in the area, I tried another mode for getting in touch. I asked Tony to get me family first class tickets and naturally, I would pay the cost for the same. He said if I gave him my personal details, he would register me as his dad in the company records and then get me the tickets.

A few days later, he telephoned me and asked me where he could drop off my ticket. I informed him I was on my vessel the 'La Buttana' at the local marina. He came over and gave me the ticket in a sealed envelope. As we had not seen each other for over twenty years at that time, I was looking forward to catching up with him. However, Tony seemed very uncomfortable and just said his family was waiting for him in a mall and he had to rush to pick them up. That was it. No conversation or even pleasantries at all. Considering he had also never ever seen the 'La Buttana', I wanted to show him around the vessel. But he never asked any questions or showed any interest in my pride and joy either. He just got away as fast as he possibly could.

Later that evening I gave Anne the envelope which I had not even opened. Anne opened it and laughed out loud. When I asked her what was so funny, she said it was really derision rather than amusement. Tony had actually attached a copy of his credit card payment slip with the airline ticket, to ensure I paid him for the ticket. Unacceptable as I found his behaviour, my word is my bond and I deposited the money into his account the next day. Even though he obviously did not trust me to settle my debts, he had absolutely no reason to think otherwise.

Tony subsequently emailed me and informed me to dress properly in a suit and tie and not to embarrass him in any way on the flight. It saddened and hurt me to realise that he regarded me as just a low down plumber, an embarrassment to him and a person not fit to travel in first class. Can you just imagine how downcast I felt at my middle aged son's true perception of me as uncultured and uncouth, with absolutely no idea on how to conduct myself? Did he also think I could not travel in first class on my own steam? He could not be more wrong.

An incident of why I travel economy class comes to mind. Many years earlier I was travelling to visit my parents in the UK and my economy class travelling companion on the long flight turned out to be an extremely successful Emirati businessman I knew. During the flight, the principal of the Dubai English Speaking School, Bernadette McCarthy who was travelling in first class (courtesy of the school), came over to chat with me.

Her first question to me was 'why are you travelling in economy when you can well afford to travel in first class?' I introduced her to my travelling companion and said that he was a multi-millionaire businessman and compared to him, I was a very small fish in the sea. My business associate turned to Ms. McCarthy and just said 'I know I have money, I don't have to prove it to anyone'. That highly principled business associate and my travelling companion was Mr. Faraidooni, who I have always held in high regard, as we even shared very similar views.

Tony and Sharon also blame Anne for driving a wedge between them and me, saying before I married Anne, they had a good relationship with me. In 2014, Tony even audaciously put in writing in an email to me, that Anne is the cause of all our problems. Unfortunately for them, their irrational words hold no weight, as they literally divorced me around fifteen years before I even met Anne.

Much as both of them go to great lengths to say otherwise, to me it all boils down to one dirty word – 'Money'! Neither of them are happy with anyone I married other than their mother. They only think of 'I, me, myself' and in the process, my own personal happiness never did enter the equation. The fact Anne is closer to their age than mine, riles them up further, I guess. I finally informed them in no uncertain terms that Anne is my wife and if they do not accept and respect her, then they do not respect me. And, if they do not respect me then we have no relationship as without 'respect', we have nothing anyway.

I retired in 2009, and as I was turning seventy in January 2010, Anne planned a weekend party to celebrate, inviting all our family over to Lake Como in Italy. We had the space to accommodate everyone, so it was no problem. Anne was still in Dubai at that time, winding up our life there and so in October 2009, she emailed Tony and invited him and his family. Though it was three months advance notice, he declined saying he had a busy schedule at work and asked for my telephone number.

Anne next called Sharon who was living in Europe at that

time, and then called me soon after speaking with Sharon, as she could not believe a simple birthday invitation call could take such a negative turn. After Anne issued the invitation, Sharon's first words were 'I am surprised you are still together'. Sharon further said 'It is because of men like him, I cannot trust men'.

I was shocked at what Sharon had said as firstly, while she may be my daughter, she did not know me better as at that time, Sharon and I had not been in close contact or even seen each other in around twenty-five years. Secondly, as my daughter, she definitely was not privy to what happened behind closed doors in any of my marriages. And neither was Tony.

Neither of them came for my birthday, nor did they call to wish me, despite Anne giving both of them my mobile telephone number. I then felt it is best if they carried on with their lives and we lived ours, without any interference or complications from them.

It certainly seemed to me their mother was their source of inaccurate information. And, it now dawned on me as to why their mother wanted the divorce decree changed to state I was the defaulting party instead of her. She obviously showed them the divorce decree but not her lawyer's letter asking for the change in the divorce decree. They were thus of the inaccurate conviction I had wronged their mother and our marriage and that was why she divorced me.

I subsequently decided as they were adults and over half a century old, it was high time they knew the true circumstances leading to their mother's accident and the actual details of our divorce. So I wrote to each of them, and sent them copies of their mother's documents pertaining to her double life in

Dubai, as well as her request through her solicitor, asking for the divorce decree to be changed, to prove the point of my letter. However, they could not have cared at all as I heard absolutely nothing from them.

Sharon purportedly came to visit with me in 2010. I was very happy about her visit as she reminded me our meeting was over twenty-five years overdue, and I was looking forward to catching up with her. I even cancelled the plans Anne and I had to drive to London, to attend our friend Steve Lamprell's big sixty birthday bash in a fancy hotel that same weekend.

Sharon stayed for the weekend with her boyfriend Rai, but she hurt me immensely as she never bothered to spend time with me or catch up on our lives. She and Rai smoked, drank my bar dry over the weekend and just left. What her reason was for visiting me is still unclear, as it certainly wasn't to meet with me. One thing I do know is that, I regret cancelling our London plans for that weekend as I heard we missed a darn good party.

I have not seen or had contact with Sharon since 2010. And as for Tony, I have met up with him just twice in the past thirty-five plus years, for less than ten minutes in total. We last spoke on the telephone a few years ago and I don't expect any further communication from him.

Our friends from Germany were visiting us and the topic about our adult children came up. They mentioned, despite financing their eldest daughter upto a settled status in life, they do not have any contact with her and cannot depend on her now they are growing older. As such, they are pleased they are financially secure themselves till the end of their days.

Well, it seemed I was in the same boat, as we agreed the more financial assistance we gave our children, the more distant and disinterested they became with us. So I decided to check if I could rely on my children if I was down and out. Sharon is not a money minded person as she enjoys life and spends every last penny she has, and would not be a good candidate. So, I telephoned Tony who is the antithesis of Sharon, and said I needed money.

Tony's reply was firstly appallingly disrespectful, as he laughed and said 'I wondered when you would run out of money. If you need money, why don't you send your wife out to work?' That was it. No mention of the money he owes me and has never bothered to repay. And secondly, as usual he could not refrain from sending a well aimed, but unprovoked and unjustified bullet Anne's way.

That short conversation re-confirmed to me everything I already knew. I telephoned Tony again the next week and informed him of the actual reason for my call, and said I did not need any money from him. I explained to him about chatting with my friends, and my call to him was just to check if he would be there for me, should anything adverse happen to me. However, his reply answered my question.

I am glad I will never ever have to rely on either Sharon or Tony. I gave up my happiness and the best years of my life for them, as I finally divorced their mother after twenty-two years, when they were adults and in their twenties. I know both of them will turn around and tell me they never asked me to sacrifice my happiness for them.

But as a parent, I did what I had to do for my children at the time. I believe that family is supposed to be there for the family, no matter what the circumstances. That is why I stood by my sister, my first two wives and children, despite the negative treatment dispensed in my direction. Unfortunately, our relationship was not a two way street. All of them just kept taking from me materially and financially. But they gave me nothing in return. No love, warmth, caring or respect.

It was only after marrying Anne and actually enjoying my life for the first time, I realised that making myself into the proverbial sacrificial lamb for my family for over twenty-two years, did not do any of us any good. Thus from my personal experience, I would advise parents to be discerning and never blindly do what I did, as life is too short and it brings absolutely no comfort nor pleasure.

As parents we are supposed to love our children unconditionally, and I did all through their growing years. But I find it is extremely difficult for me to like the individuals they have become, or accept them as my adult children. My sacrifice was for nothing as for some inexplicable reason, we continue to have a fraught relationship.

It is disheartening I will never meet or get to know my grandchildren, and I wonder if they are aware their paternal grandfather is still alive and well. I think about them and the wonderful relationship we could have had.

Now with the global COVID 19 pandemic causing millions of people around the world to be infected and hundreds of thousands, especially the aged dying of the disease, the families of my friends are rallying around them to ensure they are safe and well. However, my two elder children have never bothered to make contact with me. In my case, they are the children I brought up with love and care, worked extremely hard and all odd hours for, just to educate them and finance their futures so they had a fighting chance in life, like I never had.

Unfortunately, their adult personas bear absolutely no resemblance to the wonderful children I brought up and gave the best years of my life for. I now admitted to myself, the time had arrived for me to clean my inner attic of the clutter of my past life as try as I may, I just cannot see any chance of the three of us bridging the great divide.

Thus, I wrote an email on 20 November 2020 to Sharon and Tony, telling them they could keep the money I had given to both of them, equivalent today to around a quarter of a million Pounds Sterling in purchasing power for each of them. They could regard it as their gifts from me, as I cannot give them any further material or financial proceeds from my estate when I finally passed on. My trips around the mulberry bush to earn a living are behind me, and what I have has to last me for my lifetime.

I also made the decision to finally inform them about the doubts I have about their parentage, and that both of them may not be my biological children. While I would have preferred informing them face to face, I knew it would never happen and I was forced to send them an email.

However, even before I could send the 22 November 2020, email about my doubts regarding their birth, Sharon wrote to me a one liner email on 21 November 2020, obviously in reply to my email of the previous day, informing me in explicitly colourful language, I was not her dad.

Reading her very hurtful email was the moment my life imploded and fragmented to the point of no return, as her short but succinct cruel words ripped me to the very core of my being. It hit me this was not just the end of the road for us, but I now also just lost my eldest daughter too. I do not think I have it in me to forgive her for the way her words reduced me from a loving Dad to just a 'nobody'.

I know there is no going back as Sharon knows how to hit below the belt. However, I am also aware, when sober, people tend to mask their feelings and the truth, as they are in control of their thoughts and words. But when under the influence of alcohol, due to the lack of mental control, inebriated people come out with the truth and their true feelings. So, I have no doubt what she said was the truth.

On reflection, I now realise with certainty, both Sharon and Tony knew about the doubts of their parentage from their mother when they were probably in their late teens as that was when I first noticed a change in their attitude towards me. I now know why Tony took the chance to take the money from me and never bothered to pay me back. I further now understand what Tony meant when he said 'we were never a family' and why he does not want me to meet his family and my grandchildren - because I am not their biological grandfather.

Though, I am mystified as to why neither their mother nor either of them bothered to inform me of this pertinent knowledge all those years ago? Why did they continue to treat me with disdain but continue to use me as their personal bank? Or have I been too blind to see the glaringly obvious reason?

What I value the most in my life are two little things we all have in plenty to give, and it does not cost us anything – 'Time and Kindness'. While I gave Sharon and Tony whatever they asked for financially and materially, I never asked them for anything in return, except maybe a little bit of their time. If they spent even a few minutes with me occasionally, they would have exhibited the depth of their caring for me.

But neither of them even spared a few minutes to chat and catch-up with me, when they not only had the chance but when they also had my sole attention. Part of their actual words in a long nasty message to Anne some time ago were 'All both of us wanted was a dad. No money no privileges, just a dad'. 'You took that away from us'. Unfortunately, the saying 'empty vessels make the most noise' rings true in this instance as both of them made their personal decision to divorce me the moment they reached adulthood, long before Anne even entered my life.

I have learned in the long time I have lived, a little kindness goes a long way and is remembered for a lifetime. I believe kindness is a luxury that can never be purchased for any price. It is not measured in just deeds, as it is basically an attitude, or an expression, a kind word, a touch or even a warm look. Kindness is anything having the ability to lift up another person.

It is strange but since they became adults, I have never been at the receiving end of a kind word, deed, a 'how are you, Dad?', 'thank you Dad' or even a miniscule show of kindness in any form, from either of them. Shocking, but sad to say, very true. So, I am sure they will understand why I can never believe all their hollow words, which mean absolutely nothing to me. Unfortunately their actions as always, speak louder than words. And their actions demonstrate that they do not think I deserve either a minute of their time, or a tiny bit of kindness in any way.

For some reason, Tony has also always treated me as though I am senile and have lost my mind. He has put the blame on me for not remembering things, like for instance when he visited my ship. Some time after his visit to drop off the airline ticket, I had spoken to him on the telephone. I mentioned to him, he did not even spare the time to either chat with me or look around my ship, considering we had not seen each other for very many years. He immediately retorted 'You showed me around the ship, don't you remember?'

He visited me on my ship when I was much younger, in my sixties and totally compos mentis. Tony is on the threshold of sixty now and I wonder if he is decrepit or lost his own memory. I am eighty-two years now and enjoying an active, healthy, full life, and my 'life story' is evidence of the fact I am still far from being either 'long in the tooth' or losing any part of my memory.

Tony had also informed me many a time not to write letters to him, but to use the telephone to speak with him if I had anything to say. Anne types my letters and emails and he does not want her involved in any way. Be that as it may, I prefer the written word to a telephone call, as my words are in black and white and cannot be either misconstrued or debated on by anyone.

My children may not like what I have to openly say here, but I feel the time for the truth to be released, has finally come knocking on our doors, and the stark truth will definitely touch a nerve and no doubt hurt. Over the years I have written numerous letters to them, asking for explanations and reasons for distancing themselves, to no avail. Both of them made their choice when they reached the age of majority, not to have me in their lives for reasons known only to them and their mother.

While I can only conjecture, I have absolutely no concrete evidence as to their reasons. Across the world there are hundreds of thousands of people searching for their long lost loved ones. And then at the other end of the spectrum like mine, people leave their families without a word and stay off the radar.

I would also like to openly apologise to Sharon for the physical, emotional and mental distress she was subjected to, by what I believe was the covert but deliberate actions of her mother, when Sharon was just a young adult. I will never ever forgive Sharon's mother for not informing me of Sharon's predicament in advance.

It was not a situation of life and death, and Sharon being traumatised by a backstreet butcher in Kenya could have been totally avoided. The knowledge that Sharon's adult family life and happiness has been truncated because of it, has always saddened me and it will haunt me to the end of my days, as she will never ever know the wonderful children she could have mothered.

Had I known in advance, I would have put a stop to Sharon's mother's back-alley plans. But since I was only in the knowledge of the truth after Sharon's harrowing ordeal, I can only apologise to Sharon for her life being ruined. Sharon was going through an immense amount of turbulence in her young adult life and looking back, I genuinely feel her anguish at the situation she was in, is what drove her to drinking.

'Sharon, why did you not have either the foresight or the courage to inform me of the matter? How could I have helped you if I was not kept in the loop in advance? You know for a fact I love you and would have been there for you every step of the way, though I probably would have lectured you first. We would have found acceptance of our family situation and adjusted our lives accordingly. We would have worked things out together, without taking such drastic measures'.

'At the end of the day, you were and will always be my first born and I have always wanted only the best for you. I sincerely hope the decision you arrived at, was yours alone and you were not influenced by your mother, or forced to do something you were not ready for. I truly believe the secretive actions your mother took were not in your best interest, and I have no words to express how sorry I am if you were never given a choice in the matter, and put through something you should never ever have experienced'.

Irrelevant of the great deal of good, the minuscule bad and the real ugly, after taking into account everything that has happened, it disheartens me to say this. After spending an enormous amount of time considering the various aspects of our relationship, I have made up my mind to eventually respect Sharon and Tony's wishes and stay out of their lives. Too much dirty water has flowed under our bridge and nothing can purify the water and reverse the flow.

Time and life moves in one direction and once lost, it can never be recovered. My memories of them come to an abrupt halt at the time they were in their mid-twenties, when they last kept in touch with me. That is why I also have no photographs of them beyond the mid-eighties.

One of the final items on my bucket list, is to have DNA tests carried out on the three of us. Before I eventually sail away over the horizon and into eternity, I need to know with certainty whether Sharon and Tony are my biological children. The knowledge is not going to change anything for them, as they disowned me way back in the early 1980s, when they probably first learned of the controversy surrounding their parentage from their mother.

I on the other hand need foolproof confirmation, as their behaviour and the treatment dispensed in my direction, tells me they are intrinsically not like me, and I may not have fathered them. It will certainly be a very sad day for me if the DNA tests prove I did father them, as no Dad who gave up the best years of his life for his children should be subjected to any form of negative treatment from his children, like I received from mine.

Divorce breaks up many families. But, the components of the family can never change. I will never ever regret having them as my children and I will always have two empty spaces in my life where they should have been. Whatever the reality, they will forever remain my children and I have wonderful memories of their younger growing years. But the rest, I have allowed to flow under our bridge as flotsam.

I do not need their adult brand of ill will clouding my golden years. They had a chance to continue to be a part of my life, but they rejected me big time. I am finally very happy and contented, and I intend to live the rest of my life happy and at peace with myself and with peace in my life.

On Sharon's 21st Birthday in Dubai

With Tony in Dubai, in the 1980s

Chapter 20

Marie – my parents' daughter

From the time I was old enough to remember, my sister Marie and I did not get along. Being five years older than me, she either ignored me or treated me with disdain as she regarded me a nuisance of a younger brother. As a young child, I looked up to her and was proud to have an older sister to look out for me. But as I grew up, I soon realised it was wishful thinking on my part, and my mum encouraged me to do my own thing with my mates, while Marie got on with her own life.

However, from a young age, I did wonder why I was the one always helping my mum with the household chores, while Marie was out with her friends. With age, I recognised the fact she played on the affections of my dad, and she became his favourite child, which accounted for the freedom she was allowed, as well as the leniency in following house rules. I would not have cared if she had the courtesy to thank me for doing her chores. But I don't think the word has ever been a part of her vocabulary. She grew up with her head in the clouds, believing the world owed her a living and unfortunately, time and age just made her worse.

By the time I returned from my sojourn on the high seas, she had married Dave Gould, and moved out of my parents' home and I did not see much of her. We never had a close relationship and now we had practically no contact at all. I subsequently got married and Marie never liked nor got along with my first wife Phyllis and I did my best to keep them apart. But as I had my family with me when I travelled the world on overseas contracts, there was not much contact with Marie and I did not give a second thought to her dislike for my wife.

When Sharon was a toddler, I had asked my parents if I could have the rocking horse we used as children. Being a single income family, I could not afford to buy her expensive toys at that stage in my life. But they informed me Marie had taken it when she got married, as being the eldest, she regarded it as her property. And even though she knew I wanted it, she later sold it, instead of offering it to me for my young family.

Around the mid 1980s when I had my own company in Dubai, Marie's marriage had broken-up and she even lost her job in a UK bank at the same time. I don't blame either her self-suffering husband Dave for finally seeing the light, nor the bank for tolerating her more off days than work days, for as long as they did. But as she was now divorced, my dad asked me to take her out to Dubai and give her a job in my company, so she could get her life back together again.

What did I do to always deserve to be the one to pick up the pieces of all the casualities in my family? But as my dad never asked me for much, I did acquiescence with reluctance. And it turned out to be the biggest mistake I made with regard to Marie. That was when our sibling relationship turned from bad to tempestuous. There was no way Marie and I could live in harmony under the same roof, as I was now living on my own in my villa in Jumeira.

So I had my company convert and furnish the housekeeper's quarters, which was not connected to my villa but located at one end of my property, into a totally separate and independent single bedroom house for Marie. It now also had a separate entrance, so while we both had our own space, she had her independence. But at the same time, she did not have the added expense of renting a flat or paying for monthly utilities, as I handled the complete property running costs.

The second massive mistake and terrible business decision I made, was in terminating the services of the most loyal and efficient personal assistant I had in the company. I instead got her a job as a personal assistant in my friend Ed Abernathy's oilfield company, so she had another good job and was not hung out to dry. The only reason I took this action was to create a vacancy and give Marie a job in my company, paying her not only a much higher salary than my original personal assistant, but giving her rent free accommodation at my villa as well, just so she could get her life back together and make my parents happy.

I was divorced from Phyllis and on my own at this time. While I lived in my villa, Marie lived in the house I converted for her. One evening when I returned from a long day at work, there were several cars parked outside my villa and I just assumed one of my neighbours was entertaining. My houseboy Baba had left for the day and I was looking forward to a quiet evening and relaxing with a good movie.

However to my utmost horror, when I entered the gate of my villa, it dawned on me there was a party going on in my home. I found Marie was holding court in my home, entertaining the very people who owed me and my company money, with free food from my kitchen and drinks from my bar. I saw 'RED' and maybe, I should have first taken a deep breath and counted to five. But I did not, and threw the whole lot of them out of my house, including her.

I then had the locks changed and she was barred from setting foot into my property. I later learned from Baba she had entertained her guests in my house and at my bar several times before, probably when she knew I would be held up in the company. But being my sister, he thought she had permission from me and hence never said anything to me.

While Marie still continued to work in my company, I made sure she pulled her weight and worked hard to earn her salary, though she also continued to meet and socialise with our company clientele. There was no favouritism as far as my staff were concerned. But it seemed Marie was not happy nor satisfied with all I was doing for her.

In those days, my company was located in Bur Dubai. We worked a half day shift on Saturdays and on a particular Saturday after work, I met up with some friends and business associates from my social circle at the Bull Hitters pub in the Palm Beach hotel, which was just a short walk away from my company. On joining my friends in the pub, I noticed Marie was also there.

We were all having a drink and chatting at the bar when Marie announced loud enough for all to hear, that she had not only found a better job in another company, but I had her on cheap labour at my company, as she would even be getting a monthly salary increase of five hundred Dirhams. I did not say anything but just finished my drink and left.

Marie had obviously planned her insensitive onslaught on

me in front of my friends and business associates in the pub, as she never said a word to me at the company that very morning. That Saturday was the last time I visited either the Bull Hitters pub or the Palm Beach hotel, as I had absolutely no interest in socialising with her anywhere in Dubai.

The next morning, I fired her from her job and evicted her from her flat with immediate effect. I did not care where she went or how she managed. That was her problem. As far as I was concerned, she was living a charmed life at my expense and she abused my trust in her. I had gone all out to help her through a tough time in her life and she repaid me by insulting me without any justification, in front of my friends and business associates, and just stomping on me with both her feet without any scruples.

Now she was on her own and I realised, she never even figured out she would have to cover not only her living expenses from her salary, but also her rent, utilities and conveyance, as when she worked for me her salary was totally her own. However, I felt no regret at my actions, as I could not understand how anyone could repay their sibling with such ungraciousness, unkindness and ingratitude for all the good deeds extended their way.

Meanwhile, I employed another efficient personal assistant. Not long after Marie left the company, my office staff informed me when chasing outstanding payments with the debtors, many clients informed them, they had made the payments to Marie in cash. I was shocked to learn that she collected the oustanding payments for the company in cash, when she entertained these very people in my villa at my expense.

But she never issued any official payment receipts nor

deposited the payments into the company. Instead she pocketed thousands, thus indicating the payments as still outstanding in my company records, and swindling my company in the process. If any other person swindled me, I would have taken legal action immediately. But being my sister, I paid the company out of my own pocket to regularise the company records and clear the payments she swindled me of, and never thought of it again.

However, I did update my parents as to the facts of the matter, and why I wanted nothing more to do with their daughter. But I also knew whilst she was out of my villa and my company, she was not out of my life. She would surface like a bad penny, and I hoped it would be later rather than sooner. But I was wrong.

Some time later, Sharon was going through a bad patch and she came to stay with me, to figure things out and put some perspective to the personal upheaval in her life. During this same period, my parents were to visit Dubai and stay with me. I explained to them my predicament with Sharon, and asked my parents to postpone their trip for a month. Sharon was at the lowest ebb in her life. She was my priority and I had to concentrate on getting her back to her usual self. My parents agreed and I said I was looking forward to see them in a month's time.

Marie did not enter the reckoning, despite the fact she knew of the whole situation through my parents. It did not concern her since our parents would be staying with me, as she did not have suitable accommodation to have anyone stay with her. However without saying anything to me, and despite my parents apprehension at staying with strangers, instead of being at ease in their son's home, she coerced them to book their tickets and come out to Dubai, as she had already made arrangements for them to stay at my friend Rita Biro's home.

Marie had done this without my knowledge, since she knew her plans would annoy me no end, as firstly, I wanted our parents to be comfortable and at 'home away from home' with me. And secondly, she knew Rita and her husband were my friends and though they did not know her, Marie also knew they would do anything for me. Why did she approach my friends who were strangers to her, and take advantage of their hospitality? Should a daughter not put the welfare of her parents above all else? Did getting me riled up take precedence over my parents' comfort?

Marie has always had a deep sense of insecurity where I am concerned. As a child, she resented me for joining the family as she had to share my parents attention. As an adult, my success has always brought out an unappealing side in her, irrelevant of the fact I worked darn hard at achieving my success. Any chance she got, she tried her best to knock me back. But at the end of the day, she was still my elder sister and I turned a blind eye and tolerated whatever she spewed out, for the sake of my parents.

Marie's daughter Carina and son Graham wanted to visit Dubai and Marie asked me if I could pay for their return air tickets, as they could not afford it and neither could she. And I blindly did. To my astonishment, Carina and a lad named Jim Pendergast, who worked in a private Insurance company in Dubai, got married in a civil ceremony at the British embassy, and had a wedding reception Marie had planned in town. But neither Marie nor even Carina informed nor invited me. I found out after the event and was made to look a nincompoop by being openly used just for a totally free holiday by my sister and her family.

Marie's son Graham later became a publican in the UK and Marie had invited our parents to the opening of Graham's pub. As they were proud of their grandson, they went to join in celebrating his good fortune. They stayed for a while and after a drink and a meal, they decided to leave as it was getting late and being octogenarians, they followed a rigid schedule. However, I was extremely surprised when my parents' called me in Dubai later that night. They returned home but were too upset to go to bed and called to tell me about Marie and Graham.

It turned out just as my parents were thanking Marie and Graham, and wishing Graham all success in his venture before they left, Marie presented them with a bill for their drinks and food. To say my parents were shocked and disheartened their daughter would treat them in such a shoddy manner, would be putting it extremely mildly. As my dad said, they were pensioners and their own daughter invited them to the pub opening and then charges them for accepting the invitation. My parents paid the bill but Marie and Graham could not have stooped any lower in their view.

While Graham had some money, he did not have enough to keep the pub running. Marie approached me to give him the money, so he would not face foreclosure and lose the pub. I informed her while I could not give him the money he needed, if he gave me his business plan, I would look at it with the option of investing in the pub. However, Marie expected me to just give him the money with no strings attached, as I never heard from either of them again and he was eventually forced to let the pub go.

In mid December 1990, Marie informed me my dad was terminally ill. I immediately called my mum as I was alarmed at this news. She said that the cancer had moved into stage four and he unfortunately, did not have long to live. This was the first I heard he even had cancer. I called my parents every Friday and neither of them mentioned it to me. When I questioned my mum as to why they never said anything before, she said my dad was diagnosed shortly after my last annual trip to the UK to visit them, and she had informed Marie nearly a year ago and asked her to give me all the information.

My parents never said anything during our weekly telephonic chats, because they wanted our chats to be happy and positive, and they just presumed I thought the same way as I too never mentioned anything. It was only now we all realised Marie's resentful nature towards me was out in full force, and I was furious with Marie for not passing on this information to me nearly a year ago.

She very well knew if I had known about my dad's critical illness, I would have gone immediately to the UK and taken my dad to a private specialist, instead of him waiting to get treated on the health service. While the health service today is fantastic, in 1990 it still had a way to go to get to where it is today. May be private treatment could have extended my dad's life, or yet again may be not. But it was a decision I was not able to make, as Marie took that right away from me by not informing me.

What kind of daughter would not want her dad to live as long as he possibly could? What kind of daughter would prioritize knocking her brother back, over the life of her dad? What kind of daughter would think nothing of breaking her dad's heart, especially considering she was his favourite child?

Without a second thought, I informed my parents I would see them in the next couple of days. The Gulf war had started in August 1990, and most companies had already sent all their employees out of the country, and closed down their companies for the duration of the war. I did no such thing and was one of the very few general maintenance companies still operating in Dubai. As such, my company was functioning as normal and we were extremely busy, as we were picking up the slack left by the rest of the companies.

Marie heard of my travel plans from my mum and called me, asking me to delay my trip and travel with her later in the month, when she was returning to the UK for Christmas and to sit out the war. She was unbelievable. But my dad was my priority, and I organised the company affairs with my general manager, kept him in charge of the company and left immediately for the UK as I had planned.

My dad was at home and my mum was doing her utmost to care for him herself. I could not believe the state my dad was in. The cancer had ravaged his body to such an extent, it was difficult to recognise my dad in his emaciated body. My dad was also having an extremely bad reaction due to the sluggish flow of blood through his body.

On checking what could be done to make him more comfortable, I was informed that a company in Birmingham manufactured a machine which would help with the blood flow. So though I was tired after just flying in from Dubai, I immediately drove overnight to Birmingham, purchased the equipment and returned to Kent the next morning with the machine, and it was a relief to see my dad was feeling much calmer once he was hooked up to it.

The next day I had a meeting with a senior oncologist and private specialist. However, on checking my dad's records, he advised me to just make my dad as comfortable as possible as it was now too late to do anything else medically for him. May be something could have been done earlier, but not at this late stage. Till my dying day, I will never forgive Marie for pulling the plug on my dad's life support, so-to-speak. I blame her for deliberately not informing me about my dad's disease, and denying him the right to maybe live a while longer.

Marie returned to the UK for Christmas, and visited Dad, but not to spend time with him. Everytime she went out with her friends, she just stopped by and my dad informed Mum and me, he was immensely unhappy with her for visiting him with strangers. Dad said it was utterly depressing for him to have us close family see his cancer riddled body. But to be seen by Marie's friends who were total strangers, made him feel like a man with no dignity. My mum advised Marie to visit on her own but she never listened. I too gave her a piece of my mind but she paid no heed and continued her visits with her friends, with no thought spared for our dad's wishes and how he felt.

My dad knew his end was near and I am sure he was reliving his life in his mind. One day when I was talking with him while he rested, he reached out and caught hold of my hand in such a strong grip, it belied his frailness. He looked straight into my eyes and said in a clear voice 'I am sorry son, I was all wrong about you'.

My dad said he finally saw the light, and hoped he was not

too late to make amends for blindly taking Marie's side and believing her version of incidents, over me. He said he now realised the wrong he did by asking me to overlook her many weaknesses, since he knew I too turned a blind eye to the extremely unkind and hurtful treatment Marie threw my way, just to keep him and my mum happy.

However, he said he now knew he could not leave without clearing the air and admitting he was wrong to take Marie's side, even though he was aware it was she who did wrong. He said he idolized the ground she walked on but like all parents, he believed he too had a responsibility to take more care of the weaker of his children and in his eyes, she was weaker because she was very insecure in herself. It seemed like a weight had lifted from my shoulders at my dad's disclosure. Yes, I still had to overlook Marie's weaknesses for my mum's sake, but I no longer had to put up with her.

My dad also said he was worried my mum would not have enough money to last her lifetime and he made me promise I would get Marie to return the six hundred Pounds Sterling that Marie had borrowed from my mum sometime back. While I was not aware of it till my dad brought it to my attention, I now learned Marie had the habit of borrowing money from my mum and not returning it without her constant follow-up. I did however, assure my dad I would look after my mum financially, should the need arise.

During the second week of January 1991, my dad was moved into a hospice. We were made aware it was just a matter of time now, as my dad had unfortunately reached the end of his road. All anyone could do for him now was to keep him as comfortable as possible. Since he entered the hospice we could not communicate with him at all, as he was heavily sedated for the pain and he was not conscious most of the time. Much as I wanted to stay with my dad during the final moments of his life, we could not stay with him in the hospice, and we were asked to return the next morning. However my mum received a call from the hospice during the night, informing us he had peacefully passed away in his sleep on 11 January 1991.

My dad's funeral was being held on 15 January. But it was unfortunate the Gulf war's Operation Desert Storm was starting on 17 January 1991. My general manager called me from Dubai and informed me I had to return to Dubai immediately. Thus the war prevented me from accompanying my dad on his final journey on earth, as I was forced to return to Dubai on the last flight before the Dubai airport was closed to all international commercial traffic, as the airport was to be used by the coalition air strike force.

In the United Arab Emirates, it is a criminal offence to abscond from a war zone, leaving dependent people behind. I may not have been absconding but it amounted to the same offence, as I had all my employees in Dubai. Their families depended on them, and they naturally in turn relied on me not only for their jobs, board and lodging, but for their very safety and security, as they were my personal responsibility. Though I had made a conscious decision to take responsibility for all my men and return to Dubai instead of staying for my dad's funeral, I will always regret not being by my dad's side on his last journey.

Before I left the UK, I informed Marie to purchase a grave plot for my dad to be interred in, and said I would pay the full cost of the plot. All I wanted was for my dad to have a permanent peaceful resting place and somewhere I could visit him whenever I was in town.

However, Marie never did as I had asked. Instead, she said my dad's ashes were scattered around the tree in my mum's back garden, at my mum's request. When I asked my mum why she did not want Dad to be interred in a grave, she very sadly said she did not have the money, and Marie never informed her I was paying for the full cost of a grave plot for my dad.

I will never understand the complexities of the human mind and why Marie did what she did. Why she never bought the grave and further, why she lied to the whole extended family about my dad's ashes being scattered on my grandparents grave, while my mum says otherwise, I will never know. Nor will I understand why she informed all and sundry that I did not care enough for my dad to remain in the UK for his funeral, when she knew the facts of the matter and why I had to leave the UK.

I had also committed to donate the blood flow machine I had bought for my dad, to the hospice where he lived during the final days of his life. However Marie took it and gave it away without consulting with me, making me loose my credibility with the hospice and in the process, extremely annoyed with Marie as it was not her property to give away in the first place.

Before my dad passed away, he had made Marie and me promise to never ever put our mum in a 'care home', and to ensure Mum lived her life to the very end in their own home at 23 Cherry Gardens, and I intended to keep my promise to him. After he passed away, I advised my mum to ask her youngest sister, my aunt Nell, to move in with her, as they would be company for each other since they got along well. While they did not live together in the UK as they both valued their independence, I did take my mum and my aunt Nell for a well deserved rest and relaxation vacation to Dubai. They had a wonderful stay at my villa with Baba at their beck and call.

My mum continued to live alone and as I was still not happy about her solitary living arrangements, I tried every idea I could think of to convince her to have a bit of home help. I next informed my mum I would get her a live-in housekeeper instead, so she could take it easy and was not alone. She declined this suggestion as well, and preferred to live alone in the house where she and Dad lived for so many years, and where her memories were fresh and green.

In 1998, when Anne and I made our weekly call to my mum at her home, there was no response. We called again the next day and got the same result. I then called Marie, who informed me she had my mum moved from my house to a 'care home' in town, as Mum could not cope on her own.

I was disturbed by this news as my mum wanted to live to the end of her days in her own home, where she and Dad had wonderful memories. I was not consulted as Marie knew I would hire a day and a night nurse to care for Mum at home. But Marie did not want the added problem of keeping an eye on Mum, as it would interfere with her personal life and constant travel plans. So she just moved Mum into St. Clement's Court retirement housing.

Anne managed the companies while I rushed back to the UK to check on my mum. While the 'care home' was a very good one and the service excellent, my mum was not pleased at leaving her own home. It was the fact she did not say anything when I asked, that gave away her true feelings at being pressurised by Marie to leave her familiar surroundings, and the comfort of her home. But Marie running true to form, was oblivious to Mum's feelings.

Now that my mum was in the 'care home', I eventually sold their house at Cherry Gardens as she would not be going back to living on her own, and I had absolutely no intention of living anywhere near my sister. Around seven years later, my mum was moved to White Birch Lodge, which was a 'full care home' as she was developing the early signs of Alzheimer's. I used to make frequent short trips to the UK to visit with my mum, while Anne kept the wheels of the companies turning smoothly.

It was during the period my mum was living at White Birch Lodge, that she left the residence on three occasions, to go to her home at Cherry Gardens. I cannot understand how my mum who was a dementia patient, could leave a 'full care' facility on three separate occasions on her own, without the staff being aware of her disappearance.

On one of these excursions, she could not find Cherry Gardens, and knocked on the door of my cousin Tony's wife Thelma's home instead. They were shocked to see her and took her back to the 'care home'. When I heard of this from Thelma after my mum passed away, it saddened me to learn my mum just wanted to get to her home where she and Dad were so happy, and where she felt very close to Dad. It seemed to me she just wanted to die in her own home too, as not long after she passed away.

Not having been in the UK for very many years, I could not remember the location of my grandparents resting place. As I had decided to have my mum interred with her parents, I needed to find it quickly as well as sort out the arrangements with the registrar of cemeteries. I thus met Thelma and she very kindly showed me the grave as Tony's mum, my aunt Counge's memorial is also on the same grave. Thelma and her daughter visit the cemetery frequently, as they visit Tony's resting place too.

As a 'thank you' to Thelma for her kindness, Anne who was in Dubai, suggested I take her out for a drink or a meal. I did invite Thelma but she declined my invitation. When Anne arrived the next week for my mum's funeral, I took her to visit with Thelma and Anne was not only enamoured with Thelma's rare and interesting collection of dolls' houses, but she said she was happy to finally meet the normal side of my extended family.

On one of my previous visits, I met up with Tony, who was gravely ill at that time, and fully aware he did not have long to live. He said he needed someone to talk with and I was privileged he felt he could speak with me. During our chat over a Markaris ice-cream at the waterfront, Tony mentioned he was worried not only regarding leaving Thelma behind, but also about how she would cope on her own. He asked me to drop in and check on her whenever I visited the UK. Unfortunately I never did get the time to check in on Thelma during my flying visits to see my mum.

However, our mutual cousin Peter Gaiger, the self-appointed 'Godfather' of the Italian side of our extended family, interfered and wrote a nasty letter telling me to leave Thelma alone as I was hassling her and she was not 'interested' in me. He further demanded Anne and I leave the UK and threatened us with police arrest if we ever returned to the UK.

When Anne read his letter, she could not stop laughing but at the same time she said 'I just cannot believe you are a part of this extremely disfunctional family. These folk should get a life of their own'. Yes, I unfortunately have the misfortune of being related to people like Marie, Peter and his sister Jean. I wrote back to Peter to get his mind out of the gutter and that we don't take kindly to unjustified threats. Thelma was kind enough to take me to my grandparents resting place as neither Marie nor my cousin Jean Reeve or her brother Peter Gaiger knew where it was. However, I am sure Tony is looking down on us and having quite a chuckle at our 'Godfather's' malarkey.

Marie had tried many times to get me interested in several of her English friends over the years since Phyllis and I divorced, but I had no interest in any of them. When Anne and I married in 1996, Marie was not at all pleased at me marrying a total stranger and that too, from the 'subcontinent', as she described it. She wanted me to marry an English divorcee Claire, who was a friend of her's and my cousin Jean, as Marie was under the falsehood she would then have control over me and my finances, through her friend. She took an instant dislike to Anne, although Anne went out of her way to befriend her, and even include her in our wedding arrangements.

But after our marriage, we found out Marie showed her true colours when she said loudly at our wedding reception 'this marriage should not have taken place, David should have married Claire'. However, our close friend and Anne's bridesmaid Big Red, fortunately happened to overhear Marie and without mincing her words, Big Red put Marie in her place in front of our guests at Marie's table. But Marie's shocking and blatant diatribe at my wedding reception opened my eyes to what my sister is really like and I now realised why she did not like my first wife too.

Anne cooled off towards forming a relationship with Marie. But for my sake she gave it a go many times and never stopped me from communicating with her, though I had no intention of having a relationship with my sister either. However crazy though it seemed, I still wanted Anne and Marie to form a relationship. I told Anne I would finance the start-up of her own Public Affairs company, and it would be a good idea to take Marie on as a partner. Whatever our relationship, I still wanted Marie to have a good life, and to ensure she was financially secure in her retirement. However, being a person who says it as she sees it, Anne just said 'if you want to finance your sister in any venture, you are free to do so but I want no part in it'. As such, I said no more.

When we had the launch party of our Oman oilfield engineering company, Marie happened to be visiting her friends in Oman. Being my sister, she was invited by my Oman partner Chris Green's wife Karen, even though neither Anne nor myself invited her. Though we were co-hosting the launch party, unknown to me, Marie totally avoided Anne at our party, but caught up with me during the evening.

When she was leaving, she came to say 'bye' to me. I was with Anne and a few guests and I turned to Anne and informed her that Marie was leaving. I had a hard time suppressing my laughter at the stupefied look on Marie's face, when Anne politely excused herself from our guests, turned around and looked directly into Marie's eyes and responded 'you came to my party without saying Hi, you can leave without saying Bye'. Then Anne turned back to our guests and continued conversing with them as though she was never interrupted. That was a unanimous and undisputed knockout to Anne.

Some time the next year, Marie telephoned me and said she was on vacation in Dubai with Dave Gould her ex-husband, as well as his step-daughter and her husband, and she was bringing them over to our home to visit with us. Anne was not happy at having Marie in our home, but as she had no axe to grind with the rest of the guests, she relented.

Dave had subsequently married a lovely lady Eve after he and Marie divorced. When Anne and I visited the UK after we got married, Eve and Dave invited us over for a meal at their home, so they got a chance to meet Anne. Unfortunately, Eve passed away a few years later and Dave was on his own again. Marie then decided as Dave was now on his own, she would get back together with him and move into Eve's house, to save on rent and utilities.

Dave was a good but quiet man, and probably just went along with Marie's scheming as he did when they were married, just to maintain peace in the house. I always liked Dave and got on well with him, but I did feel sorry for him when he was married to Marie. Now it was great seeing Dave again and meeting Eve's daughter and son-in-law.

Though Anne was the perfect hostess, everyone noticed Marie's hostile attitude towards Anne. Marie never acknowledged Anne's presence from the time she entered our home, till they left. That was the last day Marie was allowed into our home. Anne point blank said to me 'if you want to meet your sibling, do it somewhere else as she is barred from within a mile from my home, anywhere in the world'.

Anne also told me it was the first time she noticed I did not have a backbone where Marie was concerned, as Marie disrespected her in our own home, and I turned a blind eye and did nothing about it. Anne said my relationship with Marie was more akin to Stockholm syndrome. Yes, Anne's words did touch a nerve and caused me immense mental anguish. But, 'home truths' always hurt and I definitely deserved her censure, no two ways about it.

I could not argue with Anne on that fact as from a young age, I had looked up to Marie as my elder sister and always went out of my way to help her. I know I should have put the brakes on our relationship, after frequently being at the receiving end of her unkind and insensitive ways. But I kept turning a blind eye for the sake of my parents, and now it was second nature to me and too late to reform my way of thinking.

Marie had also been trying to make my parents disinherit me for as long as I can remember by lying and fabricating such far-fetched stories about me. Even my parents realised what she was up to, and started keeping their distance from her. However as all her plans to discredit me with my parents was not working, you can just imagine the shock my parents, Sharon and myself had when we found out Marie went to such great lengths to spread malicious falsehoods about me with her worst agenda yet.

Marie had returned to Dubai some years after her first trip when I evicted her from my villa, to find another job and as she had no place to stay, I allowed her to stay at my villa. Yes I know. You don't have to remind me of the fact I was a total 'idiot' for letting her walk all over me. My dad had asked me to overlook her numerous faults and try and get on with her, as I had just one sibling, and he would like to see us on good terms. And that was the sole reason why I put my best foot forward and always forgave her, till the next time she ill-treated me. She eventually got a job and moved out of my villa.

This time she really had crossed the line though, and went too far when she said I was a disgusting person as I tried to molest her when she lived at my villa. None of us could believe she would go this far to malign my name. People thought she moved out of my villa, because I tried to molest my elder sister. What kind of a person would come up with that scenario? Why was she deliberately doing her utmost to destroy my name? And what in the world was wrong with me for subjecting myself time and again to her machinations?

A short while later, Sharon visited me and I told her what had happened. Being a person who hits first and talks afterwards, Sharon was at Marie's office in the blink of an eye. She went straight for Marie's jugular and ripped through her verbally using the most colourful language, in front of all her colleagues.

My parents were shocked at hearing what Marie did, but did not believe a word of it as they knew her better than anyone else, and they also knew of her habit of speaking ill about me from the time we were kids. However, a couple of years or so after Anne and I were married, Marie tried to break us up once more, and brought this story out again for good measure. She was visiting Dubai this time and staying with her friends, as Anne said she would never have any members of my disfunctional family under our roof.

But by now, Anne was totally fed up with my sister's interference in our life and asked me to get Marie to drop by. Anne went at her like a dog with a bone and questioned her at length about what she had said about me. Anne said that an attempt to molest anyone is a very serious offence of great magnitude, which no woman should sweep under the carpet, irrespective of who the molester is.

Anne asked Marie why she did not take the information, if true, to the Dubai police and get me arrested for my so-called offence? Anne further asked Marie if she would really keep quiet if she or her daughter Carina was actually molested, and allow the perpetrator to get away scot-free to commit his crime again?

Eventually after a grilling from Anne, Marie admitted I did not molest her or in fact do anything so terrible. Anne then just said 'Oh! I know you were lying and David did not molest you. I just wanted to hear you say it, for myself. The fact you were so desperate for your friend Claire to marry David, was all the proof I actually needed'. Anne also showed Marie a small recording device she borrowed from the office, and said she had recorded Marie's confession.

After my mum passed away on 31 December 2007, my cousin Peter, our extended family's self-appointed 'Godfather' as I now call him, again interfered in matters he knows absolutely nothing about. He visited Anne and me in the UK and I was really surprised to see him, and wondered what he wanted from me, as he reminded me that we only met twice in the last sixty plus years. He soon answered my silent query, when he informed me I was in serious legal trouble for cheating Marie out of her inheritance. As I had absolutely no clue as to what he was talking about, I asked him to explain himself.

The story started when my parents were living at Oxendon Park Drive but were not happy there. They wanted to move to Cherry Gardens but they did not have the finances to buy a house in the area. So I registered with a local estate agent, to inform me when any property in Cherry Gardens came up for sale. When 23 Cherry Gardens came on the market in 1980, I bought it for them.

I then went to the UK to finalise the purchase. When I received the keys to the house, I hired a Rolls Royce and took my parents out for a five-star meal. I then drove to 23 Cherry Gardens, stopped the car, and asked them to come for a walk with me. When they were outside, I gave them the keys to the house and informed them the house was theirs. Both of them were extremely pleased, though my mum was in tears throughout.

However, as I was married to Phyllis at that time, my parents were troubled about her, Sharon and Tony throwing them out and taking back the property. Hence, I had my solicitors draw up an agreement which confirmed that though the property was just in my name, I was giving it to my parents to live in for rest of their natural lives, and no one could evict them. My mum and my dad were thrilled and moved into the property.

I also advised my parents to either rent or sell their house in Oxendon Park Drive after they moved to Cherry Gardens, bank their money and maybe use some of it to go on a cruise on the QE2. They had a hard life and never really experienced the joy of either travelling the world, or enjoy living on the other side of the track, so-to-speak. My parents did eventually sell their house and bank their money, but they did not go on the cruise as they regarded it as a total waste of money.

However, Peter told Anne and me, Marie had informed all our relatives I had cheated her of her inheritance, as I had sold my parents house at Oxendon Park Drive, and used the money to buy 23 Cherry Gardens in my name only. Marie was hoping my parents would live till the end of their lives at Oxendon Park Drive, as then she would naturally get fifty percent of their estate, which included the house.

But as my parents sold their house after they moved into Cherry Gardens, they used the money from the sale of their house to support themselves in their retirement till they died, and Marie did not get half of a house or her inheritance, as she called it. But just to make her the wronged person who was robbed blind by me, she fabricated the story of me selling my parents home.

We did hear Peter out but I was really surprised at his interference without justified cause, firstly for believing Marie. Considering the facts of the matter, if what she said was the whole truth and nothing but the truth, she could have legally dragged me through the courts system to get her so-called inheritance way back in 1980, when I had bought the house for my parents. I was surprised at her and Peter spreading this false information after twenty-eight years, as he visited me in 2008.

Secondly, without even getting his facts and ducks in a row, he blindly took Marie's version as gospel truth and lodged an objectionable verbal assault on me. Finally, from my personal experience at being on the receiving end of my sister's agendas, I know that Marie gets third parties like Peter, to fight in her corner, and while they are officially conferred with a tarnished image for their interference, she goes through unscathed.

In February, 2007 Marie informed me she was visiting Dubai with her friend Harry, and asked if we could put them up at our place. Anne's answer was just one short flat word 'No'. Anne used to work daily from her work station on the 'La Buttana', while our crew and I got on with our usual maintenance tasks.

As I thought I would help Marie save on expensive hotel board and lodging while in Dubai, I asked Anne if it would be fine for them to stay on the 'La Buttana', which was moored at the Jebel Ali hotel marina. While Anne did not like the idea, it was my vessel and she said she had no problem with me 'blundering on my turf', as long as she did not have to meet Marie.

Anne got two cabins ready for them and even stocked the galley fridge with breakfast items. But she worked from home as she had no intention of bumping into Marie. On the first day of their holiday, both Marie and Harry went out to visit the various sights in Dubai. However, the next day onwards Marie went out on her own, while Harry remained on the 'La Buttana' and kept me company. As we were meeting for the first time, we chatted while I worked on various jobs with my crew.

I informed Anne of the situation and she brought us lunch every day when Marie was out. Anne inquired as to why Harry was not going out with Marie after travelling all the way to Dubai. He informed us that due to his age, he was not quick on his feet and unable to walk fast to keep up with Marie, who kept losing her patience with him because he was much slower. Yes, that was my sister alright.

On the final day of their holiday, Marie and Harry wanted to take both Anne and myself to dinner at one of the restaurants in the Jebel Ali hotel itself. Persuading Anne to come to the hotel was not an easy task for me. But she eventually agreed and joined us at the restaurant. Marie was decked out in thousands of Dirhams worth of gold, and knowing for a fact neither she nor her family had the resources to own so much jewellery, Anne asked her directly how she could afford to purchase so much jewellery.

Marie informed us that her daughter Carina did not keep her jewellery for long as she liked to keep changing her jewellery for the latest trends. Marie said Carina gave her the jewellery to exchange in Dubai. Knowing their tight financial situation, Anne just laughed openly at Marie's answer as she did not believe a word Marie said, but she did not say anything further either.

My mum passed away in the UK on the 31 December 2007, and I was thankful to be with my mum during the end of her days. As I wanted Anne to be with me at my mum's funeral, I organised the funeral for the 12 January 2008, to give Anne who was in Dubai, the time to organise matters in our business and the 'La Buttana' as well as celebrate our daughter Coral's tenth birthday, before leaving for the UK.

My mum passed away around 6 am, and Marie telephoned me half an hour after my mum's demise with the news. I told Marie I would accompany her to the 'care home' to help clear all my mum's things later in the day. But she informed me her daughter Carina had already removed all my mum's possessions from her room.

I could not believe Marie and Carina had gone and cleared all my mum's belongings overnight, even before my mum passed away and her body had gone cold. Obviously insensitivity ran in the family. I did not even have a keepsake which belonged to my mum. They had taken everything which was fine as even though I had purchased all the jewellery and expensive electronic items for my mum, I knew my mum had not passed away intestate as she had her 'last will and testament' in place.

So I informed Marie that at the moment all I wanted was an old small ordinary laminated crucifix, my mum had at home ever since I could remember. As it was of literally no monetary value, Marie had absolutely no problem asking Carina to give it to me, and while I may not be religious, this old crucifix has since held a pride of place in my home ever since.

I had ordered a new car which was unfortunately only being delivered the day after Anne was scheduled to arrive in the UK. As I did not have a car to pick Anne up at the airport, I asked Marie to take me to the airport and she agreed to pick me up at 11 am, as the estimated time of arrival of Anne's flight was at noon. I was actually extremely surprised Marie had agreed to take me to the airport, as she hates Anne's indomitable guts. But as time passed awaiting her arrival to pick me up, I began to wonder if I was about to cross paths with yet another hidden agenda from Marie's bag of tricks.

My assumptions were proved correct as running true to form, and considering my request involved Anne, Marie arrived at my place only at noon, with an implausible excuse she had to go elsewhere and could not take me to the airport. After all I have done for my sister, she could not even reciprocate in assisting me with one small request, proving my point that Marie is only for Marie and she has always used me at will, to suit her agenda. Eventually, my mate John Crippin, a retired police officer, took me to the airport and to our good luck, Anne's flight was a couple of hours late, so we were actually on time.

Anne wanted to know the funeral arrangements as neither Marie nor I am religious and the service was in the Catholic faith. Hence Anne and I met with father Patrick, the parish priest, to check on the schedule for the service. She then telephoned Marie and informed her I would be saying a few words at my mum's funeral service before my cousin Jean.

Marie was furious at Anne for making changes to the arrangements, but Anne informed Marie in no uncertain terms, my mum would most certainly prefer me to give the eulogy at the service, rather than my cousin Jean whom my mum neither liked nor ever spoke with when she was alive. Actually, Marie only asked Jean to speak as being an actress, she was used to public speaking. Anne said that irrelevant of whether Marie liked it or not, I was speaking at my mum's funeral service and she had better get used to the fact.

Not to be outdone, Marie then said she had invited over thirty people to the funeral and as we were out to cause trouble, we were not welcome at the Bun Penny pub where everyone was meeting up for drinks and a meal after the funeral. Gloves off, Anne further told Marie people are not invited to a funeral. People are informed of the funeral arrangements and those who would like to pay their last respects to the departed, attend the funeral.

Marie was using the funeral as a platform to entertain her friends for free, considering my mum was paying for everything from the residual of her estate. Other than all my cousins, many of the people at the funeral did not even know my mum, as they were Marie's friends.

On the day of the funeral, my mate John Munt drove to our place from Rainham. John, Anne and I drove in my new car to the funeral parlour. The funeral director had informed us, the family would form the funeral cortege from the funeral parlour to the crematorium. However after waiting for over forty-five minutes, Marie did not arrive. The funeral director telephoned her and she said she was already at the crematorium to be with her invited guests.

Everyone was totally shocked at Marie's callous behaviour though I was not, as she cared for no one but herself. If John, Anne and I were not there, my mum would have left on her final journey on earth absolutely alone. I did speak at my mum's funeral service and as Anne and I had decided not to go to the pub after the service, we stood at the exit of the chapel and when everyone filed out, we thanked each one personally for attending my mum's funeral. While Anne never knew anyone, I knew my cousins and recognised a few others.

When Marie came out after the funeral, Anne touched Marie on her arm and invited her to stand with us to thank everyone. We were totally shocked at the venom in her voice when she forceably moved her arm away and said 'Don't touch me'. Anne just looked at her and then said to me 'My colour doesn't run, does it?' and then ignored Marie. And that was the last time Anne and I either saw Marie or had any form of contact with her.

John, Anne and I then went for a late brunch to a restaurant on the sea front, in full view of the pub where Marie had organised the get together after my mum's funeral, as we did not have to hide from anyone. With both my parents no longer alive, I did not have to put up with my sister just to please them. As far as I was concerned, I could look forward to living a peaceful life now that she was out of it. Yes, Marie was finally out of my life for ever and I can honestly say my life is all the more peaceful and happy without her in it. However, it is just a crying shame I had to put up with her for my parents' sake, for over half a century.

I instructed my solicitors to handle my mum's 'last will and testament', and Anne and I returned to Dubai. I then ordered a marble plaque for my mum's grave and had it couriered from Dubai to the funeral home in the UK. The funeral home forwarded the plaque to my solicitors, as Marie together with my cousin Jean and her brother Peter, were causing problems and as such my mum could not be interred into her final resting place.

My solicitor informed me that all was not going smoothly with regard to the terms of my mother's 'last will and testament', which was lodged with the solicitor. They said that after my mum was forced out of her home and put into a care facility by Marie and her daughter Carina, my mum had informed the solicitor she had added a holographic and witnessed addendum to her 'will' and it was to be taken as her updated 'will'. But when the solicitor brought this up with Marie, she said there was no amended handwritten 'will'. It seemed the handwritten addendum page disinheriting Marie, and her children, Carina and Graham from her 'will', had mysteriously disappeared, leaving behind only the original 'will'.

My mum mentioned in her original 'will' she wanted all the jewellery I had given her during her lifetime, which amounted to thousands of Pounds Sterling, to be divided equally between both Marie and me. My mum had also left a gold necklace of hers, and the only piece of jewellery she originally owned, for Sharon. As it was my mum's wishes, I informed my solicitors I had no problem with the terms of her original 'will'.

However, my solicitors subsequently stated that when they questioned Marie, she had informed them there was no jewellery either, as my mum had given it all away long before she passed on. I knew it was not true as my mum never gave away anything I gifted to her, whatever the value.

Infact, when Anne went on a trip to the UK with her sister-in-law in December 1996, they spent a weekend in our quarters at my mum's home. At that time, my mum had informed Anne of all the jewellery I had given to her over the years, and asked Anne if she would like to have it back, as my mum said she was not wearing it. Anne thanked my mum but refused her gesture, saying it was gifted to her by me and as such all the jewellery was her's. My mum then smiled and told Anne she would leave it equally to both Marie and me when she died. So we knew in advance what my mum's intentions were, and we also knew Marie was now lying to the solicitors.

That was when Anne realised from where Marie got all the jewellery she was literally draped in, when she stayed on the 'La Buttana' during her trip to Dubai. She had taken all the jewellery I had given to my mum and then actually had the temerity to stay on my vessel for free, while she covertly exchanged it for jewellery in the latest designs when in Dubai, so I would not recognise any of it. Yes, I definitely was a blind fool yet again.

When Marie and Carina moved my mum from Cherry Gardens to St. Clement's care-home, they emptied out my mum's home and took everything, including her jewellery. Luckily my annex was locked as I am positive they would have emptied out my home as well. My mum just had a few basic necessities in the 'care-home' and probably did not give a second thought to all her personal items from her own home. Or yet again, may be she did, as she added a witnessed addendum to her 'will' disinheriting Marie and her children.

I am sure Mum also never expected her daughter or granddaughter to be so self-serving either. My mum later suffered from Alzheimer's disease and naturally did not know what was happening around her, or that her estate was being depleted during her lifetime. And the collateral damage of greed, was that Sharon too never received the necklace bequeathed to her by my mum. Shocking - but unfortunately true.

I informed my solicitors of what really happened to my mum's jewellery. I further instructed my solicitors to go ahead with the closure of my mum's estate and have my mum's ashes interred in my grandparents grave, as I had sorted the documentation out with the registrar of Cemeteries, before I had left the UK. I also instructed them to have the plaque I had sent from Dubai, fixed on the grave.

Four months after my mum's demise, she was still not laid to rest because Marie was causing further problems, as stated by the solicitors. She was demanding the solicitors first hand over her share of my mum's estate. Unfortunately for her, since only we siblings were beneficiaries of my mum's estate as indicated in her original 'will', both our signatures were required for the proceeds to be handed out.

I refused to sign off the estate until my mum was laid to rest in the grave with her parents, and the plaque affixed on it. With the assistance of the funeral home and my solicitors, Marie was eventually forced into a corner and she capitulated, and had my mum laid to rest four months after she passed away, on 24 April 2008, with photographic evidence sent to me in Dubai by my solicitors. After which, I signed off my mum's estate and Marie also got her wish to disinherit me in the process, as she received what she was after all along – all the jewellery and her share of the money.

I on the other hand, was looking forward to a peaceful future. But as the broken record of my life indicates, it was not to be. Whenever Anne and I visited the UK, we dropped in to the cemetery to visit with my parents. We always put flowers and Anne had put a couple of small stone angels and a candle lantern on the grave, alongside the small stone angel I think my cousin Tony's family put on the grave.

We were however left mystified when on our next visit to the UK, we found the two small flower pots as well as the two little angels we had placed on the grave, had disappeared. On searching the area, we found it destroyed and thrown into a bush nearby, from where we picked up the pieces. As the candle lantern was an expensive one, it had just vanished.

However, we did find it odd the stone angel Tony's family put on the grave was not touched. Who would vandalize and desecrate a grave of just the few things only we had placed there? Someone was obviously marking our card, to have stooped to such a low level to warn us off.

Some time later, the answers to our unanswered questions arrived in the form of a letter from our self-appointed 'Godfather' Peter. We were shocked to learn it was my cousins Peter and Jean and my sister Marie behind the vandalism and desecration of the grave. I had asked my eldest cousin Jean to take over the ownership of our grandparents' grave, so that my mum's remains could be interred there. However, I find their total disrespect for the dead and in this instance, for my parents and grandparents, is distasteful and repugnant.

Marie has also gone out of her way to antagonise Anne very many times since Anne and I got married. But Anne ignored her. Marie chose the wrong lady to cross this time, as Anne does not take any prisioners. Marie never ever let up on Anne and eventually in cahoots with my elder cousins Peter and Jean, they did try to cause more problems with threats in writing included.

But by now, Anne had enough of my disfunctional family – my sister, my two cousins and my children, and I do not blame her as she has had to put up with a lot of unnecessary aggravation from them. Anne thus put Marie, Jean and Peter in their place with a strong no nonsense letter on 3 September 2008 and we have never had any form of interference nor heard from any of them ever since.

At this stage in my life, I can honestly say I have absolutely no regrets about not having Marie in my life. I could handle anything when I was young, but I now prefer to live a peaceful existence for whatever time I have left. She knows I always helped her because I wanted the best for her. I decided to visit her one last time and I recently spoke to her briefly, and even left a few messages. However, I do not envisage a reconciliation between us as she has rebuffed my familial approach.

It is extremely unfortunate my only sister is no longer a part of my life. We may be of the same bloodline but our trajectories in life are poles apart. When I see the close relationship Anne has with her sister and brother, I wish I had a sibling who cared about me the same way. But sometimes, wishes just remain impossible dreams, and that is why I have always referred to my sister as my parents' daughter.

The Suvali clan at my aunt Nell and uncle Jock's wedding

With Marie

Chapter 21

The colours of my first marriage – the secrets of a scarlet woman

I was brought up with old school values, and I wanted to do the right thing by my daughter, who was born in 1962. However, I was not sure about marrying her mother as when I married, I wanted a lifelong marriage just like my parents had. Marriage was a big step, and it was not what I really wanted at the age of twenty-two years, but for the sake of my little girl, I decided to marry my girlfriend Phyllis Kingbeck in 1963.

I must admit our marriage was doomed right from the start, and should really never have taken place, as we both had vastly different mindsets with regard to the sanctity of marriage. It seemed I was the only one who did not know anything about my new wife or her past, as many men knew her much more intimately than just as a friend. What were these men to her? but more importantly, what was she to each of them?

She did not have many female friends, and I found her relationships with her innumerable male friends to be meretricious. I wondered what I had got myself into? But as they say, hindsight is twenty-twenty. And since I had now made my marital bed, I had no option but to lie in it for the sake of my baby daughter.

However in 1964, not even a year into my marriage, my

fears were realised and my marriage blew up before my eyes. I inadvertently found out Phyllis was constantly unfaithful to me during the short span of our relationship and marriage, with her paramour – Malcolm Townsend. When I confronted her, she not only admitted it, but she also informed me she had a child with him, and they had put their daughter into the social care system before she married me. I still have the photographs she gave me of the little child named Debbie, with her foster parents.

This brought to the forefront of my mind, the fact I had made the biggest mistake of my life, at the young age of twenty-two, by getting into a relationship with Phyllis. My first thought now was to 'cut loose and run', and I did run to Europe. But by the time I returned from Turkey in mid 1965, I discovered we now had not one but two very young children under the age of three, and their innocent lives were in my hands. If I divorced their mother, I could not trust her not to abandon them like she did her first child. Even though there was a fifty-fifty chance they were not my biological children, it was a possibility I was not willing to even consider.

I had grown up with friends who were in the social care system, and their early lives were lacking in many ways on a personal level, and not a happy period for them. They grew up asking questions no one could answer, leaving gaping holes in their lives. As such in the wisdom of my youth, I even tried to bring her first child Debbie out of the social care system and into our family fold. She was the elder sister of my two children, and I truly believed she should be brought up with her biological siblings as a family and not separately. I had no problem bringing up another child who was not mine as long as she was out of the social care system.

I also thought just maybe their mother would change her loose morals and become more responsible for her actions, with her three children to care for. But for reasons I will neither understand nor ever find out, Phyllis would not hear anything I had to say about Debbie. As far as I was concerned, whatever reasons she had for putting her child into the social care system were irrelevant, as she now had a chance to redeem herself and bring her child out of it and into our family unit. But she absolutely refused to discuss her daughter's situation or to bring her eldest child into our family.

What loving and caring mother would prefer to leave her biological child in foster care, rather than to bring her up in her own family environment, alongside her biological siblings, if she had the chance to rectify the situation? Why was she so secretive and adamant that she would never ever bring her eldest daughter to join our family unit? What was she hiding from me?

Were my assumptions that Sharon and Tony were not my biological children but actually Debbie's full siblings, accurate? My view has always been that if she had nothing further to hide, she would have brought Debbie who was a secret no longer, into our family. But the fact she refused to even talk about the subject proved to me she was definitely hiding some very pertinent information from me.

Phyllis' attitude bothered me, as she seemed to treat her innocent eldest daughter with total indifference, and I did not understand her way of thinking at all. Many years later I got Debbie's address and I sent her Christmas cards, just so she did not feel she was forgotten, though Phyllis did not bother. Even after Phyllis and I divorced, the cards continued to be sent till I sold my group of companies, as I had put Debbie's name on my business mailing list.

Sharon also informed me some time ago, she had asked her mother several times for Debbie's contact details. But Phyllis has treated her requests with heartless disregard, and refuses to divulge the information, as she does not want the siblings to meet or form a relationship with each other.

Thus I made the second big mistake in my marriage in 1965, by taking Phyllis back for the sake of the children, and trying to make our marriage work. I knew I would not be able to do justice to either the children or myself, if I took sole custody of both of them. Sharon was a toddler so I could manage caring for her and doing a full day's work at the same time without a problem.

However, Tony was not even a year old, and I definitely needed assistance in caring for him. In my mind, the only way out of my predicament was to stay married to Phyllis so she could care for, and bring up the children, while I concentrated on bringing in the bread and butter.

At that young age, I hoped I was doing right by our children, by sacrificing my happiness and putting them first. It did not hit home immediately that trying to keep my family together for the wrong reasons, did not mean either a happy marriage, or self-contentment with my life. How could we have a relationship without communicating with each other? She constantly disrespected me and in my book, where there is no respect there is absolutely no love. I most definitely believe without trust there is no reason to continue with a relationship, as it is better to live a short but happy life than a long and miserable one. However, I made peace with my decision as I could never let Sharon and Tony down the way Debbie was let down by Phyllis.

It takes love, commitment and communication to make a marriage succceed, all what we did not have as she was a very secretive woman and as I now knew, one that led a double life too. But I figured it was better knowing the devil for what she was, than living with a devil in disguise. My decision made, I continued to stay faithful throughout my marriage, and worked at having as regular a family life as one could possibly have, so the children who were growing up, did not suspect the tensions floating around our home.

A negative aspect of the long hours I worked, was that Phyllis had a lot of free time on her hands, to indulge in her own special brand of entertainment. She took up reception jobs in hotels or office work to keep her busy or so she said. But as I provided very well for the family and as she did not need to go out and earn her own money, I did doubt her.

As they say, her roses bloomed in every port of call we made. Yes, I knew she found a pair of trousers in all the countries we lived in, to keep her entertained. She frequently went out on her own and quite often never even returned till the morning. She never volunteered any information, and I really did not care as even if I asked, she just said she was out with friends. And yes, I turned a blind eye first because the children were young and later because they were growing up.

But then, so many years of her constant promiscuity had taken its toll on me, and I found I preferred being out of the house working long hours, rather than being in the home where uncomfortable silence reigned as we did our own thing, unless we were out at a social gathering with friends.

I had reached the end of my tether, as all my efforts to get her to change her loose morals was in vain. Well, a leopard never changes its spots, does it? Looking back, I wonder how I kept the marriage going for as long as I did, as our communication if at all, was limited and unlike her, I was a louzy actor.

There were instances when I even saw her with the men she was involved with, but I never confronted her nor did anything about it. I initially put it down to folly on my part. But mainly, I did not want to disrupt the happy and carefree lives of our children. Phyllis on the other hand, obviously took my silence of her cheating, as the green signal to continue cheating on me without a guilty conscience.

Normally, it is us men who are said to be philanderers, with the women being the injured party. But I can vouch for the fact this is not always the norm. In my case, I was the wronged partner, and yet I continued to stay faithful to my cheating wife.

Frequently I questioned my own acceptance of her actions. What was wrong with me? Did I have no self-respect? Was I not entitled to happiness? Why was I still with the woman who had such callous disregard for my feelings? And everytime, the answer came back 'I had to put my children first, my parents second, and me only after them'.

Phyllis thought she could do what she wanted and get away with it, because I loved her too much to let her go. Unfortunately for her, she was totally off the mark, and I was not going to be the one to set her straight. Yes, I fell in love with her when I first met her. But she killed it when she consciously destroyed our marriage in 1963, even before the ink was dry. My mum always said 'what goes around, comes around' and 'everyone gets their comeuppance' and while I laughed when my mum used these phrases, I now genuinely believed it.

After taking Phyllis back in 1965 and moving into our own house at 24 Blyth Hill, I thought she would change and concentrate on the children. But who was I kidding? She would never change. One day a local man she was having an affair with, had the temerity to come to our house and start a fight with me over her, as he wanted her back. While she was not worth fighting over, she was still legally my wife.

So though he was physically a larger man than me, I took him on. I had a pile of bricks remaining from the building work, lying by the front door outside the house, and when he came at me I just picked up a brick, aimed it at him and threatened him with it. He walked away and I never saw him again. Phyllis took her usual stance and played the innocent party. However, I now knew if I wanted my life to change, I had to move Phyllis and the children away from the UK.

I love Mauritius and I still keep in touch with friends there from days of yore. If there was any place I felt at peace during my marriage to Phyllis, it was in Mauritius. I guess the reason was I had friends I could go fishing or diving with and just forget my turbulent life for a while. The children loved it there and while Phyllis socialised with my friends she also had her own friends.

We had a maid in Mauritius to care for the children, home and even cook our meals. This to me was a luxury, as Phyllis was not proficient on the culinary front. Over the years, many times when I returned home after a hard day's work, she was not at home and there was neither a meal ready and waiting for me, nor any food stores in the house for me to rustle up a quick meal for myself. She had access to the house keeping expenses but what she did with it I did not know as she never cooked us meals. I know she fed the children and I hoped they were nourishing meals.

Phyllis wanted to learn driving and instead of asking me to teach her, she sidelined me and made her own arrangements with a local Mauritian policeman she was friendly with, and who I knew just by sight, to give her private driving lessons. I did wonder why she never asked me to teach her, and I had a suspicion her driving lessons were her excuse to be with this man. But as I was busy with work, the children, and enjoying my time on this beautiful island in the Indian Ocean, I did not want to bring the topic up with her and make my life hell again. I preferred to turn a blind eye to her escapades as the children were growing, and they were at the age when they needed stability.

On another occasion when I was on contract in Uganda, as was our daily schedule, I had left the house as usual in the morning for the work site, while she dressed and left to take the children to school. However, one day I returned to the house unexpectedly, to pick up some site plans I had forgotten to take with me in the morning. I found Phyllis in a state of undress and in a negligee having coffee with Doctor David Aery, who also happened to be a married man.

Which of us was more surprised when I walked in - me or them, is anyone's guess. Who would entertain a person outside the immediate family unit in a state of such undress? unless ofcourse the two concerned people were in an intimate relationship with each other? The thought of her desecrating our marriage, our home and our bed by bringing her paramours into it, was mindblowing and downright disgusting. And though she was busted, he looked uncomfortable while she did not seem too bothered about it.

I had noticed Mrs. Aery looking at me in a strange way on a couple of occasions but never gave it a second thought, until I came across her husband and Phyllis together in our home. She probably knew her husband, the good doctor, was having an affair with my wife, and wondered if I knew anything about it. The fact they were having an affair was confirmed when Phyllis got extremely ill once, and Dr. Aery went out of his way and beyond the call of duty, to bring in a specialist professor to treat her at his own expense.

Even in Zambia I was not spared from her debauchery. She was involved with another English married man who worked with the copper mines, and who I knew by sight as a casual acquaintance. His wife knew he had another woman in his life, but I don't think she suspected it was Phyllis.

Unfortunately, one day this man had gone to town and had just parked his car at the side of the road. As he exited his car, he was hit by a speeding vehicle driven by a local man, throwing him with such force onto the road that he fell and hit his head on the hard tarmac. His injuries were serious and he was admitted into the mining area clinic for treatment. But a short while later, while he was in the bath in the clinic, he died of an aneurysm. The last I heard was his wife flew back to the UK with his body.

Immediately after his death, Phyllis said she and the children were not happy in Zambia any more and wanted to leave the country. I found it very surprising and extremely selfish, as I had not only started my own company, but I was also immensely successful, and I did not have plans to leave Zambia any time soon. But she said they wanted to move to Australia, and so I sourced a job there and we moved to Queensland.

Unfortunately she blindsided me, as it was only after I had closed down my company, the truth hit me head-on. It was Phyllis and not the children who wanted to leave Zambia, and the only reason was as her lover had sadly died, she had lost her secret life.

Once when on a trip to the UK in between my overseas contracts, we were driving in a hired car from the airport into Croydon, and Phyllis asked me to drive via South Norwood. On the way, she saw a used car showroom ahead, and immediately asked me to stop at the car showroom. While I remained in the car with the children, she went into the office. A long while later, she exited with Malcolm Townsend, the man who she had a child with, prior to getting together with me. The man she continued to have an affair with even after marrying me. And more notably, one of the contenders to be the biological father of Sharon and Tony.

This told me that while I was not aware of it, she was still in contact with him, as after all these years, she knew exactly where he was now working. How she could openly humiliate me without batting an eyelid, was not as shocking as the fact she was more importantly, subjecting her teenage children to witness her total lack of respect for them, by blatantly displaying one of her paramours publicly.

On seeing them together, it belatedly dawned on me as to why Phyllis did not want me to go with her to the UK, to enroll the children into their private boarding schools. I would have cramped her constantly cheating style, as she without a doubt had spent all her time with him.

It was many times like these instances, when I was on the brink of walking out of our marriage. I felt my life was empty as I had nothing to hold on to, nothing to show for the sacrifices I made, other than my children, who yet again may not be my children. Was it all worth it or was it just a farce of gargantuan proportions?

Based on my marriage to Phyllis, I can with confidence say that in any relationship, when one partner perpetuates a close liaison with a person outside the relationship or marriage, they automatically not only sow the seeds of distrust in the relationship, but are solely responsible for it disintegrating to a point of no return.

Over the years, to the world outside the walls of our home, we both exuded the picture of a loving and happy couple. We had enjoyable times with friends and with the children. There were good times too, when I blanked out the misery and enjoyed my time with my family. We even socialised and travelled together as a family. While I had married Phyllis the exceptional actress, over time I too became such an excellent actor in my own way, not even Sharon and Tony saw through the smokescreen we created.

Other than the three or more people involved in my marriage at any given time, no one suspected our marriage was anything but normal. Phyllis even helped me occasionally with my reports. Any time I had to do a job survey report, I dictated the information I wanted in the report and she assisted me with the layout and typing, which was a great help as while I was darn good in my work, I could neither format nor type a report on a typewriter.

They say 'birds of a feather flock together' and I found the saying to be very true with regard to Phyllis. Every country we lived in, she seemed to find and surround herself with like minded shallow women, who were only interested in men, and the inconsequential things life has to offer. I never socialised with them but I tolerated them, just to keep her occupied and away from the men in her life.

In 1965 when I took Phyllis back so she could care for the children, while I worked to support the family, I did not expect her to make decisions singularly, and of life changing proportions with regard to their lives. Anything involving the children had to be done in agreement between the two of us. However, running true to form as the secretive person she is, Phyllis also made decisions with regard to the children without my prior knowledge, or even discussing the matters with me in advance.

Being excluded and kept totally in the dark till after the facts, I unfortunately have no option but to hold her solely responsible for being instrumental in ruining their personal lives. Sharon and Tony could have had a vastly superior education, if she did not mindlessly uproot them from their expensive boarding schools in the UK. I am sure they would have turned out to be much better and well rounded individuals, with their heads firmly screwed onto their shoulders, if they had the boarding school discipline and foundation to back them.

I also blame Phyllis, but more importantly, I can never ever forgive her for knowingly destroying Sharon's life as an adult woman, when she took Sharon with her to Kenya. When we were living in Dubai, I went home after work one day to find both Phyllis and Sharon not at home, which as a rule was not unusual, as both of them were living their own lives and were hardly at home. I went for days at times without seeing either of them. On the other hand, as I never had a social life outside work, I was always at home after work. As such, you can imagine my absolute shock, when the two of them were suddenly at home after a while, and Phyllis informed me of the true reasons for their absence together from the home. They had taken a trip together to Nairobi.

Going to Kenya ostensibly on a mini break with her daughter, would normally not have been an issue. But who leaves the home whatever the reason, and disappears abroad without informing their spouse? I could not and I still cannot understand, how a mother could deliberately subject her young adult daughter to such mental and physical trauma. How could Phyllis live with herself knowing she solely contributed to, and is responsible for Sharon being scarred for life? How can grave and momentous family decisions be taken unilaterally by just one parent? Especially when it concerns the future well-being of the children?

The independent decisions and actions Phyllis took regarding the children, gave me the feeling she was certain I was not their biological father. By my very noticeable exclusion from important decisions pertaining to Sharon and Tony, it seemed Phyllis was really driving home the fact I was only wanted for a roof over their heads, their bills paid and money in their bank. Yes, I obviously had my uses, though I was excluded from everything else.

In 1983 matters came to a head with Phyllis, when we were living in Dubai. While I was running my own company and worked extremely long hours, she was working at the reception of a hotel in the Deira area in Dubai. I did not expect Phyllis to continue collecting either notches on her bedpost or skeletons in her closet while in Dubai, where extra marital relationships are strictly frowned upon and infact illegal. But I did not take into account the fact she was an addict and like any addiction, she always found a way around hurdles to satisfy her cravings. Her job in a hotel meant she came in contact with people all the time, and she took advantage of the fact not only was I always working, but the children were now adults.

On a normal busy morning when I was at the company, I received a call from the police, informing me my wife had met with a road accident, and asked me to go to the Bur Dubai police station. I asked them where she was and if she was alright, and they just said they would give me all the details at the police station.

Having rushed to the police station, I was ushered into the chief's office. He explained to me Phyllis was driving on the main highway going towards Sharjah, when she was involved in a serious accident. She was removed from the mangled car and rushed to the Sheikh Rashid Hospital.

I found it extremely odd when they asked me vague questions, as to whether we were still married and if she lived with me. Having answered in the affirmative, I told them I had to get to the hospital immediately, to see how she was doing. They then handed me her handbag, saying nothing was removed from it when they checked for identification.

When I went to see Phyllis in the hospital, I found she had suffered brain damage, and her recovery would be extremely slow. I was informed she would get back to normal, but she may never regain the full functions of the damaged part of her brain again. When she was eventually brought into the ward post-treatment, the doctor said she was getting the best medical care and there was nothing I could do by her bedside. I could visit her at any time, and they confirmed they would call me should her condition change.

As I was busy at the company during the day, I went to visit Phyllis at the hospital every evening, after we closed the company for the day. One morning, I had a bit of free time in between client meetings and decided to go to the hospital. However, I was totally disconcerted when the ward nurses who knew me by now, refused me permission to go in to visit with Phyllis. After arguing with them for a while, I decided to just muscle my way in to her ward. On going in I realised she already had a male visitor by her bedside, and it was not me - her husband.

It dawned on me why the nurses did not want me to visit with Phyllis. The nurses then told me that her boyfriend visited her every morning, and I visited her every evening. They thought they would spare me the heartache when I arrived unexpectedly during the morning hours. But it was more than that. I was furious with myself at being totally blind to what was obviously happening for a very long time. Blinded by anger at being made a total fool, I rushed out of her ward and blindly walked right through the hospital main entrance manual glass doors, shattering the large door to smithereens in the process.

The hospital entrance security personnel got hold of me for damaging hospital property. They called the onsite police, who bundled me into the police car and took me to the Bur Dubai police station. Unknown to me, the nurses had briefed the arresting police as to the reason for the damage I caused. At the police station, it seemed every one but me, knew all the details about my cheating wife. They were very understanding and said they were not taking the matter any further, as they knew the circumstances. All I had to do was to pay for a new main entrance glass door.

The reality of what Phyllis had done struck a chord in me, driving me to the edge. I reclused myself from the world. I did not go into my company nor handle any business, and I never did visit Phyllis in the hospital again. I stayed in my bedroom for a week wallowing in self-pity at being taken for an idiot with a capital 'I'.

She had obviously asked the hospital to inform her lover to visit her there, as he would not have known about her accident otherwise. My male pride took one heck of a battering. It is one thing for me to turn a blind eye to what was going on in our marriage for the sake of our children, but quite another at knowing people around me were in the knowledge of her cheating too, and silently commiserating with her oblivious fool of a husband.

In between sleeping, my mind was being dynamited from every angle, thinking of all the countries we lived in and the men she might have been with. I was now recollecting times when on contracts around the globe, even colleagues silenced their chatter when I walked into the room, her flirtatious closeness with some men, and even the times she disappeared for hours, saying she was with friends or window shopping. I concluded people everywhere were pitying me, the blind unsuspecting husband.

Eventually, it was Tony who kept telling me to pull myself together as the company needed me. He probably thought I was in this state because of his mother's accident and medical condition, and I could not correct his assumption. There were business decisions to be taken that my men naturally could not make, and I finally knocked sense into me, got my act together and forged forward.

It was at this time I remembered the police had given me Phyllis' handbag. I found it just thrown into a corner in my room. I opened it and went through its contents which were a shocking eye opener. I now knew how the police were aware of her double life, and why they asked me those questions about our marriage.

In her handbag were original documents in her name and with her signature on it. But she put herself down as 'Miss' and not 'Mrs' or even 'Ms'. A rent agreement on a flat in Sharjah, invoices for living, dining and bedroom furniture as well as bills for general household items. On the day of her car accident, she was actually leaving me permanently, for her lover and their newly set-up love nest. The car I had bought her was a write-off, and I did not bother to follow up on it or claim it back.

After the enormity of what was going on in my life sank in, I decided I now had to make personal decisions that would effect my whole family. Phyllis was a nymphomaniac and it was high time I finally said it out loud and made a clean break. However, though Sharon and Tony were now adults, I could not bring myself to tell them the type of woman their mother really was, nor the fact she was leaving our family when the accident happened.

My decision to divorce Phyllis without delay was now a foregone conclusion, as I finally saw absolutely no reason to prolong the inevitable, which was already twenty years overdue. Children or not, I should have divorced her twenty years ago when it came to light she believed in variety to spice up her life, and a normal monogamous relationship meant absolutely nothing to her. I know ending a relationship is always tragic, especially if young children are in the equation. But like I regrettably did, it is worse to stay in a dead relationship for the wrong reasons.

I would not be made a fool by her constant unfaithfulness any longer. I also did not have to take into account the repercussion of my decision on Sharon and Tony, as they were now kids no more. The personal sacrifices I had made for them for twenty-two years was for naught, and I had nothing to show for it.

The long years of my marriage was mostly a black period of my life, with a few bright and colourful rays of light when I masked my situation and blocked out the bleak, depressing and empty life I lived. I was no longer going to martyr myself for anyone. It was my decision and mine alone to finally break free. Sharon and Tony no longer had a hold on me, or a say in my life from now on. Each of us in this world has the right to live and enjoy our life to the fullest, and my long overdue wish had eventually been fulfilled.

Every cloud has a silver lining and the one good thing to come out of this saga, was the fact I found out who my genuine friends were, and who would be there for me in times of trouble. My good Emirati friend Toufiq was the largest jeweller in the Middle East, and an absolutely great gentleman of the utmost repute. After Phyllis' accident, he came to my company one day and while chatting, he casually handed me a bulky sealed envelope. When I opened the envelope, I found twenty thousand Dirhams in it. He just said matter-of-factly, it would help me with the very large hospital bills I would have to pay. I was extremely touched not only by his thoughtfulness but also his kindness, and ofcourse I did repay every Dirham back to him. This is one man I continue to be good friends with, hold in high regard, and will always be there for him, come what may.

Phyllis eventually was out of hospital and returned home. While she was physically recovered, she still had slight problems with her brain and was on medication. I further gleaned she was having a long time affair with her hairdresser, a very much younger Palestinian man, and they had set up house together in Sharjah.

Phyllis had the gall to call her lover over to our home after she returned from the hospital. He came to my villa one day and when I opened the gate, I came face to face with the man I saw by her hospital bedside. He said she had called him to do her hair. I informed him she was in no fit state to either meet him or have her hair done, and slammed the gate on him. And that was the last I saw of him, though I do not know what transpired between him and Phyllis after his visit.

I then informed her about my decision to divorce her and finally get on with my life, as I did not see the point in delaying the unpreventable end to the sham of our marriage. I also told her I had bought her a wonderful flat on Canterbury high street, overlooking the river Stour in the UK, as I thought in her condition, it was better to have the convenience of all the facilities on her doorstep.

Considering the fact she was constantly unfaithful during the twenty-two years of our relationship, which included the twenty years of our marriage, for the life of me I will never understand, why she seemed so shocked at me finally divorcing her. I guess she also did not expect me to divorce her now, because she was just out of hospital.

However while I was not burnt at the stake, I had blindly martyred myself for my family who did not appreciate me, and I was now mentally exhausted and totally burned-out. There was no two ways about it, I wanted out now to finally live the life I had only dreamed of. Phyllis knew exactly what she had done and though she did not argue with me, I could practically see the wheels of revenge turning in her mind. But it finally hit home her scarlet life had caught up with her, and she moved back to the UK and into the flat.

Divorce proceedings were on course and going full steam ahead through my solicitors in the UK. Sharon and Tony could not understand how I could divorce their mother so soon after her accident. But then, they did not know the truth and it was better they though badly of me, and remained none the wiser to the reality of her accident, the unhealthy and toxic marriage their mother and I had or that I was now looking forward to my belated freedom.

I finally began socialising again and entertained with a vengence and even dated a bit as I was now single. By now everyone knew about Phyllis and me and I was not short of female company. I was older and wiser now and I hoped I would never make the same mistakes I made with Phyllis.

Phyllis did not live for long in Canterbury. She wanted a larger flat in Croydon. She told me to buy her the flat she wanted in Croydon, after which she would sell the Canterbury flat. My blinkers destroyed, I informed her through my lawyers she had to first sell her Canterbury flat and pay for the Croydon flat with the proceeds, as I would only pay the difference in the purchase price. She knew by then I was now playing hard ball and as she had no options, she did as I suggested through my solicitors and she moved to Croydon.

My divorce proceedings were in its penultimate stage, when my solicitors from the UK called me in Dubai with the shocking but not surprising news, that after the to and fro communication over the past few months, and agreeing to all the divorce details, Phyllis was now at the last minute, refusing to sign the divorce papers until I complied with what she wanted. And there it was! the revenge I had seen formulating in her mind.

Against my solicitors strong sensible advice, I informed them of my agreement to her request, if her request came in writing from her solicitors to mine. Her solicitors put her request in writing and my agreement was sent back, and thus I obtained a speedy divorce. This document from her solicitors proved the genuine truth about our divorce, as the details in our subsequent actual divorce decree is a total eyewash. It seemed to me nothing had changed, and she was still the scheming woman she had been before the accident. She failed to rip me off on the Croydon flat, but she nailed me to the stake in the divorce.

My life story proves that since I met Phyllis, I have blindly done a great deal of things under the guise of doing it for the right reasons. This request of hers took my blindness to new heights, but it definitely was the best decision I ever made in my life. Our original divorce decree stated I was divorcing her due to her constant unfaithfulness throughout our marriage. But Phyllis wanted it changed to read, she was divorcing me because I was unfaithful to her. Her written request through her solicitors to mine to change the divorce decree, is my solid proof of the fact I had filed for divorce due to her unfaithfulness in our marriage and she had agreed to it, but changed her mind at the eleventh hour.

She did not want the children or her family to know she was the cause of the divorce, or the type of woman she really was. Some people would say my acceptance of her request, would be considered as absolutely foolish. But I beg to differ, as to me, it was the smartest move I made. If I did not agree, I would not be able to get a divorce, quick or otherwise, and I would be saddled with her for ever. That was something I would never allow to happen as after over twenty-two years, I was emotionally and mentally drained, from being manipulated by her and the children for far too long, and my freedom from her was now all the more valuable to me.

Secondly, what difference would it make if she told Sharon and Tony she was divorcing me because I was unfaithful? She was their mother and she wanted them to keep looking up to her. While I on the other hand, was their dad but possibly not their father. This change in the divorce decree was not something I wanted, but it was a hundred percent better than the alternative of having her in my life.

As far as I was concerned, Phyllis was finally out of my life. She was relegated to the realm of my ignominious history and could have her moment of glory, as I on the other hand ultimately had my liberty, peace of mind and total closure from this day forward.

I had married Phyllis in 1963 for the right reasons, I took her back in 1965 and stayed with her for better reasons, but I divorced her in 1983 for the best reasons. I was now at that place in my life, where I just did not care any more what my adult children or anyone else thought about me. I knew the truth, I had the proof, and it was all that mattered. I could finally draw a line through the past twenty-two miserable years, and move on with my life on my own terms. And what a life I was planning on having!

With Phyllis in Mauritius

Chapter 22

The colours of my second marriage – my blindness creates blunders!

My company handled all the maintenance work at the Dubai English Speaking School (DESS). While my men sorted out the work problems, I visited the school to check out and estimate general maintenance jobs for approval by the headmistress, Bernadette McCarthy, prior to my men commencing the work.

Some time in early 1990 on one of my visits to the school, I first met Patricia Cox who was a teacher in the school and around my age. As the headmistress was part of my social circle, Patricia or Trisha as she was known as, also joined my social circle and we got to know each other over time, and meeting at a few social gatherings. We had a modern but strange relationship. She lived in her own flat and never moved in with me. However, she and her overnight bag occasionally visited me for short spells.

I think unconsciously, I was looking for a woman who was the antithesis of my first wife Phyllis. The only issue with this way of thinking, is that it is liable to stray off on a tangent to the other extreme end, bringing with it a totally different set of concerns.

When I first met Trisha, I found nothing specifically wrong

with her, and she was friendly enough with my friends. She was not promiscuous like Phyllis was, and we got on pretty well in general. I had a hectic social life and she accompanied me to all the functions I attended. Her cooking skills were negligible and her housekeeping as bad. But as I had my house boy Baba to look after the housekeeping of the villa, she did not have to lift a finger in that department, whenever she was around. We both worked full time, and only interacted with each other when I had a social evening, or on the weekends. That was the reason why I presume our relationship lasted as long as it did.

I soon realised she was with me for material gain. News spread by her mother's unfounded joy at her daughter finding a well-heeled business man, trickled back from the UK. As I had not met her parents, the only information they received was from her weekly telephone calls to them.

She did not live under my roof, and though she was working and earned a very decent salary, she never spent any money of her own. I had a monthly charge account at a neighbouring large supermarket. Since she was in a relationship with me, she raked up triple the amount of my monthly bills and sometimes even more, going into the thousands.

She purchased all her personal items and fashion accessiories there too, and I was surprised, as I was under the impression women bought their fashion items from specialised outlets and not at a supermarket. But then, what the heck do I know about women? As I either ordered food in or we ate out, the excessive bills I paid were proof of her making hay while the sun shines. I guessed the sole reason she was with me was so she did not have any personal monthly overheads.

I had gone to England in December 1990 as my dad was

terminally ill. The Gulf War's Operation Desert Shield had started on 2 August 1990 and as the schools were closed, Trisha had already left for the UK. However, she never made any attempt to contact me, inquire about or even visit my ailing dad, She also did not bother attending his funeral. Considering I introduced her to my parents during my last visit, her lack of family bonding did make me wonder about her suitability as an ideal life partner.

Another dilemma I had with her was being a school teacher, she had long summer and annual school holidays. She went on her own to the UK to visit with her parents for the duration of the holidays. While I certainly did not mind her visiting her parents, I found it extremely strange I was never included in these trips. I had the responsibility of my company and could not take long vacations. But I was never even asked if I could take some time off to accompany her. She just made her plans and left.

On one occasion when I made the effort and joined her for a fortnight's vacation, we decided to stay at her parents place for a week, after which we would stay at my home for a week, before she went back to her parents home for the duration of her holiday, while I returned to Dubai. Atleast, that is what normal happy couples would do.

However when we reached her parents home, I was firstly surprised to learn her parents were not living together and only her mother lived at the address. Why did she not mention in all the time we were together, that her parents also had a strange relationship? My first wife had secrets she kept from me and it seemed history was repeating itself. Anyway as planned, I stayed with Trisha at her mother's home for a week, uncomfortable though the visit was. But at the end of the week, she flatly refused to accompany me to my home, and I had to go alone. This was not the kind of relationship I wanted. I had been there once and got burned. Something needed to change.

That was when I made the biggest blunder in my relationship with Trisha. Like a fool, I thought if we were married, she would change and we would do things together including holidays. Obviously, I had not learned any lessons from my first marriage. She was what she was and being a spinster, no matter what drastic steps I took, she was set in her ways at her age. I certainly could not change her to suit me. What was I thinking?

But obviously I was not thinking clearly, as on her return to Dubai from her summer vacation, I asked her to marry me. She agreed without even blinking, or giving my proposal a second thought. So in late 1993 we had a small wedding ceremony at the Holy Trinity Protestant Church with just us and a couple of witnesses.

However, from then on our relationship just got stranger. I asked her what she wanted for a wedding gift and her answer totally floored me. She said she wanted me to buy an English 'Lordship' as she wanted to be a 'Lady', and I certainly wondered what the heck I had got myself into.

Well she definitely married the wrong man, as I was just 'Dave the plumber' and no 'Lordship' would change that fact. Although I was certainly very comfortable financially, her grandiose ideas were totally pretentious and did not belong in my humble home. And further, I certainly did not think a 'Ladyship' title would transform her into a 'Lady'. It seemed my marriage was yet again doomed for failure, before it even started.

Marriage to Trisha did not change my life, as my new wife never lived with me under my roof. She and her faithful overnighter continued to make sporadic stopovers to our marital abode at will. I still worked long hours and she continued with her life too. We met up in the middle occasionally when we went out together to social gatherings.

Her monthly expenditure actually increased considerably after we got married, though she still never lived with me, never ever cooked me a meal, nor lifted a finger around the house, as she now considered herself a 'Lady'. All she knew to make was a cup of tea and as I never drink either coffee or tea, she did not have the honour of making her 'Lord' a cuppa either. However, I never once questioned her about her expenditure and just let it slide. My company was very successful and as such, so was I. Money to me is only a means to an end and not the end.

For her birthday I asked my close mate Toufiq, to send over a few watches for her to choose from. He sent a selection of gold and diamond high end watches. I did not check them, but she saw all the watches and immediately picked out a very simple watch without hesitation. I asked her 'are you sure? would you not prefer a diamond encrusted one?' She said she was extremely happy with her choice, and I returned the rest back to my mate. When I told him I was surprised she had picked out the most simple watch of the lot, he laughed at my 'blindness' and just asked me 'did you not see what brand of watch she selected?' I had not, and he informed me she had chosen the most expensive watch out of the lot. A Piaget.

In early 1994, not even a few months into our marriage, I was not feeling very well and as I kept getting worse even after a month, I decided to get myself checked out. I could not fail to notice that Trisha was not bothered I was under the weather for such a long time, and carried on with her normal routine.

I went to the Computerised Medical Diagnostic Centre in Satwa for a test, and the young Indian technician there, immediately advised me to go to the UK and meet with my doctor. He did not tell me what the matter was, but just said I had a very serious condition and it had to be sorted out without delay, for me to continue to live a normal productive life.

As I was in the United Arab Emirates since 1977, I did not have a personal doctor in the UK. However on mentioning my predicament to friends, Dr. Empey in Harley Street was highly recommended by a friend of mine Brian Challis, who owned Modern Freight in Dubai. As I did not know anyone in the medical profession in the UK anyway, I promptly made the appointment.

I then informed Trisha but she showed absolutely no interest in my illness. She also said she was busy and could not accompany me. So I left for the UK alone, armed with all the xrays and diagnostic test results, but without a clue as to the seriousness of my condition.

On arrival in the UK, I went straight to my mum's home and stayed for a day with her, while I got my Rolls Royce which was left in her garage, serviced and fueled. I did not want to worry her and hence I just packed a small case, and informed her I was going to visit friends in London.

Dr. Empey was expecting me and I drove straight to his office. After he checked me and my Dubai tests and xrays, he carried out a few more tests. He then said without preamble, I had to admit myself into the Princess Grace hospital immediately. I could not go home and I could not pass 'GO'. His office made a few quick phone calls, confirming all the arrangements for my admission into the nearby private hospital, on priority.

I drove directly to the hospital, parked in their underground parking and got myself admitted. It seemed I had contracted drug resistant Tuberculosis (probably from one of my workmen who I knew had some sort of a problem). It was now apparently clear I had an extremely serious life threatening medical problem no known drugs could cure. As such, the only curative option for my survival, was a lobectomy to remove half of my infected right lung immediately, before the tuberculosis spread to my left lung, causing my untimely death.

Being major invasive surgery, the hospital asked me for the contact details of my next of kin. The question got me thinking in earnest. It seemed that other than my aged mum, who I did not want to worry, I had absolutely no genuine kin significant or otherwise, I could rely on in times of trouble.

The few kin I could think of, right from my elder sister Marie, who I had no sibling relationship with; my two adult children Sharon and Tony, who never kept in touch with me and who I could not rely on, even though I sacrificed my happiness and half my lifetime for them; and ofcourse my wife Trisha who was already bleeding me dry; were all individuals who cared tuppence for me, and would only be interested in my residual estate should I not survive the operation.

Hence, I signed the surgery form informing the hospital I had no 'next of kin', and should I not survive the surgery, my solicitors were to be notified. I then telephoned my solicitors, and asked them to visit me at the hospital without delay, as I needed to sort out my 'last will and testament' before my operation, incase I neither outlived the disease or the procedure.

To my good luck, the surgeon, anaesthetist and the operating theatre professionals were excellent, and I came through the operation with the loss of half a lung, but with no spread of the tuberculosis. I had to remain in the hospital for ten days to recuperate from the surgery, after which I was discharged.

As I had my car in the parking lot, I just drove the hour and a half trip to my mum's home in Herne Bay, and gave her quite a scare when I explained where I was, and the events of the past ten days. I had to stay in the UK for a month longer, as my lung and the external sutures had to heal. I also had to see Dr. Empey for regular weekly post-operative checks, to confirm the healing process was positive and with no collateral damage.

Since I did deserve some rest and relaxation, spending quality time with my mum was the way to go. We bonded on leisurely drives along the coast and through the country side, sampling the food at obscure but quaint little village pubs. In the early 1990s seeing a Rolls Royce on the streets of the small seaside town of Herne Bay where my parents lived, was unheard of.

One day I had to purchase some items from a hardware shop in town, and took my mum for a drive. I parked my Rolls Royce in a roadside legal parking bay opposite the shop, and left my mum comfortably ensconced in the rear seat, relaxing with a white fleece throw over her knees. When I returned to the car about fifteen minutes later, I found three or four raw eggs splattered on the rear windscreen of my car and dripping all the way down over the side of the car.

When I asked my mum what had happened, she said two senior citizens were walking on the pavement alongside the car, trolleying their shopping bags. They looked at the car and at my mum who was also a senior citizen. When they were alongside the car, one of the women opened her trolley bag in full view of my mum and took out a six pack of eggs. She looked directly at my mum and then walked past my mum's window. The next thing my mum heard was a few cracks on the rear windscreen behind her. She turned and saw the eggs streaming down the windscreen.

Those women probably did not appreciate the fact they had to trolley their shopping while my mum, who they erroneously thought was a lady of privilege, was being chauffeured around in luxury. But it was their actions which was carried out of prejudicism, that is absolutely atrocious and unspeakable. This incident proved there are people who do not relish the thought of others being more successful than them, even though their success came through hard work, sweat and toil.

While I do not live the high life, I believe that as my hard earned money is of absolutely no value to me in my after life, what better way could there be for my family and myself than to use it to enjoy our life, and make our every day more comfortable. If that means having something that makes others envious, so be it.

As is usual with time and an idle mind, I also had a lot of empty hours to think about my marriage. Trisha did not call me even once, though I was away from Dubai for well over a month. I was very clearly married to a woman who did not care about me. Right from the time my problem started, she was not bothered about the seriousness of my medical condition.

Though I was paying my villa telephone bills, she made weekly telephone calls to her parents in the UK, but she never did waste either her time or my money to call me. As such, her lack of empathy and concern was most definitely not lost on me.

What is the use of being in a marriage if the couple have nothing in common, don't live together and don't do things together? I had been on that journey before and it did not end well for me, and it was not working for me now too. Here I was having major surgery, and my wife could not be bothered about me, be at my side or even keep in contact with me. That in itself spoke volumes about where her loyalties lay within our marriage - with my money and not with me.

For the past thirty odd years, I craved the love and closeness of a tender and genuine woman, who would put me first. Unfortunately, my two wives during this period have proven to be the wrong women for me. The problem it seemed, stemmed from the fact neither of them believed in the reality of a marriage, but in the illusion of one. I on the other hand do not believe in illusions, as being a red blooded man, all I need is a warm and caring wife by my side.

Right then, I made up my mind to end my marriage to Trisha, when I returned to Dubai. I did not benefit in any meaningful way from the marriage, as there was no love, no closeness, no togetherness and definitely no caring or commitment on any level from her side. All I experienced was materialistic coldness. While we had been together for a while, we were only married for approximately six months, and I guess just like my first marriage, I knew it was a mistake the moment I said 'I do'.

As I expected, Trisha did not take kindly to my decision to divorce her. But divorce her I did, through the Dubai Sharia courts. And even though divorcing her cost me dearly, in addition to paying the rent on her flat and giving her a brand new BMW car she wanted, it was worth every penny. Yes, there was one beneficiary in the marriage, as Trisha entered our marriage with nothing, she gave me absolutely nothing but she left as the financial victor.

While I thought that was the last I would hear from Trisha, I was totally wrong. 'Anger is one letter short of danger' came to my mind when she and her family a couple of years later, tried to disrupt my wedding ceremony to Anne, on 12 June 1996, at St. Mary's Catholic Church in Dubai.

Not having succeeded in causing turmoil at my wedding to Anne, Trisha tried another tactic a few weeks later. She and her mother went to my mum's home in the UK, two years after I divorced her. Unkown to me, she informed my elderly mum I had told her she could collect all the things left behind when she was married to me. Considering the fact she never ever stayed with me in my home in Dubai or at my parents home in the UK, she did not have any of her things there. But that thought did not strike my mum and at her age, she can be forgiven for her memory lapse.

My mum let them in as she did not know what else to do. They cleaned out my part of the house, taking everything they could, all of which did not belong to her. Actually, some of the things they took belonged to my parents too. It was daylight robbery, but that did not stop Trisha.

At the weekend I made my usual weekly call to my mum, and she informed me Trisha had collected all the things as I had instructed her to do. Needless to say I was shocked and furious. But Anne went off into gales of laughter, asking if they brought Delboy Trotters yellow three wheeler van to pick up the stuff, a reference to Anne's favourite British TV sitcom 'Only fools and horses'.

Anne may have found it extremely funny, but I was not amused. As Anne said to me later, it was only stuff and if important, it could be replaced. So, I wrote a letter to Trisha and informed her of my utter disgust at her stooping to the lowest rung on her ladder of life, when she conned my elderly mum and stole blind from us.

Well, I guess she probably needed the items she had purloined, more than we wanted it, as I never heard from her again, which was terrific as Trisha was out of my life permanently.

with Trisha

Chapter 23

The colours of my third and final marriage – the best is saved for last!

By the time I crossed half a century, my life was coasting on a high. With my company prospering and no family financial responsibilities, I was literally living the 'life of Riley'. I not only had two bad marriages and two equally bad divorces behind me, but two adult children who had divorced me too.

However, I am not one to turn into a cynic based on my negative past experiences. So I instead invested my money in expensive high octane toys, guaranteed to give me a lot of pleasure, make me extremly happy, and though they were extraordinarily high maintenance, I never had any grievances against them, and I loved every minute I had them in my life.

While my toys were a boon and a great distraction for me, it was also the bane of my life. With a plane, a multitude of boats, bikes and luxury sports cars, there was no dearth of single disingenuous women around me. Anytime I had to go to a formal function, I had no problem finding a companion to accompany me. But I was under no illusion they were anything other than just arm candy, and none of them struck a chord or meant anything to me romantically. I knew they were with me just because I treated them well, splashed out lavishly on them, and because they wanted to make the gossip circles. I figured, as long as I knew the score, they could not throw me under the bus, figuratively speaking.

On 26 April 1996, my excessive lifestyle in the fast lane changed for ever. My day started as usual with the morning at the company. For some unfathomable reason, I returned home earlier than I normally did on a Friday, and was relaxing at home as I had no plans as yet for the rest of the weekend.

Not long after I returned home, Big Red arrived out of the blue with two of her gorgeous friends. Anne her close friend who she also worked with and Anne's sister. Introductions made, we all chatted easily with drinks at my bar, and as it was just past mid-day by then, I told them I was taking them out to lunch. It was a spur-of-the-moment invitation, and as I was genuinely enjoying myself, I did not want to see them leave. And, something that had not happened to me before - me pursuing a woman instead of a woman pursuing me.

A good friend of mine, Bernadette or Big Red as I call her, was an ex-Manchester (UK) police sergeant and recently divorced. She accompanied me several times to official functions, when I did not want to be bothered with anyone in my virtual little black book. She is a tall beautiful red head with a heart of gold, and I had nicknamed her 'Big Red'.

Big Red left her car at my villa and we all got into my daily work wheels - Mercedes 320CE, and I drove us to the Hatta Fort hotel, about an hour and a half out of Dubai on the Oman road, just shy of the Oman border. We stopped enroute by the side of the road in the desert and took a few photographs, never realising that life had just dealt me a fresh set of cards.

We were all in good spirits and with the car hood down, the warmth of the summer sun engulfed us as we drove through the desert, with the wind playing at blowing around us to see which of us reached our destination with the worst windblown look. It was Anne and we all laughed when she looked at us and said with exaggerated exasperation 'have you desert dunes never seen stylized windswept chic?'

Conversation between the four of us was lighthearted and non-stop. The ladies were busy doing all their weekend household chores, when Big Red who was at a loose end and restless, turned up at their flat that Friday morning. She dragged them out for a drive as the weather was too good to miss out on, and definitely wasted by doing chores.

While driving by Jumeira, Big Red said a close friend was living around the corner and she wanted to stop by. The angels in Heaven were definitely smiling down on us, as just that day I broke my workaholic rule and returned home from work earlier than usual, and thus I got to meet Anne and her sister. While Anne calls it serendipity, I just call it fate.

The afternoon passed all too quickly with scintillating company during an enjoyable luncheon, and much as I did not want it to end, we eventually headed back to Dubai as dusk was setting. On the drive back I invited Anne for dinner the next evening and to my extreme pleasure, she said she would love to join me. I hoped it would be the first of many dates, as I was looking forward to get to know her.

The next evening I picked Anne up at her flat in Deira, and we went to the 'Don Corleone' Italian restaurant at the famed Metropolitan hotel on Sheikh Zayed road. For a first date, there were no awkward moments of silence or uneasy conversations about the weather to pass the time. Anne has a way with words along with a heck of a sense of humour, and our dinner date overflowed with interesting conversation and gales of laughter. We connected in a way I have never ever connected with anyone else. On the whole, without a doubt, our evening was superlative.

Before our evening ended, I totally surprised Anne and myself, by asking her to 'Marry Me'. She was saying something in conversation and was dumbstruck mid-sentence, when I asked her my question. I know the norm would be to date and get to know her, but the timing seemed totally propitious to me and I have never ever regretted blurting out the question. After a minute or so, she asked me with laughter in her eyes 'you're not serious?' When I answered I was never more serious or sure where marriage was concerned, she just said 'may I have a few days to think about your surprise question?'

It was not the answer I was hoping for. But then, what did I expect? we had met only twenty-four hours ago and I guess when Anne accepted my dinner invitation, she did not anticipate a 'marriage proposal' for dessert. It now meant I had to resolutely pursue her till she gave me the answer I wanted. From the moment I met Anne, I was sure she was 'the one' and I was determined she would never get away.

I invited Anne out the next evening, but she said she had to go to Sunday Mass after work and would not be able to meet with me. Undeterred, I surprised her by arriving at her office in Deira at closing time, to pick her up and take her to St. Mary's Catholic Church. There were three factors in that equation, which was an eye-opener and totally uncharacteristic for me.

The first was being a workaholic, I never left the office early. The second was when I was working, I lost all track of time. I only made it to all my appointments with time to spare, because my personal assistant had strict instructions to remind me of my meetings well in advance. But in this instance, I did not ask my office for a reminder as I did not need one. Finally, though I am a Catholic, till that day, I had never been to St. Mary's Church. Considering I was living in Dubai for the past nineteen years, my relationship with God and the Church was suddenly thrown into the spotlight.

You would think God would be pleased with me and get us to the church on time. Absolutely not so. We had just driven from Deira, off the Maktoum bridge and onto the Dubai side, when my car spluttered and stalled right in the middle of heavy traffic at the roundabout.

It turned out I had run out of petrol. I have never run out of fuel before. Why now? I was doing my damnedest to make a good impression on Anne, and I messed up big time. Someone up there was looking down at me with uncontrolled mirth, but I was definitely far from amused.

My only recourse was to push the car to the nearest fuel station and to my good luck, there was a fuel station near the roundabout. To my bad luck, while Anne could drive, she could not drive yet on her current driving licence in the UAE.

To my extreme embarrassment, Anne gamely jumped out to help me push the car, while I controlled and guided it through the open driver's door. Anne found the situation so hilarious, she was laughing more than she was pushing the car, and we caused quite a stir as the drivers of passing cars were honking and waving with a note of levity, and Anne was actually waving back.

A few labourers from a building site were walking by the side of the road on their way home, and saw Anne in her business suit and high heels not really doing much good behind the car. They immediately rushed over, laughingly handed their lunch boxes to her and started pushing the car to the fuel station, with Anne following behind, her arms full of empty lunch boxes. Needless to say, the lads were well rewarded for their welcome and timely aid and we made it to church with seconds to spare.

Since I messed up, I invited Anne out the next evening for a quiet dinner, and we had another great evening at the Dubai Marine hotel in Jumeirah. I then asked Anne to accompany me to a dinner at my friends home the following evening and understandably, she was hesitant at meeting anyone from the social circle I moved in, so soon. She did say it felt like she was going to be scrutinised by my family, but she did agree to accompany me.

However when we got to my friend's home, I found that our expected quiet evening of four, turned out to be a bigger affair than I anticipated, as my business partner Derek was instrumental in lighting the match. The news had spread like wild fire within my social circle, with curiosity getting the better of all my close friends. They were intrigued about the woman who obviously was more than just a passing fancy to me.

To my dismay, the evening did not go as well as I had hoped, as my friends expected a woman more my age and not a gorgeous young lady nineteen years my junior. I guess Anne made all the older women feel extremely inadequate and jealous, the men rather envious and me bursting with pride at my good fortune. Now, all I had to do was get her to say 'yes'. But after this disastrous evening with my so-called friends, that was a big task and highly doubtful.

In 1996, Dubai was still growing sideways into the desert,

with new residential houses and villas being built, though there were no roads to these developments constructed as yet. The houses were just surrounded by soft desert sand and my friends lived in a house in one of these newly developed areas.

On leaving the dinner that evening, being a low slung convertible, I could not get my car out of the soft sand next to my friends house, and onto the harder ground even after trying for some time. Eventually, some great young local lads from a house nearby, brought their souped-up beast of a four-wheel drive, and pulled my car out of the soft sand effortlessly. Could things get any worse for me? On the other hand, Anne did not seem fazed either by my stuffy friends or the catastrophes I suddenly seemed to get myself into.

The next evening I picked Anne from her flat after work and we had a quiet dinner at my villa, which I had ordered in as I do not cook. I apologised profusely for the mishaps of the past few days since we met, and to my utter surprise Anne laughed and said she had better marry me as it seemed I was utterly useless at trying to emulate 'the elegible bachelor', and she did not think she could survive any more hilarious but calamitous dates.

Naturally at her acceptance, I was on cloud nine. Since we met, we had talked easily with each other, on any and every topic of conversation. Anne knew by now I came with a load of unappeasing baggage, and the fact she was not flustered by my inglorious past was a very positive sign. I may not have known Anne for more than a few days but it felt like she was my best friend and I had known her my whole life. I had finally found my other half.

Without delay, I contacted my close friend Toufiq, and told

him I needed wedding bands made but first, I wanted the best diamond engagement ring. We made an appointment to meet at his office the next day and I took Anne to choose her ring. Toufiq brought out a tray of the best diamonds in different cuts and weights.

Anne immediately dismissed the larger diamonds, though I advised her not to go for anything less that a carat as it would not have much value. But Anne said she has never cared what people thought, as she did not have to prove anything to anyone. She said she wanted something that was not ostentatious, since this was one piece of jewellery she would be wearing constantly, along with her wedding band. Before we left, my friend whispered to me, 'Anne does not need diamonds, she is a diamond' and I could clearly see my future with Anne was going to be a spectrum of bright multifaceted colours.

Anne is totally different from every woman I knew, married or dated. Yes she is beautiful but her beauty is not just skin deep. Her internal beauty shines through and when she smiles or laughs, her face lights up and several people have even mentioned it to me.

On Friday, 10 May 1996, we had a small engagement party at our villa, with just Anne's family as well as Anne's close friend Azhar Mohammed, a successful business woman and her family. I did not want a long drawn out engagement and so we decided on a wedding as soon as Anne could organise it as being in public relations, her clients also included the top hotels. With decisions made, Anne designed and had the invitations printed through her local printing company and we sent them out, sending shock waves through my social circle at the swiftness my relationship had taken.

Anne is an Anglo-Indian but refers to herself as an Indian christian. While she did not grow up in India, she absolutely loves all things Indian, right from its culture, food, fashion and most of all the people and the beauty of the country. Though I worked with and had several employees of Indian origin on my staff, and while I have socialised with them at our office parties, they were not a part of my personal social circle, as I kept my company and private life totally separate. As such, I had never actually experienced the ever so gracious hospitality of the Indian people, till I met Anne. Or as Anne jokingly says, I moved with the wrong crowd.

The prejudiced comments from my so-called close English friends in Dubai was out in full force, saying I was marrying a woman from the subcontinent and I would soon lose all my friends. When the shards of their racist gossip trickled to Anne, I was upset but she just laughed and turned her back on them. She said what my friends said could not hurt her, and she infact felt extremely sorry for people like them and their lack of global cultural education.

We were getting married in just over six weeks, on Wednesday, 12 June 1996, and I would not let anything stand in my way. I realised as Anne's work kept her in the media and public eye, she ensured her private life was extremely private. She did not even want a large wedding, as then our guest list would increase to include her friends in the media. So we decided to have the reception at our villa, and we hired the Hilton hotel who was a client of Anne's, to set up and decorate our villa as well as to cater our wedding reception for around a hundred guests.

Anne's bridesmaids were her sister and Big Red and her page boy and flower girl were the children of her friends. I on the other hand, had never had a proper wedding, as my first marriage was an unplanned spur-of-the-moment quick civil ceremony in the UK, with just us and one witness. My second one was again an off-the-cuff marriage with just us and a couple of witnesses, but held in the Holy Trinity Protestant Church in Dubai. This time I was going for the gold, and I had five of my close mates as my bestmen, and they even organised a stag night at my villa. So while I was doing things the wrong way around, as this was my final foray into matrimony, there was absolutely no stopping me from enjoying it to the hilt.

My school mate John Munt, who was one of my bestmen, and had also been the witness at my first marriage, arrived from the UK two weeks before my wedding and stayed at my villa. The wedding arrangements were moving forward without any hitches considering the short time frame, and that was due to Anne's organisational skills.

However, my life has never been smooth sailing, and the devil threw in his oar for good measure. Four days before the wedding, the parish priest of St. Mary's Church, where we were having the wedding ceremony, called us to meet with him as he was troubled about our wedding. John, Anne and myself went to meet with Fr. Daniel Cerofolini who had known Anne's parents well, as they were part of the expatriate community in Bahrain since the mid 1950s, from where they moved to Abu Dhabi in 1970. As such, he knew Anne since she was a child and did not want anything adverse to happen at our wedding.

Anne is a staunch Roman Catholic and to get married in the Catholic Church, both of us had to submit our documents and in my case, documents of my previous marriages and divorces, which were all in order. Since my two prior marriages never took place in the Catholic Church, and my divorces were totally legitimate, the parish priest had no concerns officiating at our marriage in the Catholic Church. I was thankful for that as I had wanted to marry Anne from the moment we met. By now, I also knew with certainity, Anne would never have married me in any ceremony other than in the Catholic faith. And as she is not the 'live in' kind of lady, it was marriage or nothing.

The parish priest explained he had a visit from my ex-wife Trisha's family, with a complaint I was a bigamist, as I married Trisha in the Holy Trinity Protestant church, and as such, I could not get married again. The parish priest knew the truth from the documents I had submitted to the church. But, he felt Trisha and her family could cause a problem at the church during the ceremony.

So Fr. Daniel spoke with the bishop of the Apostolic Vicariate of Southern Arabia, based in Abu Dhabi. The bishop gave his permission for us to have the church marriage ceremony at the St. Mary's Catholic Church in Al Ain, with the Al Ain parish priest officiating at the ceremony, after which we could return to Dubai for our wedding reception.

But both Anne and myself decided we were not going to let my disgruntled ex-wife and her family disrupt our well organised wedding plans, which was going ahead as scheduled at St. Mary's Church in Dubai. Anne was understandably perturbed at this eleventh hour development and I who was not religious, was actually winging up a prayer, that she would not be my runaway bride.

That evening was Anne's bridal shower at their flat and my bachelor's party at my villa. Big Red had also invited my sister Marie and the few women from my close circuit of friends to

Anne's bridal shower, but they all declined. Anne subsequently told Big Red she was glad they refused the invitation as they definitely would have put a damper on the party.

Anne also informed Big Red of our meeting at the church. The next day, Big Red went to the Dubai English speaking school where Trisha worked, and informed the headmistress Bernadette McCarthy, who incidently was to be a guest at our wedding, about what had happened. She advised Ms. McCarthy to keep her staff in line or she would personally do it for her. And knowing Big Red, she definitely would have taken great pleasure doing it too.

Big Red also asked two of our Scottish friends Hamish Duncan and Graham McAllister, to stand guard in full Scottish regalia with ceremonial swords included. They stood on ceremony at the entrance of the Church to prevent any troublemakers from entering, and it worked as we did not have any uninvited guests.

Our wedding ceremony was beautiful, and the reception was a lot of fun and an extremely informal and memorable evening for us. All my five bestmen Derek De Wilde, Ed Abernathy, Tim Lamprell and John Munt, raised a toast while Brian Keller read out a personalised poem he wrote for our big day. Not to be outdone, Big Red raised a toast to us too. All our guests had a great time and the Hilton hotel went overboard and did a fantastic job all around.

Anne changed into a sari before dinner was served, much to my surprise and pleasure. She later laughed and told me it was only the second time she had worn a sari in her life. But this was a momentous occasion as she did it just to put the noses' of my snobbish inner circle of close friends' out of joint. She certainly did that alright.

Anne and I however, missed having her mum and sister Melanie as well as my mum to share our life-changing day with us. But I had finally met and married the woman of my dreams within a span of six weeks, and I was now looking forward to years ahead of all I never had from my previous two marriages. As they say – 'better late than never'.

In order to introduce each other to our parents, we first spent two weeks with Anne's Mum and Melanie in Bangalore, and had a wonderful holiday with them. On chatting with Mum one evening over dinner, I casually asked her how much dowry I would be receiving from her, for being brave enough to marry and take her daughter off her hands. While everyone at the table was laughing, without saying a word, Mum just gave me a look resembling one that a stern teacher gives a wayward pupil. She then started laughing heartily, and told me to dream on as I had joined the wrong family. Anne obviously gets her lightheartedness from her mum who also had funny bones, often sending her into gales of laughter. It is a great disappointment we never got the chance to meet and get to know each other's Dad's though.

We had a hectic social schedule in Bangalore, as we were also wined and dined by several of Anne's close friends. Their genuine and no-holds-barred Indian hospitality is second to none, and I thoroughly enjoyed meeting her friends, as well as our stay in Bangalore, on every level. While we have hosted several of Anne's friends at our home over the years since, we also enjoy catching up with them on their home turf, whenever we visit India.

We returned to Dubai and after a few weeks, we went to the

UK so Anne could meet my mum. We stayed in the UK for a month, as the moment Anne agreed to marry me, I contacted my cousin Tony in the UK to have an extension built to my mum's house. It was completed and in the process of having the finishing touches carried out during our stay, so Anne and I could move in.

My mum and Anne got on well together and to my surprise, my mum even asked Anne to accompany her to town on a few occasions when she had some odd jobs to do, and introduced her to several folk they met. She showed Anne how to cook my favourite foods, and Anne continues to make these comfort foods for me. Anne however says my mum was reserving her judgement, and we still have a good laugh about my mum's opinions, with regard to her latest daughter-in-law.

Whatever her views, they got on well and my mum trusted Anne enough to confide in her many a time over the years. When Anne visited the UK some time later with her sister-in-law, my mum asked Anne to inform me about Marie not having returned the last six hundred Pounds Sterling my dad had mentioned to me on his death bed. And, that she had infact recently borrowed another six hundred Pounds Sterling from my mum. Anne then advised Mum not to lend Marie any more money, however small the amount. Anne also told Mum not to tell Marie I would be looking after Mum financially, so Mum could have peace of mind and live the rest of her life without any financial worries.

A few days into our stay, we had some clothes to be washed and Anne took it to the kitchen which had an integrated washing machine. Clothes washed, my mum told Anne she could dry the clothes on the line in the back yard as there was no clothes dryer. Anne went to hang out the clothes and found the clothes line was ever so high and stretched tightly between two poles, that there was no way she could reach it. Anne says she surveyed the line, and wondered how my mum got her clothes up there as compared to Anne, she was a pint sized woman.

Meanwhile, my mum was watching Anne's antics from the kitchen window, but did not intervene. Anne laughingly says she was probably pitying me, and my bad choices in wives. Eventually, after about five minutes, my mum joined Anne in the garden and without saying a word, she went to the left pole and lowered the line by unwinding the end which was secured to the pole on a hook, that was hidden from view. Anne gaped at my mum for a few seconds and then just sat on the lawn and rolled with laughter. And that was when I came in from the garage and found Anne on the grass and my mum standing next to her, arms akimbo with a game, set and match victory smile on her face.

Anne was brought up with maids to look after her siblings and herself right from Bahrain, as well as maids to do all the household chores and laundry in Bangalore. And she is also used to modern washing machines and clothes dryers, not some archaic apparatus called a high-wire outdoor clothes line. My mum smiling just said that life certainly changes through the years.

My mum mentioned a week later in conversation, about the rear lawn requiring mowing. As I was out with my cousin Tony sorting out the final paperwork for the building work, Anne decided to redeem herself by playing the good daughter-in-law, and told Mum she would mow the lawn. After all, as Anne later said to me with laughter in her voice, 'it is just pushing a lawn mower across the grass. How hard can it be?' But considering she did not know one end of the lawn mower from the other, and still does not after twenty-six years, that was a question soon to be answered.

Anne went to the garage to get the lawn mower and found that instead of a modern lightweight model, a very heavy, ugly, antiquated contraption from years gone by, was smirking back at her. Anne found it too heavy to even move, and the very thought of pushing it up and down the rear lawn, small though the lawn was, just to please her mother-in-law would definitely be asinine. So, she did the next best thing. She did not bother with it, as she decided she would get me to do it on my return. Decision made, she went inside and relaxed with a book in our new quarters.

However half an hour later, her quiet solitude was rudely disturbed by a loud harsh sound in the rear garden. On checking through the french doors, Anne was amazed to see my mum pushing the heavy lawn mower up and down the lawn. Having found that her obviously incapable latest daughter-in-law was not going to get the job done, she decided to do it herself. When I returned home, Anne told me what had transpired and instructed me to buy my mum a new lightweight lawn mower. Anne said if she could not move the lawn mower, we could not expect my mum to handle it at her age. But my mum was not having any of it, since she was used to her old faithful ugly as it was, and she did not want any modern pretty but unreliable replacement.

My mum was as tough as they come despite her dainty physical appearance. No job was too hard or out of her reach to handle. During a visit to the UK after my dad had passed away, I was shocked one day to find my mum who was an octogenarian, high up on a ladder in the rear garden sorting out a maintenance job herself. I asked her what she was doing up there at her age and she just turned to me and said 'what am I supposed to do, you are not here!' That was my mum alright. She did not complain about her life but just got on with what was given to her. I guess I am more like my mum than I realised as without a doubt, I inherited her abundance of inner strength.

Before returning to Dubai, Anne and I stopped off in Malta for a week's break. Well, it was to be our honeymoon, but we spent most of our time being entertained by several friends living there, which made for a very enjoyable and fun vacation. We loved the island so much we even found the time to go house hunting for a home with a granny annex for my mum. But once we returned to Dubai and started expanding our business, we did not have the time to follow up on our Malta plans and it died a natural death.

Anne is neither a smoker nor a drinker and the one thing she did not like about me was my smoking. I have been a chain smoker since I went to sea and it just got worse over time. I was informed not to smoke after my lobectomy when half my lung was removed in 1994. But as all smokers know, smoking is an addiction and I was most definitely an addict. Infact, I had actually increased my daily quantity since then. Anne could not handle the cigarette aroma and she complained that the curtains, carpets, bedlinen, our clothes and even her hair carried the terrible odour. I switched for a while to pipes and then cigars as they had a much more aromatic scent, but I missed the familiarity of a cigarette inbetween my fingers, and

I went back to my old but faithful mistress.

That was when Anne allowed me to smoke only in the garden, when at home. She also informed me it was not fair I had an expensive addiction and she did not. She said since we married she had developed a passive smoker addiction. So for every packet of cigarettes I bought, I had to give her the same amount of money in compensation. I took it as a big joke and humoured her. But in a few days I figured a packet of cigarettes which costed six Dirhams, now costed me twelve Dirhams and as I smoked no less than three packets a day, my addiction now costed me around thirty-six Dirhams a day. Food for thought and unfortunately, that is where it just remained. I continued smoking and Anne gleefully kept collecting the money from me. But as she put it towards the housekeeping, I just paid up.

There was a joke doing the rounds in Dubai at that time, informing anyone who wanted to stop smoking to 'ask Dave Forrest as he has done it a million times'. Yes, I had tried the anti-smoking patches, Nicotinnel, acupuncture, hypnotheraphy and even Zyban, which Anne ordered for me from the USA. But as you can guess, nothing worked and my addiction continued.

Then in 2007, I had visited the hospital for a checkup and I was informed in no uncertain terms that if I did not stop smoking at once, I would be on a breathing machine for life. Anne was with me and added to the doctor's censure, which she continued as a non-stop monologue, till we reached home. The next day I quit smoking cold turkey. I cannot say for certain whether it was the thought of dragging around a breathing ventilator, or having Anne haranguing me for the rest of our lives, that made me stop smoking, but I have never smoked ever since, so I will never know.

Unfortunately, the first few years of our marriage was a big test of inner strength for Anne, though she took it in her stride with her usual lightheartedness and stoicism. Yes, she knew I came into the relationship with baggage in the form of two adult children – Sharon who is just four years younger and Tony who is just six years younger than Anne, and she had absolutely no problem with them, as her younger sister and brother are the same ages. But the soiled baggage she had to deal with was my ex-wife Phyllis and a couple of other women, one of whom was instigated by my sister Marie and cousin Jean.

While I never informed Phyllis of my marriage to Anne, I have a feeling she found out from one of the children, though neither of them ever mentioned it to me. However, she kept writing frequent short letters and also phoned me regularly. She never bothered with me when we were married, and she ripped through me in the divorce. Now after thirteen years, what were her reasons for trying to mess up my life?

Though I did not have to continue giving Phyllis additional finance after the divorce settlement, she always said she was low on funds and hence I sent her payments twice a year. This carried on even after Anne and I married and infact, Anne wrote out the cheques. However when I retired, I informed Phyllis I could no longer send her any further payments and to my horror, she turned around and asked me 'what payments? you have not sent me anything'. I was so angry, I asked my office to make out a statement of all the payments I had made to Phyllis since I divorced her, which ran into thousands of Pounds Sterling, and I sent it to Phyllis to refresh her conveniently selective memory.

In 2008 when Anne and I made a trip to the UK, I visited Phyllis on my own and gave her some photographs and a painting of us which was in storage and which I had no use for, and that was the last time I saw her. But she continued to phone me even though I asked her not to. Eventually when she last called me in 2017, Anne answered and Phyllis had the audacity to give Anne a false name. Anne transferred the call to me along with the name given. When I answered, I found it was Phyllis, and I informed her without mincing my words that I was very happy with my life and she had to leave me alone, as I wanted nothing to do with her. I have since not heard from her and that is a blessing.

A few months after Anne and I were married, when we returned home from the company one evening, we found a message on the answering machine from my maternal cousin Jean in the UK. She said her friend Claire who incidently, my sister Marie had wanted me to marry instead of Anne, was in her house and in a terrible state of upset due to my marriage to Anne. Jean also asked me to return her call immediately. I knew Marie was definitely behind this and needless to say, as I had absolutely no interest either in the woman or in returning my cousin's call, I ignored the message and they obviously received my answer loud and clear as I never heard anything more from any of them.

The final soiled piece of baggage was also an English divorcee Diane who I had dated for some time in Dubai. She wanted to get married but as I was not interested, she moved with her young daughter to Hongkong. However, she kept sending me personal faxes, to my office. I never replied them but she was thick skinned and never got the message. Then one day

I received a call from a couple visiting Dubai, who said they were Diane's friends from Hongkong. I had no option but to invite them over for a drink. It seemed Diane had asked them to check Anne out and give her the feedback. After their visit, there was silence finally from her end.

However in 2008, out of the blue I received a call from her when I was working on my 'La Buttana' at the Jebel Ali hotel marina. She informed me she was in town and wanted to catch up. I told her I was working with my crew and could not leave the vessel, but if she wanted, she could drop by for a quick drink. She did and probably stayed for about an hour and left, while I got back to working with my onboard crew. I intentionally did not mention her visit to Anne when I got home later that evening, as I knew Anne would give me the third degree. 'Big Mistake!' That was the first and last time I kept anything from Anne, as she somehow has a knack of finding things out anyway.

Anne did not work daily from her office on the vessel, as she handled all the company's government and legal matters, and she was always on the move. But the next day Anne had to complete some paperwork at her work station on the vessel, before she left for a meeting at one of the government offices.

As she was sorting her paperwork on her desk, she came across a business card. Anne looked at the card and casually asked me if I had any visitors the previous day. Without thinking I said 'no'. Anne then gave me the card and said 'well, she says she was here'. Totally confused I took the card and could not stop laughing. I had forgotten all about Diane's visit the previous day. And running true to form, the scorned 'bitch' in her, surreptitiously left her card on Anne's work station, knowing Anne would find it. At that moment, there was never a truer saying – 'Heaven has no rage like love to hatred turned, nor Hell a fury like a woman scorned'.

I have never ever stepped out of line nor kept anything from Anne since we met and got married. She is a smart and sharp lady with an extremely efficient inbuilt radar system. Till today, she knows even when I sneak a piece of candy to satisfy my diabetic sweet tooth. Anne trusts me implicitly, but she did question the desperate lengths that my ex-wife and these two women went to, just to break up our marriage and get their feline claws into me. Well being materialistic women, it was my money they were really after.

Anne laughed and mentioned that it seemed they just wanted to be 'kept women', and I was probably the only 'MUG' they knew. I was thrilled when I was finally shot of my first wife, and there was no way she was darkening my doorstep ever again. I had also never had any interest in, or wanted to marry either of the other women, or infact any other woman when I was single, so why would I want to ruin my marriage for any of them now?

Over the years Anne has to my immense regret, also had to put up with my inner demons. I should never have given in to my pent-up frustrations over Marie, Sharon and Tony. On the rare occasions whenever I spoke to Sharon and Tony, it always left me depressed and harrowed as they are not only rude, but also downright disrespectful. Talking with them or receiving nasty messages from them, put me in a vile mood, and with Anne constantly within firing range, she has taken the brunt of the full blast of my exasperation everytime. However, Anne tolerated these occasional black moods of mine over the years, and then one day she decided enough is enough, and blasted right back.

Anne informed me with crystal clarity, my adult children obviously had a toxic relationship with me for some reason I was not aware of. She said though they were my children, they were now first and foremost adults who had crossed half a century. As such, I had the option of either working at changing my relationship with them for the better, or making a tough decision for the worse.

Anne would have let the incidents slide, but unfortunately Sharon and Tony along with my sister Marie, were the sole contributers to my deteriorating mental health. It was a case of psychological self-flagellation as I used to beat myself up mentally, thinking I was in some way responsible for the appalling treatment being meted out to me by Marie, Sharon and Tony. Anne was worried since it was also affecting my physical health as insomnia became my best friend.

If Anne was not with me to stay on top of my health, listen to me as well as be my sounding board, and in the process keep my sanity intact, I can say with absolute certainty that Sharon, Tony and Marie would have sent me six foot below in the blink of an eye. I faced the facts and knew if I did not put a stop to my unhealthy relationship with my now practically senior citizen children and octogenarian sister, I would be dust long before I had planned, or even had the chance to finish all I wanted to do, as my bucket list is pretty exhaustive.

And thus my 'life story' has finally come to fruition, with Anne's help in putting my stories and words into print. Reliving my life has certainly been therapeutic, and it has not only reinvigorated me but it also dammed the haemorrhagic erosion of my mind, destroying my demons, leaving my sanity intact and giving me utter peace of mind.

Over the years I never did entertain much, other than drinks at my bar. However as Anne is a professional on the culinary front, after we married we frequently entertained, having atleast four cocktail parties and two silver service formal dinners every month. Needless to say, there was no catering involved as Anne prepared all the food, with Baba assisting her by handling the butler service. We also had a large party with a buffet dinner for about fifty to sixty people once a year, which again Anne handled herself. With Anne handling the catering and the bar under my mastery, how could we go wrong? Unlike most people, I constantly mixed business with pleasure and our parties were always a merry fusion where people had an enjoyable evening, that was talked about for a long time.

One difference between Anne and me is my love for all animals. Like my toys, they never ask for much, in total contrast to the previous women in my life. All our pets want is someone to love and care for them and in return, they show their love and loyalty by being man's best friend. I have learned a dog is the only creature on earth who loves you more than he loves himself. When Anne came into my life, I had a German Shepherd named 'Tiger'. I had him from a puppy and he was a lovely and affectionate pet though as he grew up, he was like a frisky bull in a china shop and I could not have him in the house as he used to break items daily.

Right from the first day Anne and I met, I had to share her as Tiger took a shine to Anne and it only grew over the years. He was extremely protective over Anne, and while Baba fed him and cared for him, Anne had the habit of talking to him and playing with him whenever we were relaxing by the pool or in the garden.

Anne never let him or the cats into the house as she did not like their fur everywhere. But Tiger had unconditional access to his very own extremely comfortable crib, in one of our permanently airconditioned garages which housed my high-end cars. During the hot and humid desert summers, he refused to leave the comfort of his airconditioned quarters even for his daily walk with Baba.

On one occasion, for the first time since I started my company about seventeen years previously, I did not go in to work due to illness, as Anne was the 'boss' at home and laid down the rules. Since she would be managing the business in my absence, I knew the companies were in good hands, and I rested and relaxed at home with Baba around if I required anything.

A couple of days later, Derek, my partner in my general maintenance company, came with Anne after work to discuss some business matters with me. The moment Anne opened the gate and walked in with Derek, to everyone's surprise, Tiger who was not only an extremely friendly canine, but also knew Derek well, aggressively pounced on Derek and luckily Anne and Baba who was working in the garden, were there to hold Tiger back.

On another occasion, I had gone home directly from a meeting with clients, while Anne returned home after closing the office at the end of the working day. My partner in my security company, John Wiegold, informed me he was coming over for a chat and a drink after work. He arrived home at the same time Anne did, so they entered the villa gate together.

This time too, Tiger was irate at Anne coming home with another man, and went for John with a vengence. However as we now knew Tiger's modus operandi, I was in the garden when they arrived and managed to get hold of him before he reached John. While I have always said Tiger was over protective about Anne, she vehemently but lightheartedly disputed this and said I had covertly trained him to keep an eye on my interests. Needless to say, Tiger's antics produced a great deal of hilarious banter between us over the years.

When I had gone on a two week job to Turkmenistan to commission an offshore labour camp in the Caspian Sea, Anne managed the company for me. A few months earlier, I had taken home a little stray dog who used to visit our company daily for food. Anne named him 'Roamer' as he was street smart and roamed all over the drydocks getting fed at several companies. Roamer was good company for Tiger and was Tiger's constant shadow. One morning Anne locked the villa and went to the garage through the garden to her car. Absentmindedly, she placed the house keys on the roof of her car before getting in and opening the remote controlled garage door. Forgetting her keys, she reversed out, closed the garage and drove to the company.

The keys slipped off the roof of the car when she drove away, and what Anne did not know, was the keys were found by a prospective neighbourhood thief. Anne only realised her keys were missing when she returned to the villa in the evening. Fortunately Baba was still at home so she was able to enter the house. Anne asked Baba to phone our company purchaser and have him buy new locks for the gate as well as for the villa main door, and return to the villa with the company carpenter to change the locks immediately, as she did not want to give any thief the chance to break in.

The next day Anne left for work and around mid-day Baba called her at the company, with the news that Tiger who was a good swimmer and could get in and out of the pool by himself, had fallen in and could not get out. Roamer raised the alarm by barking continuously and alerting Baba who was doing chores in the villa. Tiger was also not breathing very well and was frothing from the mouth, which was a sign of poisoning. Baba managed to get Tiger out of the pool and while he was talking to Anne on the phone, Tiger breathed his last.

Anne was upset and told Baba they would bury him when she returned home after work. Anne chose a tree where Tiger frequently relaxed under its shade, and he was laid to rest there. The shade of the tree became Roamer's favourite spot after Tiger died. Though I spoke with Anne daily from Turkmenistan, she never mentioned what happened to Tiger as she knew it would not only sadden me, but I would also worry because she was alone at the villa with Tiger not there to protect her.

When I returned to Dubai, Anne informed me about her lost house keys. It seemed someone found the keys and wanted to break into the villa. However, knowing there was a large dog in residence, the person decided to get rid of the dog first, and threw poisoned meat over the high fence of the villa. As Tiger was a big dog, he obviously managed to get to the poisoned meat first, since Roamer was absolutely fine.

Unfortunately, a few months later, some visiting guests did not close the gate properly on their way out and it was the last we saw of Roamer. We scoured the area and further afield but could not find him. Considering he was a stray and street smart, we hoped he would be able to continue to fend for himself till a kind soul found him and took him off the streets. Anne has since refused to have any more pets at home. Currently our livestyle is unconducive to having a pet. But I am sure I will convince Anne to add one to our family in the not too distant future.

Anne is not like the other women in my life in another aspect. She does not believe in big gestures or pricey gifts. On special occasions she is happy to have a nice quiet dinner at home for just us or maybe with family and a few close friends. I remember before I met Anne, Valentine's was a day I was never allowed to forget by my ex-wives and subsequent women friends. While Anne is not immune to romance, she does not believe any one particular contrived day like Valentine's day, boosts a relationship in any way. She says love and romance should be a part of every day in a relationship or marriage. I could not agree with her more, as we do everything together and never go out or travel anywhere without each other.

The first Valentine's day after we were married, we went to the supermarket directly from the company as Anne was cooking me my favourite dinner, and she did not have a couple of ingredients. While in the supermarket, she picked out a beautiful Valentine's card, gave it to me and asked me to read it. When I had read the card, she laughed, wished me a Happy Valentine's and put the card back in the rack. I was so surprised, I could not stop laughing. Anne just laughingly said it did not make sense for me to pay for a card for myself.

I am not good at remembering dates. Normally Anne's brother and in recent years Coral too, calls to remind me for Anne's birthday or our anniversary. Once on Anne's birthday a couple of years after we were married, my brother-in-law called to remind me and thus jogged my memory. So on the way home after work, I rushed into the supermarket and picked out a large bunch of red roses. They were so fresh, they still had water droplets on them. Extremely pleased with myself, I went home with my gift for Anne.

When I gave the bunch of roses to Anne, she more than thanked me, and was surprised I even remembered. Then she laughed out loud and asked me if the shop I purchased the roses from, did not have fresh flowers. I told her it could not be any fresher as even the water droplets were still on the petals. Anne could not contain her laughter, and she explained the flowers I purchased were a fantastic and realistic imitation right down to the dew drops. Infact, though Anne dislikes roses, she still has that bunch of roses on display at home, just to rub me up the wrong way, and they are still as fresh as the day I purchased it, nearly twenty-four years ago.

Another time Anne was ill and at home. Derek reminded me at the office that it was my wedding anniversary. So on the way home, I dropped in at my friend's Damas jewellers shop in Jumeira to buy Anne a gift. The manager showed me a selection of jewellery, but also brought out a twin necklace and bracelet set, saying Anne had shown interest in it a while back, when she visited the shop to buy a gift for a friend.

So I bought the set and as Anne was alseep when I went home, I placed the bracelet in the safe. I woke her up and presented her with the necklace. She was surprised at my gift and immediately asked, 'was the matching bracelet not available?' I could not stop laughing as she caught me at it yet again. I had locked the bracelet away, deciding to present it to Anne on another occasion, but I should have known she has the memory of an elephant. And yes, without further ado, the bracelet and necklace were happily reunited once again.

When Anne first told me we were expecting a child, I panicked inititally and could'nt think straight as I was a wreck with the turmoil of my inner demons, as well as my mind churning in confusion. It was not because I did not want a child with Anne, but because I was terrified I would lose another child. I had been there twice before and both my children did not grow up as I expected. Obviously I was not a good father to them, as all the decisions I took and the sacrifices I made for them, did not yield the results I wished for. Instead, I lost a son and daughter. If I had messed up twice before, what guarantee would there be I would not do so again?

I have genuine empathy with parents who have lost a child to death and the heartbreak they go through. While there is no comparison with my situation as my two elder children, are living and breathing somewhere in our world, there are similarities. When a parent loses a child, whether to death or due to life's mysterious ways, the heartbreak the parents go through is the same. I have no contact with my children, I do not see them and will never know their families or my grandchildren. All I have are a host of memories which are fading with the passage of time, memories that unfortunately, do not bring me solace and are best left in the attic of my mind.

No one knew what I was going through except Anne, and she told me at the very beginning, our child was a beautiful and precious gift from God, being sent into our lives to give me another chance at being a Dad. Someone to cherish and help me erase my dark perspective about my two elder children, change my attitude, and to prove my prior experience was not a reflection on me, as I had done no wrong by my children. With Anne's positive outlook and confidence in me, I too slowly changed my belief and I have never second guessed myself ever again.

On Thursday, 8 January 1998 at 1125 hours Dubai time, our beautiful bundle of joy Coral, came into our world making her presence felt. I had chosen her name before she was born, as my love for the sea and its most colourful and precious living organisms will forever be nature's beauty to behold. Anne loved the name too as in Hebrew Coral means 'luck' and 'destiny'.

Over the weekend, our friends kept popping over to our villa when they heard the news of Coral's arrival, to join me in 'wetting the baby's head', which was nothing other than an excuse to enjoy some raucous alcohol drenched fun at my bar.

With Anne also working extremely long hours with me at our companies, neither of us were around a lot and it was extremely difficult to blend our business and family lives. As such, Anne was pleased her sister, Mum (nana) and the maid were also there to look after and care for Coral. It was not the ideal situation, but it was the only option we had and as I did not interfere in her upbringing, there was no chance of me messing up a third time. I always say Coral has three Mums as nana and Anne's sister waited on her hand and foot. There was certainly no contest as to who was pulling the strings ofcourse, but they doted on her and even spoilt her rotten as she is the only next generation addition to the family.

Anne said we were very fortunate to have close family to help us bring Coral up in Dubai itself. She said her parents were not that lucky, as she and her siblings were brought up with strict rules and regulations at the various private residential boarding schools they were educated in, just like all the other children in the UAE in the 1970s. Though she does confirm, boarding school life did them absolutely no harm and infact, it contributed to moulding them into the positive thinking, strong willed, optimistic personalities they are today.

Unfortunately, very often children view the decisions their parents make from their own tunnel visioned perspective, which has absolutely no bearing on the reality of life. Reality only kicks into their lives when they are adults and parents themselves, and by then, it may be too late. Parents on the other hand have to do whatever has to be done to earn a living, and while it may not always be the best decision or liked by the children, most often it is the only viable one for the family. I would have liked another child, maybe a son, so Coral grew up with a brother. But Anne said she was not prepared to have any more children at that stage in her life.

Time has gone by and Coral has since forged ahead towards making her own mark in the world. I have absolutely no doubt she will blaze a trail on her way to reaching the shining star at the end of her rainbow. With her family wishing for her all the 'luck' in the world, I am confident a great and very happy life is her ultimate 'destiny'. I may not have played a central part in Coral's upbringing but I have never stopped loving and supporting her unconditionally in my own way. I sure hope I get to know and have atleast one of her children in my life in the not too distant future.

After my mum passed away in 2007, I have regarded Anne's family as my only family. As I no longer have any close family of relevance, they have from the beginning accepted me into their close knit fold. Anne and I have been extremely happy together and thoroughly enjoying our married life. Every day is a novelty and we are never bored in each other's company. We always find lots to laugh about together, and we never run out of interesting conversation.

Though we may not have the same point of view on various subjects, we inevitably accept the other's views and opinions with grace. Like all couples we have the occasional arguments, but we never let it build a wedge between us and keep us apart. We have no secrets and no hidden aspects of our earlier lives, as our past is an open book to each other. We never go anywhere without each other and still have a very close marriage, which I know will take us to the end of our days.

After we married, I wanted Anne to run the companies with me as her shrewd business, legal and finance acumen, would be an asset to our companies, and complement my technical expertise of the business. However, several friends dissuaded me. They said we would head for disaster, and we had to make a choice as to which was more important – our marriage or our companies, since we would never be able to make a success of either, if we worked together.

Anne and I decided to give it a shot and if it did not work out, Anne would cease working in our companies and concentrate solely on our family. The first week was 'hell', considering both Anne and I are very strong personalities, and we had our own views and modus operandi on running our companies.

The next week turned out to be 'Heaven on Earth', as we spoke about our working together and Anne said to me 'this is your group of companies and I will respect and accept you as the boss, for all the hours I work here. However, when we go home, while you will always be the 'head of our home', never ever forget I am the boss'. While we laughed at that time, I must say this adage has worked ever so well for us since that day way back in 1996. We have been together all the hours God has given us, with absolutely no problems to concern us. Without a doubt, Anne and I are defined by the paradox of the immovable object and the unstoppable force.

When Anne initially started working at the companies, she had her own office. She not only helped me in running the companies, but she also handled all the company's legal matters, as well as dealing with the various government offices. As I needed to constantly talk with her on business issues and clarify various legal points on matters of interest, I asked Anne to move into my office since I hated talking with her over the telephone. I always had a large double size desk, and from then on, we sat side by side at the same desk in the same office, and never ever had a problem, other than her refusing to sit on my lap and discuss company matters.

I always tell Anne I wish I had met and married her first. Oh! I know it is something that could never have happened considering the difference in our ages. But believe me, what ever trials and tribulations we go through, we should never lose hope or give up on our dreams, as the best is always saved for last.

Anne however says from my track record at the young age of twenty-one, she definitely would not have been the type of woman I went after anyway. Yes, I was blind as most young men are at that age, and from my personal experience, I do believe age and wisdom does reap rich rewards.

All I went through in my past, was like doing my penance

on earth, before the scales fell from my eyes and I began to live my life. But Anne's take is my past has made me the internally indestructible person I am today. She also quoted Oscar Wilde when she said 'men always want to be a woman's first love, but women like to be a man's last romance'. She said while she was sorry I missed out on the first part with my previous marriages, she is extremely pleased with my last romance. Well actually so am I, as I finally got it all.

My so-called friends had taken bets our marriage would not last even a year, due to the vast age difference between us, and the fact we did not know each other well, since we married within six weeks of meeting each other. My elder two children too had their doubts for similar reasons. We have happily proved them all wrong. Age is only a number that does not have any bearing in a good marriage, where love, honour, caring, respect, trust and commitment hold centre stage, surrounded by constant communication, good humour and heaps of fun and laughter.

Someone once asked Anne why she married me and if the age difference has a negative bearing on our marriage. Anne laughed and replied 'well, David and I married each other for better or for worse - he could do no better and I could only do worse!!!' And she further said – 'age - what age? like a classic vintage, David just gets better with age'.

The fact that at eighty-two years I am still enjoying my life, confirms Anne's response. The other day I told Anne, I plan on sticking around a long while, to ensure she never has another man in her life. She roared with laughter, looked up to the Heavens and said 'you're having a laugh ain't you? he has already given me blood pressure and a silver crowning glory'.

Based on my past track record, I am not the best person to turn to for marital advice. However, from my personal experience, do believe me when I say you should never settle for anything in life, be it love, career or anything else of importance to you, as it will never bring happiness your way. Don't ever make a martyr of yourself for anyone like I did, as time will prove it brings no rewards. There is no such thing as second best. We all deserve only the very best for us.

I also do not believe in perfect love. To me, love is as perfect as it can possible be, when a couple don't expect each other to be perfect, but they see each other perfectly. I have found love is not a destination but a journey, and a great life long adventure with our road strewn with an abundance of flora, fauna and a smattering of jaggered rocks along the way to keep us grounded.

When it comes to the people you love and care about, never ever put off saying what you need to, or delay doing something for them, as tomorrow may never come. While we may treasure our memories, we must never live in the past. I am of the personal belief, we should always live a rich life in the present, as tomorrow is but a dream that may never materialise.

Anne and I can certainly vouch for the fact that there are no perfect marriages. While we are definitely not perfect as individuals, we are perfect for each other and compliment each other. That makes us an absolutely perfect match.

I am now in my 'golden years' with my 'golden girl' by my side. Yes, after twenty-six years together, we are ageing in sync. Her beautiful face has matured and her perfect body has blossomed, but she continues to be the fantastic person she was when we first met, and I know intrinsically she will always be the same.

She loves and accepts me for the vintage but classic model I am now, despite my middle aged spread and thinning mane. My 'get up and go' may have 'got up and gone', though she still sees in me the man she met and married. Anne's friend once asked her if she felt cheated at being 'wife number three', she just replied 'they may have had the young man in him, but I have the best of him'.

Yes, Anne is not only my rudder, but she keeps me young mentally, physically and also literally on my toes. She not only wants the best for me, but also brings out the best in me. We are emboldened by our ever increasing laughter lines, as we continue to anchor each other and enjoy life. We never cease to embrace what life has to offer, and make the best years of our time together count for us. My life has finally come full circle and Anne is and will always be my wife, the love of my life and my best friend till the end of time.

Chapter 24

Conclusion: A life worth living – (you know what I mean?)

With time and age, the colours of my life have changed several times over the years. I look back on my life and wonder about the various good, bad and regrets I have about my past and 'what if' I had done things differently?

Regrets at not being there more often for my mum and my dad. Regrets during my first and second marriages which should really never have taken place. Regrets about not being more firm when bringing up my two elder children. Regrets at blindly taking all that was aimed at me by my only sister. Regrets about the people I got into business with. That is a heck of a lot of regrets in the short span of my life.

I learned very early in my adulthood that all the mistakes I thought I had made, were not really mistakes at all, but decisions I had consciously taken, which had a profound influence whether positive or negative, on my life. Unfortunately, while I made every effort over the years to review situations and arrive at the correct decisions, sometimes circumstances over-ruled my head and the outcome was maybe one I had wanted at the time but not what I needed in my life.

But that is now in my past and since banished from my memory. When Anne and I married, unlike Anne who was never married before, I entered our marriage with a truckload of unappealing baggage. However being a person with a sanguine disposition, I realised what's done is long gone and I could not live our future based on my checkered past experiences or regrets. Life is too short for recriminations and I do believe 'It's better to light a candle and move forward in the light, than curse the darkness and live in the past'. If I dwelt on the past and did not move forward, I would not be able to enjoy the rest of my life with Anne, and that would be the greatest regret I have no wish for.

With Anne by my side, I have conquered and attained the impossible. My life through these years has surpassed my earlier life by a long stretch and could never be any better. It has been a 'life worth living'. Do we have our marital spats? ofcourse we do - no one and no marriage is perfect. Is there a winner at the end of our spats? ofcourse there is - take a wild guess!

I have lived through many a dark period when there was no colour to brighten my days, uplift my drooping spirits or chase away my solitary blues. But I never let it dictate my tomorrow and what was yet to come. I believed in myself and what I could achieve to be a self-made man, with no monetary assistance or handouts from my parents, family or friends.

I entered our world with a resilience par excellence, which enabled me to move forward and out of the confines of my shadowed past. It has always stood me in good stead and is also responsible for the courage I garnered to take that step into the unknown from a young age. A positive outlook has always held the top spot in my life as what good can cynicism and negativity get me, or how far can it take me?

I cannot change my personality, and being blind to the

negative treatment meted out to me by the people close to me, did not mean I was a doormat. Far from it. I believe if given a chance, people can change. Unfortunately from my personal experience, I find some people, family or otherwise, sometimes do not conform to this particular thesis. Family like my sister and my elder two children, have the tendency to take advantage of other family members and even take them for granted, while treating friends and total strangers to their kind and courteous side.

I started out with faith my first family unit would persevere and survive. But I soon realised everyone in the unit should have the same belief, and that was why my marriage and family was doomed from the start. However, my faith has finally come to fruition and my new family and my life has weathered and out-lived our new beginnings, and our lives could not be any better.

As a child growing up during the war, I naturally missed out on a lot. That has made me a person who will never say 'no' to a request for help, be it for my work expertise, for my life experiences or even for financial assistance. If I have it I will willingly give it, as I was that little boy once, who knew what it felt like to have nothing. I genuinely believe the credo, 'in life there will be times we may need a helping hand and sometimes, we may have to lend a helping hand'.

However, Anne put a stop to me helping people financially as when we got married, I had over half a million Pounds Sterling given out to various people in personal loans, and no one seemed too bothered about paying it back. Anne started getting the loans back by using her excellent public relations skills and in a few cases, even the long arm of the law.

My mum frequently said – 'if you give to others you will always have, as it is the law of nature', and I have kept it at the back of my mind. And while I have helped very many folk, some appreciated me but many just used me. I now know with absolute certainity, no one other than my sister-in-law would be there for me, if I ever needed assistance in any form.

Money in my opinion does not bring happiness. It's just an aid for a comfortable life as contentment comes from within. To me, the beauty of life does not depend on how happy I am but rather, on how happy I can make others. I used to work myself to death just so my first wife and children and my second wife led a charmed life.

But I don't have that issue with Anne. Money or no money, we are happy and content anywhere in the world as long as we are together. Anne said to me a long time ago, I did not have to prove myself to her with expensive material gifts, and the fact we are very happy together, confirms the old adage 'It's not what we have in life, but who we have in our life that really matters'.

My way of looking at life now is – if it were not for the thorns that messed up the illusion of my bed of roses, I would not have woken up to appreciate the fragrance of the roses. All the colourless times in my life have made me cherish the good times I have now and I value every passing minute. While I cannot change the past, I know I can most certainly ruin a perfectly great present, by worrying about a future I have absolutely no control over. With Anne, I have learned to let my life take its course and live each day to the fullest, as if it were my last.

Since I first travelled at the age of fifteen years, I have

traversed the globe several times, and each time seeing the same countries and its people in a different light. I have also experienced the various facets of their cultures in the glory of all its colours. There is an old Moorish Proverb I believe in, and which is ever so true 'he who does not travel, does not know the value of men'. My travels have made me the open minded person I am today. It has made me see in myself what I see in the world I have travelled through, and the people I have come in contact with. What better education could I have had than that?

My blindness encompassing race, colour, caste and creed, age, sexual orientation and financial standing, defines me as a person. When I look at someone, I do not see anyone other than a person like me. Everything else is of no consequence, as are we all not cut from the same multicoloured fabric? Why should ethnicity or any other factor be a source for discrimination as don't we all belong to the same humankind?

Unfortunately my blindness did not end there. As you know by now, I also chose to be blind to various situations in my first and second marriages under the distorted view I was doing the right thing and my life would get better. Blindness with regard to Marie was unfortunately constantly forced upon me just to please my parents. But where Sharon and Tony are concerned, my blindness was genuine, as I erroneously believed as a parent, I am supposed to love, trust and accept my children unconditionally, till the end of time.

However, it took my innumerable follies for me to belatedly realise, that loving someone does not mean I have to like who the person is or has become. Further, irrelevant of who the person is, trust is not free for the taking, as it always has to be earned. I have learned the hard way, I cannot live my life on anyone's terms except my own. And finally, I should never pander to the pressures, emotional or otherwise, exerted by those around me as at the end of the day, I have to take personal responsibility for my actions and answer to no one else but myself.

While I never discriminate, I have experienced my fair share of discrimination. As a white Englishman, no one would believe me if I said I have been discriminated against several times during my life. While all people are not prejudiced, from my personal experience, I can without hesitation say that prejudicism is prevalent in every corner of our world. No country can state their people do not discriminate in some form or the other.

After Phyllis and I got married, we experienced a few incidents of prejudicism in the UK. Once in the 1970s when in a supermarket, Phyllis had just reached the checkout to pay for our purchases, while I was just behind with the two children, and she was subjected to some degrading prejudiced remarks due to her dusky skin tone. A customer ahead of Phyllis bobbed her head towards Phyllis and said to the checkout counter staff 'they're even getting down here now'. I heard the remark and it shocked me to the core but before I could give the person a piece of my mind, Phyllis just took our purchases and walked out of the supermarket and motioned for us to follow her.

When Anne and I got married, my so-called English friends in Dubai excelled in their open prejudicism against Anne. But Anne also very correctly said these 'friends' were not genuine friends of mine as we had nothing in common, and they were in my life just for what they could get out of me, as I always gave expensive jewellery and gifts to my friends, their spouses and families.

But after Anne came into my life, I discontinued my practice and my friends did not appreciate it. Infact, one of my friends made the mistake of calling me at the office on Valentine's day with the complaint she had not received any gift from me. Unfortunately for her, I was not in the office so the reception connected the call to Anne. What transpired I will never know as when I asked Anne, she just laughed and said with dripping sarcasm 'what does one bitch say to another?'

My inner self has struggled to keep up with our times. When I grew up in the 1940s the gay culture was not an open common topic of conversation as it was still a very closeted secret. To me no folk should be given a tag just because they have a different view from me. Anne has had many gay friends over the years. One of Anne's close gay friends was the first gay person I was closely associated with and I wondered what the heck all the fuss was about. He was a perfectly normal great guy, just like me or my mates.

Infact, Marc became my close mate too and we all spent many happy hours together, before he sadly passed away in 2018. But he was discriminated against and treated differently by very many people over the years. What hetrosexual or gay couples do behind closed doors is their private business and does not concern anyone else. We are all as normal as anyone will ever be. Are any of us perfect? certainly not. But then, despite what you would like to believe, no one in this world is even near perfect, and that definitely includes you and me.

Through the years I have learned, it is extremely unfortunate many people despite their professed academic education, are blind to the fact we do not live in a monochromatic world. Their whole life can be changed for the better, by keeping an open mind, knowing right from wrong, a bit of cultural education and, not forgetting eradicating the deplorable habit of giving derogatory labels to people.

I have always lived my life honestly and to the fullest, and I intend to continue in the same colourful vein and go out with a BANG! Yes, there was a time when I surrounded myself with flashy toys to perk up my lagging spirits. But I learned that just like the 'Moon', it is okay for us to go through phases in life, and I make no excuses for my excesses, global homes and my high octane toys. All this superfluity helped me during the empty period and filled the excessive chasm in my life.

I took charge of my life at a young age, accepted my fate and worked towards my destiny. With hard graft I rewarded myself along the way as while I always gave a hundred percent to everyone around me, no one returned the favour. I would be lying if I said it did not bother me. Initially it did. But I learned to rise above them and I did not let the behaviour of those around me control me or my future relationships.

My personal experience has taught me there are three types of people in our world. Some people are given a financial start in life like my elder two children, but they never learn the value of money nor the art of giving. Some people like my sister Marie think the world owes them a living. And then like me, there are a vast majority of people who work extremely hard their whole life, just so they can enjoy their retirement as they do not want to rely financially on anyone else. When I was young I was poor. Now after years of working hard and achieving success, I am unfortunately, no longer young. But don't ever pity me, as age has never prevented me from enjoying and living my life to the fullest.

Within my family, a multitude of lies, secrets, deceptions and unjustified accusations have been held, hurled, spread and compounded further by all of them. This has resulted in an excessive amount of unfounded, unnecessary and unhealthy resentment being held within each of them for ever so long. As such, I feel the time has come for me to tell it as it is, since I may never get another chance to do so. I may be too late to wipe the slate clean but atleast, I am confident in the knowledge the whole family is now in possession of the truth.

From a young lad with just a high school education to nothing more than 'Dave the plumber', my success story is not a novel one. I have had to reward myself for my success and achievements and I make no apologies for doing it with gusto. However, when Anne entered my life and totally destroyed the void and emptyness, I learned to be discerning with the fruits of my hard graft and still be able to enjoy my life.

Our world is such a fascinating place to live in, only because of the wide spectrum of people that populate it. If we were all identical in this world of ours, we would be extremely boring and lacklustre, with our lives bordering on hell on earth. Our time here is short and the only way to ensure we live a happy and productive life is to accept everyone for who they are.

We will all face our battles in life. I have taken wild swings at life and at times it has swung right back at me. Yes, I have also stumbled several times but just like the 'Sun', I believe however many times we go down, we should keep rising for tomorrow is a new day and like me, you will win some and lose some.

My tidbit of worldly advice is 'what you cannot change,

you can control by embracing it'. However, never ever forget 'everything that happens is for a good reason and anything that doesn't happen is without a doubt only for a better reason'. My life has taught me happiness is not about getting all I want, but rather, it is about enjoying what I have. For me, life is not measured by the number of breaths I take but by the moments that take my breath away. Despite the clouds that have sometimes obstructed my rainbow, the 'Stars' taught me if I live my life well, my innermost vision will shine through brightly.

I have never claimed to be a saint and as you know by now, certain experiences in my life turned me far away from faith in my religion too. But after a major tussle with my conscience, and difficult as it is, I finally made the decision to forgive all the people who have done me wrong. However, my life story does bear testament to the fact that the one thing I can never do is forget. Well, I did say I am no saint!

I am sure my 'life story' will resonate with you on several levels, and I hope you will absorb the value of life's lessons I belatedly learned, from the innumerable erroneous but conscious decisions I made. May you achieve all you aim for in your life and may you never lose faith or belief in yourself, to know you are strong enough to endure whatever journey your winding road ahead may lead you on.

Though I have viewed life through my blind spot, my life has without a doubt traversed through a gamut of colours with time, and has unequivocally been a life worth living. *'You know what I mean?'* I am living and enjoying my life to its fullest and I have reached exactly where I want to be in my life.

Right Here!
The End